"KING ARTHUR LIVES
IN
MERRIE CARLISLE"

Carlisle in the Arthurian Literature
of the Middle Ages

for Alexander and Amelia

Stephen Matthews

BOOKCASE

The Romantic view of Carlisle: detail from Nutter's retrospective picture of a walled Carlisle viewed from Primrose Bank in the west. From Carlisle in the Olden Time *(1812)*

Preface

Carlisle is the setting for many of the greatest stories of the Middle Ages. Its name was known throughout Europe as a city of chivalric deeds and the home of King Arthur.

In this book I have sought to retell some of these stories and show something of the role Carlisle played in the medieval imagination.

I have quoted considerably from the original works or translations and such direct extracts are printed in italics without additional quotation marks. Other retellings are my own abridged paraphrases. I have not hesitated to standardize spelling and other matters, since my object has been to make works as readily accessible as possible and yet retain something of the savour of the original. The spelling of names varies considerably from story to story, and often within a story, and I have used standardized forms where it has been convenient.

The picture on the cover is a detail of the poster for the 1951 Historical Pageant. The medieval king is not identified, but might be Edward I or Edward IV or Henry II or even King Arthur himself.

ISBN 978-1-904147-41-1
First edition: 2009
Copyright: Stephen Matthews
Published by Bookcase, 19 Castle Street, Carlisle, CA3 8SY
01228 544560   bookcasecarlisle@aol.com; www.bookscumbria.com
Printed and bound in Great Btitain by CPI Antony Rowe, Chippenham and Eastbourne

The romantic Carlisle of the imagination.
Detail of 1780's engraving by B Ralph after the Buck print of forty years earlier.

Contents

"King Arthur lives in Merrie Carlisle"   7

Gildas, Nennius, Taliesin and Others: The Origins of the
   Arthur Story   13

Geoffrey of Monmouth: the Fiction of History   27

Marie de France and the Enchantment of Romance   34

Chretien de Troyes and the Origin of Romance   46

The Story of the Holy Grail, and Some More Worldly
   Romances   57

Fergus of Galloway: a Border Burlesque   65

The Alliterative Morte Arthure: Arthur moves from
   Caerleon to Carlisle   77

The Awntyrs off Arthur at the Terne Wathelin: a Ghost
   and a Joust in Inglewood Forest   91

The Wedding of Sir Gawain and Dame Ragnelle: What
   Women Most Desire   106

The Avowyng of Arthur: Further Adventures in
   Inglewood Forest   116

Sir Gawain and the Carle of Carlisle   134

The Stanzaic Morte Arthur: Lancelot and Guinevere   143

Thomas Malory and Morte Darthur   158

Bishop Percy and his Reliques   194

The Real Arthur in the Carlisle of the Imagination   215

Further Reading   226

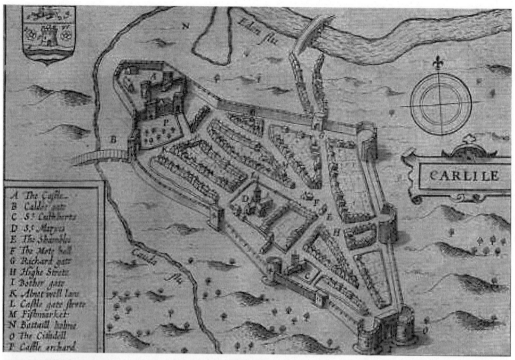

Above: Bird's Eye View of Carlisle: Detail from John Speed's map of 1611.
Below: Carlisle from a map of 1624 by Thomas Meissner.

"*King Arthur lives in Merrie Carlisle*"

King Arthur lives in Merrie Carlisle.

Every word of this title is false or questionable.

However, this line from a medieval ballad was first presented to the modern world, in 1765, by Thomas Percy in his *Reliques of Ancient Poetry*. That challengingly indisputable statement was the opening line of The *Marriage of Sir Gawain*, one of the many old ballads that Percy published in his ground-breaking collection. These three volumes, rescued from an old and battered manuscript that was being used to light domestic fires, played their part in igniting Romanticism.

Two great sons of the Borders who did so much to change the way we thought and felt two hundred years ago, Sir Walter Scott and William Wordsworth, were also aware of Arthur and *merrie Carlisle*. Carlisle, with its fine cathedral and resolute castle and its booming textile industries and its slum housing, was seen as a city of myth and legend. The idea was recalled in the historical pageants of the twentieth century and something of the city's heritage gradually disappeared as we lost our taste for dressing up and play-acting.

The truth, of course, is not necessarily the same as old ballads, myths and dressing-up and pageants.

If there was a King Arthur, he was probably not a king, merely an overlord or a *dux bellorum*, a leader in war, commanding an army of Britons against forces of Angles and possibly Picts. He may have defeated them, he may have ushered in an era of peace, a time of respite from the persistent encroachments of the barbaric settlers in a post-Roman Britain, but there is no reason to suppose he was king.

However, we have little reason to suppose he was Arthur. Such records as there are are so scant and questionable that, if there was such a leader, he may not have been Arthur. If he was Arthur his name was not spelled out in English orthography, the language of the enemy, but would have been written *Artyr,* in his native Welsh, or *Arturus,* in the Latin that was once the lingua franca of the failing Roman Empire.

That he lived is equally questionable. If he lived, he lived in the fifth and sixth centuries A.D. in the years after the Romans had deserted Britain, withdrawn their forces to defend a beleaguered empire from the hordes that pressed across the great plains of Eurasia. But he may not have lived. Is Arthur merely the mythical creation of a desperate and defeated Celtic nation, seeking hope in a futile resort to what might once have been and still might be, *A Once and Future King*? Arthur's existence is such that he merits an aside in all respected histories of the sixth century, in some ways, the darkest of the Dark Ages. There is no evidence for Arthur, but then there is little evidence for barely anyone else.

In is doubtful. Maybe Carlisle was the site of one of Arthur's courts. There are many possible Camelots: Winchester, where a Round Table is to be found, but that was a fourteenth century construction; the craggy, precarious rocks of Cornish Tintagel and its impossible, romantic castle; Glastonbury, with its abbey and its Tor rising mystically out of the Somerset rines; Caerleon on Usk with its huge castle, now no more, favoured by Geoffrey of Monmouth; distant Carmarthen, the last resort of the beaten Celts, far to the west in Wales and giving its name to Myrddin the magician whose own name was later bowdlerized into Merlin; Chester, guardian of the Welsh Marches; and northern Edinburgh with its magnificent crags that bear the name and, some would say, the profile of Arthur himself. And there is no evidence, no proof, for any of these places except the enthusiastic assertions of poets and similar mythographers and the often mercenary enthusiasm of local patriots and hucksters.

The great virtue of Arthur and his myth is that he has swollen into a huge vacuum waiting to be filled.

And then there is *merry* or quaintly *merrie* Carlisle, redolent of bonhomie and cider and of a golden age of eternal spring and merry-making in a blessed England, equally the creation of Victorian Christmas cards and the ruddy cheeks of the Women's Institute responding to Edward German's jingoistic romp. Only Wakefield, of all other places, was regularly referred to as *merry. Merrie Wakefield* has even less resonance than *Merrie Carlisle*.

Merry is an interesting word. It has no cognate or corresponding word in other Germanic languages except Dutch, and is possibly ultimately derived from the old Teutonic word *murgjo* meaning *to shorten,* as though being merry served to abbreviate the tedium of existence. Its range of meaning in the middle ages is so wide that it could be used to describe the pleasure one has in having sight of God's face as well as the more familiar pleasures of convivial mirth.

But it seems odd that Carlisle, of all places, should be called *merry*. For centuries it was one of the most turbulent and lawless of English cities, a backwater in a buffer zone on the border between a restless Scotland and a predatory England, dominated by its military garrison and subject to the depredations of outlaws and reivers and recurrent waves of ravishing armies. And it was poor, a city of 1500 people commanding an impoverished hinterland on the road to nowhere. There might be good reason to think it was the least merry city in England.

And was it *Carlisle*? The first record of a name for Carlisle was found to date to the mid 80s A.D. The name *Luguvalium* was inscribed on a writing tablet found in Castle Street. In the fourth century the *Itinerarium Antonini Augusti - The Journeys of Antony Augustus* - talks of a *Lugovallus*. Three centuries later the monk, the Venerable Bede, from his scriptorum in Tynemouth Priory, writing his *Historia Ecclesiastica* or *History of the Church*, and telling of St Cuthbert visiting the city, identified it as *Lugabalium*. The city is also referred to as *Lugabalium* in a Latin work that went under the title *Ravennatis Anonymi Cosmographia*. However, in 1129, listing the resting places of St Cuthbert's corpse as it was transported by monks around what is now the north of England and the south of Scotland, Symeonis of Durham talked of *Lugabalia, id est Luel nunc dicitur Carleil*. By then the place that was once known as *Lugabalia* or *Luel* was called *Carleil*. Another document from the early twelfth century refers, in Latin, to *Luel which is now called Carleol*.

During the Middle Ages, the name of the city is found in a confusing array of forms. Sometimes it is simply *Luel* or *Lues*. *The Register of the Priory of Wetheral* employed the forms *Karlioli* and *Karleoleum*. Layamon, the thirteenth century poet from Worcestershire, wrote of *Kaer Leil* and in *The Calendar of Patent Rolls,* in 1217, the city is grandly referred to as *urbem Carleolensum*. Elsewhere it is found as *Carlol, Carlel, Chaerleolium, Caerleolio, Kaerleoli, Caerlyle, Karlel, Carlel, Carlelle, Carlil, Karlehill, Karlisle, Carlesley, Carleslee, Carduill, Kardoyl, Karduil, Kardoil* and even *Charduil*. The coins that were minted in Carlisle in the twelfth century were variously stamped with the inscriptions *On:Carli*; *on Cardi*; *n Crd*: and *oncar*.

It is interesting that the name is *Carleil* and not *Luel-* or *Leil-caster* or *-cester*. Other Roman towns in England took the same form as Lancaster, Leicester, Cirencester, Winchester and Chichester. Towns in Wales formed their names in the opposite way: Caernarfon, Carmarthen or Caerfyddn, Cardigan, Cardiff and Caerleon. The name Carlisle points to a Celtic rather than an Anglo-Saxon origin.

The modern Welsh form, and Carlisle is one of the few English places that retains a distinctive form in the Welsh language, is *Caerliwelydd*. This is very similar to the *Cair Ligualid* found in manuscripts of Nennius's history from the ninth and tenth centuries.

The Anglo-Saxon Chronicle recorded the name as *Cardeol* in the eleventh century. The name is also found in many, and even more various forms, in continental manuscripts, often in connection with Arthurian Romances. *Cardue(i)l,*

Cardeil, *Cardoel*, *Cardoil*, *Carduil*, *Charduel*, *Kardoel*, and *Quaraduel* are some of the forms occurring in French manuscripts.

The Latin name meant *strong as Lugus*. Lugus was a Celtic god and the name had been used elsewhere to give the original name to Leiden in Holland and Lyons in France. The *vallo*, *valio* or *balium* element of the name is often assumed to refer to the Roman Wall or vallum, but experts think this is unlikely and prefer the etymology that refers to Lugus's strength.

Did Carlisle actually exist in the sixth century? After Roman forces abandoned their proud Wall and retreated to defend the Imperial City against the invading Ostragoths, did the city's economy collapse? Did this important military garrison city with its paved streets and fine buildings fall rapidly into decay? Did grass grow where the troops had paraded when the soldiers and their money left and the merchants and the prostitutes had to look elsewhere for a living? Carlisle had been on the very periphery of the civilized Roman world, a Spitzbergen of culture facing a hostile world. Its urban existence would have been fragile. Would it have been a worthy city for such as King Arthur?

But our sixth century Arthur, if there was a sixth century Arthur, would not have been the chivalrous knight of our myths and imaginations. There would have been no finely caparisoned horses and flying pennons, richly decorated shields and dazzling coats of armour. There would have been little courtesy, chivalric virtues and no sophisticated bonds of brotherhood and nicely determined honour.

Sixth century Britain would have been a country afflicted by civil war. The two million or so Celts had regressed to an agrarian society. They would have been living directly off the land pursuing a pitiable and subsistence agriculture. The once busy trade routes of the Romans would have been deserted and there would have been little in the way of goods of high value. As a society they would lack the skills and the infrastructure, the supply of materials and tools, to produce any arms of any quality, let alone a sword like Excalibur. The legend itself may have been prompted by the survival of a fine weapon of earlier years, a consummate piece of the armourer's art imported from Damascus or Toledo.

The enemies the Celts faced were numerous and had not been softened by the settled life the Romans had brought. The Angles and Jutes and Saxons came from barbarian tribes who had long plagued the boundaries of the Roman Empire. They were peoples addicted to war, constantly in search of lebensraum, pushing the Celts further and further into the mountainous reaches of the west. To the north were the notoriously painted Picts and to the west were the marauding, sea-borne Irish.

There was no time for chivalry. The age of Arthur was probably the time when this country was most bereft of the civilizing virtues.

King Arthur and his brotherhood of the Knights of the Round Table is a myth. However, it is a myth of exceptional potency, one of the few secular myths that can rival the myths of religion. The events, in which whatever desperate war-lord had achieved however-limited curtailment of the onset of barbarism, became a seed that grew into a vast array of stories. These stories, true to their mercurial Celtic origins, changed and transformed themselves to become the embodiment of the self-image of many different cultures.

The Arthur of the the Welsh *Triads* and the tales of the *Mabinogion* was endowed with very different meanings to the Arthur who was used to legitimize Henry II or the Arthur who became a projection of Edward I's ceaseless military ambition. The Arthur who caused Henry Purcell to sing of England's *Immortal Isle* was very different from Tennyson's defeated, departing hero awaiting on the rocky shore for the dark barge to bear him to Avalon. The mystical chromaticism of Wagner's *Parsifal* was far removed from the simple peasant Peredur of the empty hills of North Wales and Thomas Erceldoune on the River Tweed in the Scottish Borders would not have recognized the Tristan of *Tristan and Isolde*.

The origins of the myth of King Arthur lie in the very scant records we have from the Dark Ages. The monk Gildas, who lived in the same century as Arthur, provides us with a disputed passing reference. A later *History* by Nennius, another monk living on the Welsh border, supplies an intriguing paragraph offering names of Arthur's battles, but this is several centuries after Arthur's existence. In addition,, there are tantalising references in Anglo-Saxon and Celtic annals. Otherwise, before the eleventh century, knowledge of Arthur may have been preserved orally among the Celtic peoples of Wales, Cornwall, Brittany and Cumbria.

The story of Arthur first entered literature in Geoffrey of Monmouth's extravagant history in the twelfth century. His story was repeated and developed by Wace, a Norman monk from Jersey, and was given in poetic form with mystical additions by Layamon, who was writing on the borders of Wales. Geoffrey, Wace and Layamon were the origin of a chronicle tradition which accounted for a pseudo-historical Arthur.

A parallel romance tradition goes back to the remarkable poems of Chretien de Troyes and, to a lesser extent, of Marie de France. They were both writing several decades after Geoffrey. Their imaginative world was translated, adapted and enlarged in the thirteenth century to become a vast literature found throughout western Europe from Iceland to Spain.

An English language Arthur flourished in the fourteenth and fifteenth century culminating in a work of genius, Thomas Malory's compendious retelling of *Le Morte D'Arthur*.

The romance of Arthur remained a recurrent theme in English, but it flourished again with the Romantic revival, with Walter Scott and many others. A generation later, Alfred Lord Tennyson placed Arthur and chivalry at the heart of Victorian society. Since then Arthur and matters Arthurian have been the subject of numerous poems, novels, plays, films, paintings, operas and songs.

Very few ideas have been possessed of such artistic potency.

Carlisle was, at least, the nominal location for Arthur's court in many of these works from the earliest poems by Chretien and Marie through to many of the modern novels of Arthurian romance.

Over the coming pages I will follow the story of Arthur and his association with Carlisle in some of the literature of the Middle Ages.

Gildas, Nennius, Taliesin and Others: The Origins of the Arthur Story

For a person of such renown King Arthur has left very little if any trace in the historical record. Such little trace as there is provides no adequate evidence for his specific existence and certainly no substantiating details that bear scrutiny. All seems to be surmise and speculation that arises from a possible memory, kept alive over the centuries and then magnified through the imagination of the ages.

The one possible near contemporary record of King Arthur is just one sentence: *After this, sometimes our countrymen, sometimes the enemy, won the field, to the end that our Lord might this land try after his accustomed manner these his Israelites, whether they loved him or not, until the year of the siege of Bath-hill (Mons Badonis), when took place also the last almost, though not the least, slaughter of our cruel foes, which was (as I am sure) forty-four years and one month after the landing of the Saxons, and also the time of my own nativity.*

The native Britons, it appears, had won a battle against the invading Saxons of such military significance that it had ushered in a lengthy period of peace. Arthur may have been the leader of the Britons at Mons Badonis.

The writer is Gildas, a monk in the Celtic church, whose life spanned the first half of the sixth century. He was possibly born in 505 and may have died in 570. The book is *De Excidio et Conquestu Britanniae*, a title, *On the Ruin and Conquest of Britain*, which tells us exactly where its author is coming from. Gildas seems to be talking about a period of war between the Saxons and his people, the native Britons. The battles have gone one way and then another over a period of forty-four years until the battle of Bath Hill or Mons Badonis, which resulted in the slaughter of many of their foes.

Gildas loved his country: *Its plains are spacious, its hills are pleasantly situated, adapted for superior tillage, and its mountains are admirably calculated for the alternate pasturage of cattle, where flowers of various colours, trodden by the feet of man, give it the appearance of a lovely picture. It is decked, like a man's chosen bride, with divers jewels, with lucid fountains and abundant brooks wandering over the snow white sands, with transparent rivers, flowing in gentle murmurs, and offering a sweet pledge of slumber to those who recline upon their banks, while it is irrigated by abundant lakes, which pour forth cool torrents of refreshing water.*

However, Gildas, in a true jeremiad, rails against the iniquities of the age. The writing is not an historical account of his times, but an angry preaching against the sinfulness of his fellow people and their rulers. He excoriates the clergy: *Britain hath priests but they are unwise; very many that minister, but many of them are impudent; clerks she hath but some of them are deceitful raveners, pastors (as they are called) but rather wolves prepared for the slaughter of souls (for they provide not for the common people, but covet rather the gluttony of their own bellies) possessing the houses of the church, but obtaining them for filthy lucre's sake; instructing the laity, but showing withal most depraved examples, vices and evil manners;* etc. etc.

Gildas's work is one long diatribe, larded with Biblical quotations, against the evils of his day. What is interesting is that, although he bewails the degeneracy of his society, he actually confirms the existence of a social order, a still Christian society, with established hierarchies, laws and norms, and not a country in anarchic disarray.

Carlisle may be one of the few places he mentions. He is talking about the Diocletian persecution of Christians in the years 303 to 305. *God, therefore, who wishes all men to be saved, and who calls sinners no less than those who think themselves righteous, magnified his mercy towards us, and, as we know, during the above mentioned persecution, that Britain might not be totally enveloped in the dark shades of knight, he, of his own free gift, kindled up among us bright luminaries of holy martyrs, whose places of burial and martyrdom, had they not for our manifold crimes been interfered with and destroyed by the barbarians, would have still kindled in the minds of beholders no small fire of divine charity. Such were St Alban of Verulam, Aaron and Julius, citizens of Carlisle, and the rest, of both sexes, who in different places stood their ground in the Christian contest.* This is the standard Victorian translation by J A Giles. The Latin original refers not to *Lugabalia*, but to *urbs legionem, (the city of the legions),* which modern scholarship would interpret as possibly Caerleon or Chester, but most probably as York, and certainly not Carlisle.

Gildas also mentions the Roman Wall. The Romans are called to rescue the Britons from the incursions of the Scots and Picts: *All of them were driven beyond the borders, and the humiliated natives rescued from the bloody slavery which awaited them. By the advice of their protectors, they now built a wall across the island from one sea to the other, which being manned with a proper force, might be a terror to the foes whom it was intended to repel, and a protection to their friends whom it covered. But this wall being made of turf instead of stone, was of no use to that foolish people, who had no head to guide them.*

Gildas describes a later attack on the Wall: *No sooner were they* (the Romans) *gone, than the Picts and the Scots, like worms which in the heat of mid-day come forth from their holes, hastily land again from their canoes, in which they had been carried beyond the Cichican valley, differing one from the other in manners, but inspired by the same avidity for blood, and all the more eager to shroud their faces in bushy hair than to cover with decent clothing those parts of their body which required it. Moreover, having heard of the departure of our friends, and their resolution never to return, they seized with greater boldness than before on all the country towards the extreme north towards the wall. To oppose them there was placed on the heights a garrison equally slow to fight and ill-adapted to run away, a useless and panic-stricken company, who clambered away days and nights on their unprofitable watch. Meanwhile the hooked weapons of their enemies were not idle, and our wretched countrymen were dragged from the wall and dashed against the ground. Such premature death, however, painful as it was, saved them from seeing the miserable sufferings of their brothers and children. But why should I say more? They left their cities, abandoned the protection of the wall and dispersed themselves in flight more desperately than before. The enemy on the other hand pursued them with more unrelenting cruelty than before, and butchered our countrymen like sheep, so that that their habitations were like those of savage beasts; for they turned their arms upon each other, and for the sake of a little sustenance, imbrued their hands in the blood of their fellow countrymen. Thus foreign calamities were augmented by domestic feuds; so that the whole country was entirely destitute of provisions, save such as could be procured in the chase.*

There is little doubt as to the tone of Gildas's writing or to his feelings about his compatriots, but his geographical references and his awareness of events before his own day are vague and imprecise. Is he talking about Hadrian's Wall or the Antonine Wall? When did these attacks occur? The historian is left speculating and guessing and can draw few, if any, conclusions in the absence of corroborating evidence of any sort.

Similarly, the site of the battle, called Bath Hill in the Victorian translation above, but usually referred to as Mons Badonis or Mount Badon, has resisted precise identification. The most probable location is somewhere in the south of the country, in the area that became Wessex, where the Britons were retreating in the face of an aggressive Saxon settlement. Even though this is cited as the one near contemporary reference to Arthur, the battle having taken place in the year of Gildas's nativity, Arthur is not named. The significance of this battle, which may have ushered in a period of comparative peace, is given in a much later work.

This work is ascribed to one Nennius, although it may be a composite of the work of several writers. The earliest manuscript we have of the *Historia Brittonum* or *History of the Britons* is from the twelfth century. The *Prologue* begins: *Nennius, the lowly minister and servant of the servants of God, by the grace of God, disciple of St. Elbotus, to all the followers of truth sendeth health.* In 755, St Elbotus or Elvod was the bishop of Bangor-is-y-coed, also known today as Bangor on Dee, on the Welsh border. The *History* proper opens with a chronology that begins, ambitiously: *From Adam to the flood are two thousand and forty-two years,* and concludes: *From the passion of Christ are completed nine hundred and forty-six (years); from his incarnation, nine hundred and seventy-six; being the fifth year of Edmund, king of the Angles.* Nennius was writing in the tenth century, some four hundred years or more after Gildas and the supposed time of Arthur.

He introduces himself with an extended apology, which, even though he quotes his sources, does not inspire confidence in the reliability of his work: *I, Nennius, disciple of St. Elbotus, have endeavoured to write some extracts which the dulness of the British nation had cast away, because teachers had no knowledge, nor gave any information in their books about this island of Britain. But I have got together all I could find as well as from the annals of the Romans as from the chronicles of the sacred fathers, Hieronymus, Eusebius, Isadorus, Prosper, and from the annals of the Scots and Saxons, and from our ancient traditions. Many teachers and scribes have attempted to write this, but somehow have abandoned it from its difficulty, either on account of frequent deaths, or the often recurring calamities of war. I pray that every reader who shall read this book, may pardon me, for having attempted, like a chattering jay, or like some weak witness, to write these things after they had failed. I yield to him who knows more of these things than I do.*

The references to the annals of the Romans and the Scots and the Saxons sounds encouraging, but when it comes to matters that concern Arthur, Nennius is probably drawing on ancient traditions.

In its sixty-five paragraphs the *History* traces the years of Roman rule from the time of Julius Caesar. It makes reference to the Roman Wall: *Severus was the third emperor who passed the sea to Britain, where, to protect the provinces recovered from barbaric incursions, he ordered a wall and a rampart to be made between the Britons, the Scots, and the Picts, extending across the island from sea to sea, in length one hundred and thirty-three miles: and it is called in the British language Gwal. Moreover, he ordered it to be made between the Britons, and the Picts and Scots; for the Scots from the west, and the Picts from the north, unanimously made war against the Britons; but were at peace among themselves.* His picture of Roman Britain is one of alternating rebellion and repression: *The*

Romans, therefore, came with a powerful army to the assistance of the Britons; and having appointed over them a ruler, and settled the government, returned to Rome: and this took place alternately during the space of three hundred and forty-eight years. The Britons, however, from the oppression of the empire, again massacred the Roman deputies, and again petitioned for succour. Once more the Romans undertook the government of the Britons, and assisted them in repelling their neighbours; and, after having exhausted the country of its gold, silver, brass, honey and costly vestments, and besides having received rich gifts, they returned in great triumph to Rome.

The majority of the text is taken up with an account of the years of Vortigern and the mission of St Germanus to Britain. Vortigern, a British chieftain in the years after the Roman departure, had permitted three vessels from Germany, commanded by Hengist and Horsa, to land on the Isle of Thanet. *The Saxons were received by Vortigern, four hundred and forty seven years after the passion of Christ.* Vortigern engaged them as mercenaries. He was manipulated into marrying Hengist's daughter and giving the Saxons the country of Kent. He also agreed to a proposal by Hengist: *I will send for my son and his brother, both valiant men, who at my invitation will fight against the Scots, and you can give them the countries in the north, near the wall called Gaul.*

Vortigern married his own daughter and was denounced by St Germanus. His wise men advised him: *Retire to the remote boundaries of your kingdom: there build and fortify a city to defend yourself, for the people you have received are treacherous; they are seeking to subdue you by stratagem, and, even during your life, to seize upon all the countries subject to your power, how much more will they attempt after your death!* Vortigern departed to Guinet, possibly Gwynedd in North Wales, but all his attempts to build a fortified city were in vain as the materials he assembled for the purpose vanished every night. He was told to sprinkle the ground with the blood of a boy born without a father. The boy, when he had been found, revealed a pool in the ground containing a vase in which was a tent with red and white dragons in combat. The red dragon, he told Vortigern, will overcome the white dragon which represents the Saxons, *and drive the Saxon race from beyond the sea, whence they originally came; but do you depart from this place where you are not permitted to erect a citadel; I, to whom fate has allotted this mansion, shall remain here; whilst to you it is incumbent to seek other provinces, where you may build a fortress.* The boy was called Ambrosius.

Then the king assigned him the city, with all the western Provinces of Britain; and departing with his wise men to the sinistral district, he arrived in the region named Gueneri, where he built a city which, according to his name, was called

Cair Guorthegirn.

In many an old manuscript there is not only the main body of the text, but also much marginalia, where various readers and scholars have written their comments and additions. In one such early manuscript of *Historia Brittonum,* a gloss at this point reads: *He then built Guasmoric, near Lugubalia, a city which in English is called Palmecaster.* Palmcaster is the medieval name for Old Carlisle, a large series of earthworks, that lies a mile or two to the south-west of Wigton, which was once a Roman settlement.

Much fighting is supposed to have followed between the Saxons and Britons, until the treacherous Saxons stabbed their inebriated British guests at a feast. Vortigern was spared. St Germanus, *the blessed man was unanimously chosen commander against the Saxons. And then, not by the clang of trumpets, but by praying, singing hallelujah, and by the cries of the army to God, the enemy were routed, and driven even to the sea.* Vortigern fled to his castle, where, thanks to the prayers of St Germanus: *On the third night, at the third hour, fire fell suddenly from heaven, and totally burned the castle. Vortigern, the daughter of Hengist, his other wives and all the inhabitants, both men and women, miserably perished: such was the end of this unhappy king, as we find written in the life of St. Germanus.* Ambrosius was *the great king among the kings of Britain.*

St. Germanus, after his death, returned into his own country. Octa ruled Kent after the death of his father Hengist.

It is at this point in the manuscript that we have the one and only paragraph about Arthur:

Then it was that the magnanimous Arthur, with all the kings and military force of Britain, fought against the Saxons. And though there were many more noble than himself, yet he was twelve times chosen as their commander, and was as often conqueror. The first battle in which he was engaged was at the mouth of the River Gleni. The second, third, fourth and fifth, were on another river, by the Britons called Dubglas, in the region Linius. The sixth on the river Bassas. The seventh in the wood Celidon, which the Britons call Cat Coit Celidon. The eighth was near Gurnion Castle, where Arthur bore the image of the Holy Virgin, mother of God, upon his shoulders, and through the power of our Lord Jesus Christ, and the holy Mary, put the Saxons to flight, and pursued them the whole day with great slaughter. The ninth was the City of Legion, which is called Cair Lion. The tenth was on the banks of the River Trat Treuroit. The eleventh was on the mountain Bregouin, which we call Cat Bregion. The twelfth was a most severe contest, when Arthur penetrated the hill of Badon. In this engagement, nine hundred and sixty fell by his hand alone, no one but the Lord affording him assistance. In all these engagements the Britons were successful. For no strength can avail against the will of the Almighty.

There is no further mention of Arthur in the *Historia Brittonum*. Nennius goes on to tell the story of St Patrick and to provide genealogies of Saxon kings.

That one paragraph has exercised scholars and enthusiasts considerably. Compared with much else in the work, it seems to be clear and precise. Arthur was not king, but chosen by kings to be their overall commander at twelve battles. All twelve battles are clearly named and, in some cases, we are offered alternative names and, in other cases, locations. However, none of the nine sites has been identified with certainty. The river Gleni or Glein might be the River Glen in Northumberland or the Glem in Lincolnshire. The Dubglass might be in Lothian or Lancashire or Lincolnshire. The river Bassus might not be a river but Bass Rock in the Firth of Forth or it might be the river Lusas in Hampshire. Cat Coit Celidon is almost certainly the Caledonian Forest, but this is a vast area. The note to Giles's edition suggests that it might even be *the forest of Englewood, extending from Penrith to Carlisle.* Suggestions for the identification of Gurnion Castle have ranged from Binchester in Durham to Cornwall taking in Garionenum, near Yarmouth, in Norfolk. The City of the Legion, identified in the text as Caer Lion, appears to pose no problems. However, it has been suggested that this battle was fought not at Caerleon, but at Exeter. And it is more than possible that the phrase was a later interpolation by a scribe who thought he knew better. The banks of the river Trat Treuroit might lie in Somersetshire or Lancashire and the mountain Bregouin has been variously placed at Cadbury in Somerset or Edinburgh in Scotland. Finally, Mons Badonis, Mount Badon itself, the one battle which is corroborated by Gildas, might be at one of many locations in the south of England. Arthur's single-handed slaughter of 960 of the enemy seems as though it is the product of an over-fertile imagination.

Nennius offers no easy answers. But his work is even more problematic. There is no identifiable source for his information, although the pattern of the names themselves might indicate an origin in Welsh poetry. The origin in Welsh poetry might suggest a willingness to sacrifice accuracy before the fires of patriotic enthusiasm. Welsh bards would find it acceptable, even more, desirable, to exaggerate the exploits of their heroes. A great hero's name would be a magnet for all the vague battles of the period. A name like Arthur's over a period of several centuries would attract associations and these would become established as fact within the oral tradition. We are also dealing not with the original manuscript written by Nennius himself, but with copies and transcriptions of various quality that may include scholarly or political interpolations. Certainly some phrases are found in one copy and not in others. It is possible that the paragraph about Arthur is itself an addition to the basic text. Nennius's list raises more problems than it solves.

The earliest copy we have of Nennius's *Historia Britonnum* is in a twelfth century manuscript known as Harleian 3859 in the British Library. This manuscript also contains, among other items, a copy of the *Annales Cambriae*, the *Annals of Wales*.

The *Annals* are a list of dates with events, ending with an entry for for the year 954. The early entries are brief. The compilation was probably begun in the ninth century and the two entries that relate to Arthur are therefore suspect for much the same reasons as Nennius's writing. And, all we have is a copy made a century or two later.

One entry, for a date that might be between 490 and 516, says: *Battle of Badon in which Arthur carried the cross of our Lord Jesus Christ on his shoulders for three days and nights and was victorious.* This corresponds in part with statements by both Nennius and Gildas.

The other is for a year somewhere between 511 and 537: *The fight at Camlann in which Arthur and Medraut were killed.* These tantalising entries confirm nothing other than that, three hundred or six hundred years after the events were said to have occurred, it was thought that these events had happened.

The fight at Camlann, Arthur's fatal battle, may be of interest. Again, many attempts have been made to locate its site, and it is often associated, perhaps, simply, because of its ready phonetic correspondence, with the River Camel in Cornwall. In the 1930's it was suggested that Camlann might be a form of Camboglanna, a fort on the Roman Wall, which was then identified with Birdoswald. The name contains the words *cambo* meaning crooked and *glann* meaning bank. The curving sweep of the River Irthing at the foot of the steep bank at Birdoswald has seemed for many Arthurians the perfect setting for Arthur's last great battle. The romantic back-drop was the perfect film-set for Arthur's death at the hands of his treacherous step-son Medraut or Mordred. More recent archaeological evidence has suggested that Birdoswald was not Camboglanna. The name belongs to the fort of Castlesteads, which lies further to the west in a far less transcendently romantic situation.

One of the earliest Welsh poems, *Y Gododdin*, by the bard Aneirin, is an elegy for the men of the north who fell at Catraeth. The poem, a magnificent, heroic lament, tells how a band of 360 warriors set out from Edinburgh to meet the Angles of Bernicia and Deira, approximately the areas of Yorkshire and Durham today, at Catraeth, sometime around 595. Appropriately Catraeth may well have been Catterick, for long one of the country's major army camps. Certainly Catraeth was in the vicinity, possibly at Richmond, in an area that held the key to the overlordship of the north. The position commanded the route north to Northumbria and the British tribes of Lothian and the route to the Stainmore Gap, which afforded an accessible route across the Pennines and north through the Kingdom of Rheged.

This long poem, in its extant versions, is much changed and confused by multiple copyings over the centuries. It is most readily summed-up by an extract translated and adapted in the eighteenth century by that scholarly, meditative poet, Thomas Gray. He was possessed of an exceptional sympathy with the bardic power of Wales and the wild otherness of the Cumbrian landscape.

> *To Catraeth's vale in glittering row*
> *Twice two hundred warrior's go;*
> *Every warrior's manly neck*
> *Chains of regal honour deck,*
> *Wreath'd in many a golden link:*
> *From the golden cup they drink*
> *Nectar, that the bees produce,*
> *Or the grape's ecstatic juice.*
> *Flush'd with mirth and hope they burn:*
> *But none from Catraeth's vale return,*
> *Save Aeron brave, and Conan strong,*
> *(Bursting through the bloody throng)*
> *And I, the meanest of them all,*
> *That live to weep and sing their fall.*

Despite their heroism, all except three, (or perhaps one, the bard) were killed. The defeat was a crucial moment in the process by which the native British tribes were pushed increasingly further to the west.

The poem, more than any other work, indicates the intense heroic values of the society. The male camaraderie, the ecstasy of battle, the courage that knows no physical fear, the lust for enemy blood and the desperate sense of loss and tragedy at the death of one's fellow warriors make the men of Catraeth take on the role of immortals. These values, the simplified, abstracted ideals of a passionate male heroism, possessed a peculiar justificatory force for a beleaguered and defeated nation. Their very intensity gave them an extra-ordinary mythical power. They are ideals that persisted over the centuries to play their role in the developing mythology of Arthur and the more sophisticated values of chivalry.

The poem was probably written near the time of the battle. Aneirin may well, in his young days, have known men who had known Arthur. *Y Gododdin* offers what is probably the earliest specific reference to Arthur, in a passing comparison to one of the defeated warriors:

> *He glutted black ravens on the rampart of the city*
> *Though he was not Arthur.*

The legend of Arthur was sufficiently powerful sixty years after his death for his name to have immediate and unqualified recognition as the greatest of warriors. That is, if the comparison with Arthur is not an interpolation by a later scribe.

The poem also provides the first mention of Peredur, who may have been a king of York, but who, through the processes of time and imagination, was transformed into the innocent Sir Perceval of the Grail legend and, eventually, into the Parsifal of German legend and Wagnerian opera. The men who went to Catraeth, we are told, were drunk on their lord's distilled mead and paid for their drink with their lives. They included *Peredur of the steel weapons*. When Perceval is first found as a peasant boy in the woods of Gwynedd, he equips himself with a rusty sword.

Taliesin was a near contemporary of Aneirin. Aneirin was attached to the the court of Mynyddawg Mwynvawr in Dineidin, which is still the way the Welsh refer to Edinburgh. Taliesin was the bard at the court of Urien, King of Rheged. This court may have been held in Carlisle, or in the Valley of the Lyvennet, near Crosby Ravensworth, or at Dun Reged, near Stranraer, in the extreme west of Galloway. Urien's own name may be a form of the Latin Urbgen, indicating that he might have been born in a city, which might be Carlisle.

In the earliest surviving manuscript, *Y Llyfr Taliesin*, that is *The Book of Taliesin*, there are twelve poems among the fifty-eight, that may have originated in the sixth century. They lavish praise on the heroic deeds of Urien and his son Owain in their battles against Deodric, King of Bernicia, and against a certain Hussa. This is poetry that would delight a Border reiver: stories of raids into enemy territory and the burning of homesteads and the carrying off of booty. It is perhaps not fanciful to sense a continuity between the lives and values and literature of these early British heroes and the outlaws, who were so vigorously celebrated in the ballads that Walter Scott collected in his *Border Minstrelsy*.

The poetry praises Urien's largesse towards his friends and his unremitting ferocity towards his enemies. He is (in Gwyn Williams's translation):

> *the most generous of Christians . .*
> *He is the outstanding, the supreme chieftain,*
> *refuge of the stranger, foremost in battle.*

The English are fully aware of this:

> *death they have suffered and frequent pain,*
> *their houses burnt, their garments taken.*

One stanza from the poem, *Marwnat Uthyr Pendragon,* that is, *The Death of Uther Pendragon*, gives some idea of their sheer heroic blood-thirstiness. In English it reads:

> *I have broken a hundred forts,*
> *I have killed a hundred seneschals,*
> *I have given a hundred garments,*
> *I have cut off a hundred heads.*

In the original Welsh the brutality is made to appear cultivated, but is certainly not redeemed, by the high level of artistry. The quatrain is formed from strongly rhythmic parallel phrases that employ both end-rhyme and internal rhyme.

> *Nei vi a torreis cant kaer.*
> *neu vi aledeis cant maer.*
> *Neu vi arodeis cant llen.*
> *Neu vi aledeis cant pen.*

At a later time, Uther Pendragon is seen as Arthur's father and is strongly associated with Cornwall. It is interesting to note that he was celebrated by a bard in a northern court.

There is, possibly, a third poet who belongs with the men of the North. *Gwyr y Gogledd*, the men of the North, is a phrase that has echoed down the ages expressing the deep sense of racial loss as communities were separated and then destroyed. This poet is Llywarch Hen, Llywarch the Old. He may have been a chieftain in Rheged, but in later life he was a witness to much suffering during the relentless struggle with the forces of Mercia in Powys. His name is attached to poetry that is most probably from later centuries, but which, perhaps, retains a vestige of his original work. One poem laments the death of Urien, and describes his feelings as he carries the king's head away from the battlefield:

> *My arm shakes, my breast trembles,*
> *my heart breaks.*
> *I carry a head by which I was fed.*

The poetry of Aneirin and Taliesin can with some justice take pride in being the earliest known poetry in any modern European language. Welsh is no longer spoken in Cumbria, but the county's earliest, great poets rhymed in the Welsh or Cumbric, as some would now call it, of the old North, and not in English.

The existence of Owain ap Urien is adequately recorded and his historical existence is not doubted. The name is the Welsh equivalent of Eugenus or Eugene, meaning well-born. He is probably the pre-cursor of the Owain of later Welsh legend, as found in the *Mabinogion,* and of the Yvain or Ywain of French and

English Arthurian romances. One of Chretien de Troyes's most celebrated romances tells the story of *Ywain or the Knight and the Lion.*

Several other Arthurian characters have left a possible historical or literary trace among the men of the old north.

A medieval Welsh poem *Afallennau* depicts Myrddin, who tells us that for ten and forty years,

> *. . . in the wretchedness of outlawry*
> *I have been wandering with madness and madmen.. . .*
> *After enduring sickness and grief in the Forest of Celyddon*
> *May I be received into bliss by the Lord of Hosts.*

Myrddin has worn a golden torque in the battle of Arferydd. His words are confused, but he talks of having slain the son and daughter of Gwenddyd and of having fought in the battle of Arfderydd.

A Scottish *Life of St Kentigern* tells of a homo fatuus, or madman, called Laloecen who was attached to the court of King Rederech in Strathclyde. A later manuscript talks of St Kentigern meeting *a naked hairy madman named Lailoken, said by some to have been Merlin (Merlynum).* He says that he has been the cause of the deaths of the people slain on the plain between Liddel and Carwannock

Out of this confusion of madmen and incidents a line in the development of the myth of Merlin might be extracted: a madman called Lailoken, who served Rederech, fled from the battle of Arthuret and lived in the Caledonian forest for many years. The legend became part of Welsh mythology and Lailoken acquired the name of Myrddin taken from the town Caerfyrddin, modern day Caermarthen. The word *myrddin* (mutated to *fyrddin* in the place name) means sea-fort. The legend developed and was transformed to become Geoffrey of Monmouth's prophetic Merlin, the magician of Arthur's court. In the process the name was changed from Myrddin to Merlin, when it entered the French language, to avoid its unfortunate chiming with *merde*, a not very desirable name for a magician, or, indeed, for anyone else.

The whole complex process of transmission and transformation points to one of the sources of the Merlin figure among the people of Strathclyde.

The Battle of Arfderydd was fought in 573 at Arthuret, ten miles to the north of Carlisle. The name Arthuret has naturally tempted people to see a connection with King Arthur. However, the earliest form of the name in the *Annales Cumbriae* in the twelfth century was *bellum armterid*. It is found later as the Welsh *gueith arywderit*. It is probable that the first part of the name, the *art* or *arf*, means place. The second defies easy explanation, though it is possibly the old word *terydd*. The meaning of *terydd* is unclear, but it is a word usually used in medieval Welsh to describe fire. One very appropriate use, which evokes the terrors of the battle itself, is by Taliesin, where he employs it to describe the cries of the damned on their way to hell.

The battle of Arfderydd was not against the invading Angles, but was, apparently, a very bloody incident in a civil war among the British tribes. The *Annales Cambriae* records the battle as being between Gwenddoleu ap Ceidio and his nephews, the sons of his uncle Elifer. This same Gwenddoleu might be remembered in the name of a nearby farm known as Carwinley, which might consist of the words *car* or *caer* for fort and a much-altered form of Gwenddoleu. In such a way, events that are long past and forgotten have left their trace on the landscape of today.

We have little idea of the extent of the Kingdom of Rheged, either geographically of chronologically. Speculative place-name evidence might suggest that it stretched from the west of Galloway, where there is an old fort named Dunregit, as far as present-day Rochdale. This would be an exceptionally large political unit for a time when central authority had disappeared, the economy had collapsed and an effective network of roads was falling into disrepair. There was a strong sense of tribal loyalty among the Britons, which often resulted in conflict. It is possible that there was such a sizeable kingdom unified about the Merin Reged, the Rheged Sea, (possibly the Solway Firth) referred to by Taliesin. It is also possible that the Kingdom of Rheged was confined to a small area in western Galloway about Dunregit. The tribal divisions as they were known to exist in Roman times would not have provided a basis for such an extended kingdom. The tribe in the Carlisle area were known as the Carvetii, or the people of the deer.

We can assume that the Kingdom of Rheged developed sometime after the departure of the Romans in 370. Its development might have co-incided with Urien's presence at the Battle of Cartraeth and its demise was marked by the marriage of Urien's great grand-daughter, Rhienmelth, to Oswiu of Northumbria in 632.

There is no evidence for Carlisle playing any part in the kingdom. However, Carlisle was, or had been, by far the most considerable place in the region. Its size indicates that it may have been the military command centre for the Roman Wall. It had supported two cavalry regiments, one probably on the site of the present castle and the other, the 1000 strong Ala Petriana, across the river in Petriana, which lies beneath the streets of Stanwix. There may have been a stone built forum, near Tullie House, and there were certainly some impressive houses as well as many crowded smaller dwellings. Archaeologists suggest that there may have been crowded tenements for retired soldiers in Blackfriars Street. Small workshops have been found along the line of Botchergate and there is evidence of there having been, at some time during the Roman period, gem-making, wood-turning and pottery-making within the city. The very fine tombstones found at Murrell Hill and elsewhere, and the altar found in the castle, suggest that there may well have been a local school of sculptors. Luguvalium appears to have been a busy, prosperous centre in an area that lacked the high level of civilization found in the south of the country. In Roman times, Carlisle probably had a population of between three and four thousand. This was a population larger than it was to have at any time in the succeeding millennium. A milestone found in Middleton in Lonsdale indicates that the city of the Carvetii was 53 miles distant. Carlisle was this *Civitas Carvetiorum*.

After the Romans left, the roof was allowed to fall in on the barracks. However, the fort continued to be used as there is clear evidence of a timber building constructed in the centre of the fort.

The Venerable Bede writes that St Cuthbert *came to the town of Lugubalia, which the English people corruptly call Luel, to speak to the queen who had arranged to wait the issue of the war there in her sister's monastery. On the next day, when the citizens were conducting him to see the walls of the city and the marvellously constructed fountain of Roman workmanship, he was suddenly troubled in spirit.* The walls and the fountain must have been of exceptional note for Bede to mention the citizens' desire to show them to St Cuthbert. No trace has been found of walls about the city, but there were stone walls around the fort. An aqueduct ran along Botchergate and may have led to the baths, which were on the site of the present market or to the fort where there was a sophisticated network of pipes and drains. The monastery must have been in existence in 685 and, with its royal connections, was of some importance.

Carlisle had a sufficient post-Roman presence for it to have retained a place in the mythic imagination alongside the ancient stones of Caerleon, Chester and York.

Geoffrey of Monmouth: the Fiction of History

Geoffrey of Monmouth completed the *Historia Regum Britanniae*, his *History of the Kings of Britain*, in 1138. He is the principal fount of all the Arthurian literature that has followed over almost a millennium. He wrote in a clear and artistic medieval Latin which, influenced by the vernacular languages of his day and being used as the language of learning, lacked both the formal elegance of classical Latin and the naturalness of a native tongue.

However, his influential essay in highly romantic history was a popular and literary triumph. Even today, when we are fortunate if one manuscript of a medieval work survives, there are almost two hundred copies of Geoffrey's imaginative history in existence. It is a fair testament to the success of the work.

As always, very little is known about the author and what we do know comes largely from references he makes to himself in his writing. Geoffrey wrote two other closely related books: *Prophetiae Merlini* (*The Prophecies of Merlin*) in 1135, and a *Vita Merlini* (*Life of Merlin*) in 1150. He styled himself *Gaufridus Monemutensis* and his knowledge of the Monmouth area and in particular Caerleon on Usk - he refers to the city thirteen times - suggests a close acquaintance with the district.

Geoffrey's *History* is very far from what we would recognize as history. It is an amazing amalgam of received information from the *Bible* and classic authors and the surviving works of earlier writers such as Nennius, Bede and Gildas and much else of which we now have no other record. He writes in his dedication that: *These deeds were passed joyfully down in oral tradition, just as if they had been committed to writing, by many peoples who had only their memory to rely on.*

He also tells, somewhat ambiguously and intriguingly, of an ancient book written in the British language:

At a time when I was giving a good deal of attention to such matters, Walter, Archdeacon of Oxford, a man skilled in the art of public speaking and well-informed about the history of foreign countries, presented me with a certain very ancient book written in the British language. This book, attractively composed to form a consecutive and orderly narrative, set out all the deeds of these men, from Brutus, the first King of the Britons, down to Cadwallader, the son of Cadwallo. At Walter's request I have taken the trouble to translate the book into Latin, although, indeed, I have been content with my own expressions and my own homely style and I have gathered no gaudy flowers of speech in other men's gardens. If I had adorned my page with high-flown rhetorical figures, I should have bored my readers, for they would have been forced to spend more time in discovering the meaning of my words than in following the story.

Geoffrey leaves us uncertain about the existence of the ancient book. He has felt free to 'translate' it very much into his own idiom and he seems to suggest that he has also incorporated material from other sources, both written and oral, and he appears to give precedence and authority to the learning of his friend Walter. The 'ancient book', if it ever existed, an ur-source of Arthuriana, has never been identified.

Geoffrey's *History* is a wonderful creation. His book begins with the founding of Britain by Brutus on his flight from Troy. His imaginative etymological link of Brutus and Britain is sufficient historical justification. The parallel with Virgil's Aeneas and the founding of Rome provides the weighty resonance and the flattering historical parallels that Geoffrey required.

His account of the history proceeds readily through a succession of kings and founding of cities set within a wider chronology of biblical and classical history.

However, when he comes to Arthur, the narrative expands to accommodate the magnificence of Geoffrey's hero. The story, that he builds on whatever small basis of received fact, laid the foundation for the extended edifice of Arthurian romance.

Arthur was conceived when Uther Pendragon, disguised as her husband through Merlin's magic, slept with Ygerne immediately after her husband has been killed by Uther's soldiers. Uther returned to Ygerne in the impregnable Tintagel castle and the two fell deeply in love and married.

The land was laid waste by the Saxons. The aging Uther won many victories and his enemies eventually resorted to poison. The fifteen-year-old Arthur led his troops to victory at the battle of the River Douglas. Forces from Brittany supported Arthur in defeating an augmented Saxon army at Lincoln. They were pursued to Scotland and vanquished in the battle of Calidon Wood, surrendered their treasure and agreed to become tribute to Arthur.

Treacherously the Saxons sailed away only to land at Totnes and ravage the South-west. Arthur, armed with his shield, Pridwen, which bore an image of the Virgin Mary, and his spear, Ron, defeated them at a strenuous battle on a hill near Bath. With his matchless sword Caliburn, Arthur accounted for four hundred and seventy single-handedly. He immediately went north, battling the Scots and the Picts from Moray to Loch Lomond and cutting their allies, the Irish, to pieces. Then he rebuilt York, and, finally, when he had restored the whole country to its earlier dignity, Arthur married a woman called Guinevere.

The next summer he set sail and conquered Ireland and Iceland. Gotland and the Orkneys promised tribute. He returned home and lived in peace for twelve years. The courtly, generous Arthur was famed and feared throughout the world for his bravery.

He sought to conquer all of Europe. He defeated Norway and Denmark and laid Gaul waste. He slew Frollo, Gaul's gigantic leader, in single combat with a blow that clove his head in two. He spent nine years subduing the whole country and then returned to Britain.

He now determined to call a plenary court at the City of the Legions, Caerleon. All came to honour Arthur at his coronation and marvelled at the wealth and sophistication of his court.

In the midst of the feasting, twelve envoys came from the Emperor, Lucius Hiberius, in Rome. They demanded that Arthur pay him tribute and submit to him for punishment for the damage he had done to Roman lands. At a council of war, all dedicated themselves enthusiastically to Arthur's cause and promised an army of one hundred and eighty three thousand, three hundred men ready to assemble at Barfleur and to march to meet Lucius.

When the envoys returned to Rome, Lucius called an army from throughout the Middle East and set out for Britain in the beginning of August. Arthur left Britain in the hands of his nephew, Mordred, and Guinevere and set sail from Southampton. That night he dreamt of a fierce fight between a dragon and a bear.

News was brought that a voracious giant was terrifying the country about Mont St Michel. Arthur met this monstrous man in single combat and, after the fiercest of encounters, he cut him through the brain with his sword.

Gawain was sent with an envoy to Lucius, but, being too eager for a fight, he responded readily to provocation and there was a fierce running skirmish. The Romans were led into an ambush, but, freshly re-inforced and well-disciplined, they were beating the British until Boso led a new assault with the utmost commitment. The Roman army were looted and slaughtered, apart from a small number who were kept as hostages to take to Arthur. The party of Britons taking the hostages to prison in Paris beat off an ambush by a large Roman contingent.

Lucius retreated but Arthur out-marched him and drew up his troops in battle formation in the Sauusy valley. Both leaders courageously exhorted their men before the battle.

The two armies clashed in the fiercest of combats. Fortunes wavered, but, eventually, through Arthur's heroic, savage example, and after much bloodshed, victory was to the Britons.

The British heroes were buried accordingly. Arthur instructed local villagers to bury the Roman dead and he sent the body of Lucius back to the Roman Senate, saying that that was the only tribute they could expect from him.

After wintering in France, Arthur prepared to march on Rome, when news came that Mordred had usurped his crown and bed and was living adulterously with Guinevere as his queen. He prepared to return immediately.

Mordred had leagued himself with the Saxons, the Picts, the Scots and the Irish. The armies met at Richborough. Gawain and many of Arthur's men were killed, but through superior discipline and skill in arms, Arthur was the victor and Mordred re-grouped at Winchester. Guinevere, who was at York, hearing of this, entered a nunnery. A fearsome battle followed at Winchester where there was immense slaughter on both sides. Mordred fled yet again to Cornwall. In bitter anguish at his losses, Arthur pursued him to the River Camlam.

In the battle that followed, in the midst of the thickest and most savage fighting, Mordred was killed and Arthur was mortally wounded. Arthur was carried off to the Isle of Avalon that his wounds might be tended. He bestowed the crown of Britain on the head of Constantine in the year 542 after our Lord's Incarnation.

Briefly told, that is the sum of Arthur's history as presented by Geoffrey. What my synopsis doesn't show is the enthusiasm and relish with which he writes about Arthur's fight with the giant and the succeeding battles. Suddenly, Geoffrey's long chronology of historical facts leaps into life. Here is an epic hero of courage, might and fortitude to compare with those of classical antiquity. It was no wonder that his contemporaries were so excited by his work. What had once been unknown or vague was now made extraordinarily vivid.

Throughout the centuries historians have scoffed at Geoffrey's history, even though kings and other politicians found that insisting on its veracity, particularly the evidence for the conquest of Scotland, gave legitimacy to their territorial claims. William of Newburgh, writing in 1190, some forty years after Geoffrey's death, felt no respect for his fellow historian: *It is quite clear that everything this man wrote about Arthur and his successors, or indeed about his predecessors from Vortigern onwards, was made up, partly by himself and partly by others, either from an inordinate love of lying, or for the sake of pleasing the Britons.*

The charge of inordinate love of lying seems misplaced, but the idea of the work as propaganda is not. Geoffrey probably had Celtic antecedents, either Welsh or Breton. His father was called Arthur and he styled himself using the Welsh form, Geoffrey ap Arthur. Bretons, who had accompanied the Normans, had settled in Monmouth. He dedicated the work to Robert, Earl of Gloucester, who was the natural son of Henry I. *The History*, by demonstrating the heroism and martial abilities of the Britons, would serve to glorify Geoffrey's own race that had been defeated and dispossessed by the Anglo-Saxons, and, since many Britons had fled to Armorica and caused it to be renamed Brittany, it would lend a kind of pseudo-legitimacy to the neighbouring Normans and their conquest of England. I suspect that insofar as the work disparaged the native English, it pleased their Norman overlords.

The interesting question is not so much the truth of Geoffrey's *History* as the extent to which he and his contempories felt it to be true. He authenticated his facts by reference to etymology, a favourite device of the time, which was felt to have almost talismanic properties. Thus the name Britain serves to verify the nation's descent from Troy's Brutus and the name London, once Caer Lud, confirms the existence of a worthy King Lud and Leicester that of a King Lear. He makes constant cross references to events and personages in the Bible and Classical history, and makes appeals to various sources.

His one reference to Carlisle in the *History* demonstrates the style of argument very clearly:

Leil, the son of Greenshield, a great lover of peace and justice, succeeded him. Leil took advantage of the prosperity of his reign to build a town in the northern part of Britain which he called Kaerleil (Carlisle) after himself.

This was the time that Solomon began to build the Temple of the Lord in Jerusalem and when the Queen of Sheba came to listen to his wisdom. About this time Silvius Epitus succeeded his father Alba in the kingship of Rome.

Geoffrey's suppositions lie on the page with the same weight as the received knowledge of the other great civilizations of the ancient world and their authority is transferred to his intuitions, speculations and inventions.

He also seeks authority through his remarkable, almost eye-witness, detail. Caerleon, for instance, which he seems to have known very well, is described with the patriotic and parochial pride of a native:

Situated as it is in Glamorganshire; on the River Usk, not far from the Severn Sea, in a most pleasant position, and being richer in material wealth than other townships, this city was eminently suitable for such a ceremony. The river which I have named flowed by it on one side, and up this the kings and princes who were to come from across the sea could be carried in a fleet of ships. On the other side, which was flanked by meadows and wooded groves, they had adorned the city with royal palaces, and by the gold-painted gables of its roofs it was a match for Rome. What is more, it was famous for its two churches. One of these, built in honour of the martyr Julius, was graced by a choir of most lovely virgins dedicated to God.

The second, founded in the name of the blessed Aaron, the companion of Julius, was served by a monastery of canons, and counted as the third metropolitan see of Britain. The city also contained a college of two hundred learned men, who were skilled in astronomy and the other arts, and who watched with great attention the courses of the stars and so by their careful computations prophesied for King Arthur any prodigies due at that time.

It was this city, therefore, famous for such a wealth of pleasant things, which was made ready for the feast.

The feast, which was being made ready, was the one, that was interrupted by the senators from Rome demanding tribute, that became a set-piece in many of the later chronicles of Arthur.

The passage glows with Geoffrey's pride in the presumed antique fame and splendour of his city of the legions. He is prepared to quietly elide over awkward facts in order to build the bigger picture, which accords with the sweep of his sympathies and ambitions.

Geoffrey was writing a history of a time and a place, the Britons in Britain in the years before and after the Romans, for which we today have little or no evidence, and he was seeking to construct a convincing story out of the fragments of written and oral information available to him. He had none of the scruples of the evidence-based historian, but he did have a superlative eye-of-the-imagination. His history may appear to us today, as it did to William of Newburgh, as lies and fabrication, but for Geoffrey and many of his contempories it offered the enticing possibility of a glorious near-truth.

And if its value is measured by the number of great works which are deeply in its debt, then very few books can lay claim to such a rich legacy. Shakespeare's *King Lear* and *Cymbeline*, Edmund Spenser's *The Fairie Queen* and the limitless world of Arthur from Chretien de Troyes and Marie de France through the Middle Ages to Malory and on to Dryden, Tennyson and their multifarious contemporary representatives. All are descended from Geoffrey.

In 1155 Robert Wace, a cleric from the island of Jersey, living in Caen in Normandy, wrote an adaptation cum translation of Geoffrey's *History* in Norman-French verse. It kept Geoffrey's work much as it was, but emphasized the courtly personal details rather than the martial, lending it a far more romantic air. It was known as the *Roman de Brut* and had a considerable influence on the development of the Matter of Britain, as the Arthurian stories were called, in French literature.

A further version, this time in English, based on Wace's work, was written sometime in the early thirteenth century by an obscure country monk living in the Severn valley in Worcestershire. Layamon's *Brut* extended to 30,000 lines and was twice the length of Wace's. It was written in an alliterative verse that recalled the poetry of the Anglo-Saxons. Layamon relished the battle scenes and produced a poem that was vivid and heroic and far removed from the courtliness of Wace.

Robert Wace's is the first work to make mention of the Round Table, although it is probable that the idea came from the stories of the Breton minstrels. Layamon elaborates the idea of Arthur in Avalon and introduces a faery world.

The geography of the two versions is very much as it was in Geoffrey's History with Arthur holding his court in Caerleon.

Marie de France
and the Enchantment of Romance

One of the earliest French Arthurian romances is *Lanval.* It is among the most celebrated of medieval stories. It was written by Marie de France in the latter part of the twelfth century. It is a delightful tale, poised between the real and the faery world, perfectly shaped and told in the concise teasing French of a very bright, sharp lady.

Marie insists that she will tell us the tale just as it happened. As in her eleven other extant tales, she insists on her Breton sources: the hero was called Lanval in Breton.

The story is set in the court of King Arthur in *Kardoel*, a medieval French form of Carlisle. Unusually, she supplies specific, circumstantial detail. The name does not appear to be arbitrary.

Arthur was in Carlisle because the Scots and Picts were ravaging the country and laying it waste. It was a borderland where the peace and stability that the wise and courtly king had brought to his kingdom were threatened. The time was Pentecost, when the gift of the Holy Spirit was celebrated, in the days of early summer.

Arthur was apportioning gifts and land and, even, wives to his favoured counts, barons and knights of the Round Table. It was a time of generosity and largesse, and of self-congratulation as the worthiest company in the world. Only Lanval was excluded. He was a foreigner. His father was king of a distant land, and he had spent all his substance. Arthur failed to remember him. Lanval's valour, generosity and beauty were a source of envy and none of those who were supposed to esteem him spoke up on his behalf. The worthy company of the Round Table was not as perfect as it seemed.

The penniless, friendless Sir Lanval rode out of the city into the countryside. He stopped in a meadow, by a stream. His horse trembled violently. Lanval freed its saddle and the horse rolled on its back in the grass. Lanval took his cloak and folded it for a pillow and lay down beside the stream. Two maidens were walking towards him. They were richly dressed in close fitting tunics of dark purple. One carried a finely-wrought, golden bowl and the other a towel. Both maidens were extraordinarily beautiful.

The well-mannered Lanval rose to greet them. They invited him by name to attend upon their lady, a damsel who was most worthy, wise and fair and who was to be found in a tent nearby.

This tent was so beautiful and costly that it defied all description. Queen Semiramis at the height of her wealth and power or the Emperor Octavian would not have been able to afford even its right-hand panel. The eagle of gold that was on the top of the pavilion and the poles and the guy-ropes were beyond value.

Inside was a lady beyond compare. She surpassed the lily and the newly-born summer rose. She was clad only in a shift. She lay on coverlets that themselves were the value of a castle. They were spread on a bed of exceptional beauty. Her body was finely formed and delicate. To shade herself from the heat of the sun she had a mantle of white ermine edged with purple from Alexandria. Her side was uncovered, Her face, her neck and her breasts were bare. She was whiter than the flower of May.

"Lanval," she said, "I have come from my country for you." No-one will feel such joy or happiness as he will because she loves him more than anyone else. Lanval, in chivalrous fashion, desired her love. She granted him her love and her body and promised him that he should have all that he desired: that should his purse be empty it should be immediately replenished. The more he spent, the more he would have. However, if ever he should reveal his love, all would be lost.

Lanval remained with the lady until evening, and then she told him to depart, but promised that, whenever he was alone and in a private place, she would appear to do as he should desire.

He was dressed in the richest of raiments and then dined with his lady and feasted on her lips.

He returned to Carlisle. Wealth was his. He clothed the poor and feted the rich. And day or night, whenever he desired, his lady would come to him. It seemed too good to be true.

Several weeks later, on St John's Day, in late June, thirty knights were taking their ease in the gardens beneath the queen's tower. Sir Gawain, regretting their neglect of the courteous and generous Sir Lanval, invited him to join them.

The Queen, sitting at her window, observed Lanval's welcome. With thirty of her most beautiful ladies she joined the knights in the garden. They held hands, walked about the garden and conversed in a manner that was not uncourtly.

Lanval longed for the presence of his beloved and retreated to a quiet corner. He wanted to touch her, to kiss her, to embrace her.

The Queen saw the knight by himself. She came straight up to him and sat down beside him. She spoke: "Lanval, I honour, cherish and love you. Tell me all you desire. I offer you my love. You should be pleased to have me."

"My lady, leave me alone," said Lanval. "I do not want your love. I have long served the king. I will not betray him."

The Queen was angry, wild and spoke viciously: "Lanval," she said, "I have been told that you do not like this sort of pleasure. You have no desire for women. You enjoy the company of well-bred young men." She even suggested that Arthur might have sinned with him.

Lanval was angry. He replied immediately. He was not a homosexual. He loved a lady and she loved him. She was more beautiful than any other. Even her poorest serving maid was worth more in beauty, wisdom and honesty than the Queen.

The Queen felt humiliated and rushed in tears to her chamber. She took to her bed and swore: "Never will I rise unless the king rights the wrong that has been done to me."

The king returned, well pleased with his hunting. The Queen fell at his feet, said that Lanval had shamed her, had claimed that even his chambermaid was worthier than she. Arthur was angry and swore that either Lanval would defend himself in court or else he would be burned or hanged.

Three barons were summoned to fetch Lanval. He was in his chamber. He was distraught: by revealing his love, he had lost her.

Facing the angry king, Lanval denied, point by point, each of the charges. He had not sought the Queen's love, but he did acknowledge his boast and insisted on its truth. He said he would accept the court's judgement. Arthur called his knights together to ensure fairness. A day was fixed for the trial and the accused was bailed on a surety from Sir Gawain. Lanval stayed in his lodgings and his friends were concerned for his state of mind and urged him to give up his love.

He was brought to court on the appointed day. He had the silent support of many of the knights who were aware of the real state of affairs. The king demanded the verdict from the barons. The Count of Cornwall proposed that, unless Lanval provide the evidence for his statement that had so upset the Queen, he should be banished. Lanval could not.

Just as the barons were about to pronounce their verdict, two maidens were seen approaching, gently ambling along on two fine palfreys. They were very beautiful and were dressed in purple taffeta, which they wore next to their bare flesh. The knights were pleased to see them. Gawain urged Lanval to respond, but he did not recognize the maidens. They dismounted before King Arthur's dais. Courteously, they commanded Arthur to make ready a chamber and hang it with silken curtains for their lady. The chamber was to be made ready and the maidens were led away.

Arthur was increasingly impatient, but the barons, having seen the maidens, were not ready to reach a verdict.

As they continued with the trial, two finely dressed ladies approached along the street. They were attired in Phrygian silk and rode on Spanish mules. Surely Lanval was saved. Ywain appealed to him to acknowledge his lady, but Lanval said he did not know either nor did he love them.

They dismounted before the king and many admired their bodies, faces and complexions. They were both worth far more than the Queen had ever been. They also asked for lodging for their lady.

Impatiently, Arthur again asked the barons for their verdict. The Queen was becoming increasingly angry.

They were on the point of giving their verdict when, through the town, a maiden came riding on horseback. There had never been anyone so beautiful. She rode a white palfrey. The horse, that carried her with such elegance and grace, was the finest animal on earth. The lady wore a tunic of white linen that was laced to reveal her sides. Her body was fair, her hips low, her neck was whiter than fresh snow on a branch. Her eyes were bright, her face white, her mouth bountiful, her nose well-shaped; her eyes were brown and her brow beautiful. Her hair was curled and fair and shone far brighter than the sunlight reflected from golden threads. Her dark, silken cloak was draped over her legs. On her wrist she bore a sparrowhawk and a greyhound paced behind her.

All, thrilled by her beauty, watched in silence as she slowly approached the judges. Lanval was told of the lady. He raised his head. The blood rushed to his face. "It is my love. If she shows no mercy, I care not if I live or die. My cure is in seeing her." No-one so beautiful had been seen there before. The lady dismounted before the judges. She let her cloak fall to reveal her full figure.

The king rose to greet her. All honoured her and praised her beauty. "King," she said, "I have loved your vassal, Lanval. The Queen is wrong. He never sought her love. If he can be freed by me, let your barons release him."

The king agreed to accept the judges's verdict. All agreed that Lanval had successfully defended himself. He was freed.

The maiden left. Lanval climbed onto the marble mounting block by the gate. As the lady rode past, Lanval leapt on the palfrey behind her and they rode away to Avalon.

My abbreviated account does little to show the exquisite beauty of this tale.

Its 646 lines are in rhyming couplets with eight syllables to each line. This is a very difficult form to maintain without the rhyming and the cadences becoming repetitive and irritating. Neither is it easy to keep a tight focus on the narrative and avoid introducing extraneous details for the sake of the form.

Marie succeeds magnificently. Even in the introductory lines, where she is locating the story in Carlisle with the worthy and courteous Arthur when the country is being destroyed by the Scots and the Picts:

a Kardoel surjurunot li reis,
Artur, li purz e li curteis,
pur les Escoz e pur les Pis,
que destruient le païs:

her rhyming is natural and weighted to meaning and a pointed contrast is made between the civilized Arthur and his destructive enemies. We are ushered into an apparently urbane courtly world of good manners and wealthy ease. This graciousness is a cover to the viciousness of the queen and the potential injustice of Arthur.

Similarly, in describing how, inside the tent was the maiden: the flower of the lily or the rose when it first appears in early summer touched her beauty:

dedenz cel tref fu la pucele:
flur de lis [e] rose nuvele,
quant ele pert al tens d'esté,
trespassot ele de beauté.

the rhyming of maiden and new rose and summer and beauty are enticingly appropriate.

Marie's language has a descriptive precision and a teasing awareness of playing with the ideal that creates a sensuous clarity. There is a controlled eroticism in the account of wealth and materials and in the evocation of beauty which makes a strong contrast with the social reality of the mean-minded and vicious court.

The structure of the narrative defies criticism. The scene is rapidly and evocatively set with poetic economy. The action moves forward rapidly and each scene is measured and emerges naturally from its predecessor. The meeting with the lady, the parallel encounter with the queen, the queen's lies to Arthur and Lanval's failure to verify his love to the court and, finally, the formal sequence, the procession of the ever more beautiful ladies, that results in the mounting ideal of beauty astounding the spiritual ugliness of the court.

Lanval is a finely polished jewel, an exquisite work of art, that is as perceptive as it is beautiful.

Breton lais were almost certainly sung to the accompaniment of the harp or rote, a primitive violin. *Lanval*, a piece the length of 650 lines, one might imagine providing thirty to sixty minutes of charming entertainment. Needless to say, we have no knowledge of the music or its manner of interpretation.

We know nothing about Marie de France apart from the little she reveals of herself in her work. She tells us she is Marie and from France. She is the author of the thirteen *Lais,* which have been translated from the Breton, and has also translated fables from English and *A Purgatory of St Patrick* from Latin and she may also have compiled a life of St Audrey.

She may have been attached to the court of Henry II. One speculation is that she was the illegitimate daughter of Geoffrey of Plantagenet, which would have made her half-sister to Henry II. If this is the case, this astute, sharp, worldly lady was Abbess of Shaftesbury for 34 years from 1181 to 1215. Other possibilities picture her as Abbess of Reading, or as a Norman lady, either Marie, eighth child of Waleran de Meulan, or as Marie, Countess of Boulogne and daughter of King Stephen and Matilda of Boulogne.

She may have had some awareness of Carlisle. Henry had waged several campaigns against Scotland and had actually visited Carlisle on four recorded occasions.

If Marie chose to set the story in Carlisle, then we would expect such a consummate artist to have a keen sense of the narrative requirements of her location and select a place that had the requisite resonance with her audience.

Marie's story required a place that was on the periphery of her society's awareness, a place distant in miles and years, the equivalent of a romantic Samarkand or Shangri-La, in which the manners of her sophisticated court might be mirrored and exposed.

Of course, the city that she presents, despite its position in a war-zone, bears no comparison to the real city and in a tale like this, we would not expect any precise, circumstantial detail.

On the other hand, *Karduel* may simply be a given in the oral material that prompted her sophisticated re-working. Marie probably did not know the Breton language. In one of her *Lais* the title and the name of the hero is *Bisclaret.* This is supposedly from the Breton for *talking wolf.* The actual Breton words are *bleiz lauaret.* It is not the sort of mistake that someone with a facility in the language would make. This prompts the conjecture that she received the generality of her tales, rather than their detail, from her possible oral sources.

Breton trouveres did not confine themselves to the north-west of France. They appear to have accompanied the Norman knights throughout their travels, whether on crusades to the Middle East or settling on their estates in England. *Karduel* may have been one name associated with Arthur's court in their oral tradition or, far less probably, it may have been a name they appropriated during their time in England. *Kardoel* is the Norman-French version of the city's name rather than a Welsh form. Other names in the story are in their Breton form, including the name Lanval, which Marie says specifically is Breton. This may suggest that the story itself was taken from a Breton oral source, but that the name *Kardoel* was a later addition.

Whatever the reason for adopting one of the most unlikely cities in the country for this sunlit tale delicately poised between reality and faery, the imaginative concept of *Kardoel* would not have been in conflict with either the author's or her audience's awareness of this distant city, situated in a no-man's land on the edge of the kingdom.

What was, until recent years, the only generally available English version of Marie's *Lais*, the free and flowery Everyman translation by Eugene Masson, chose to set the story of Lanval in Caerleon.

Marie is well aware of British geography. Caerleon features in two lais. In a non-Arthurian story, *Milun*, a squire, on the instructions of his knight, Milun, nets a swan in the meadows near Caerleon. In *Yonec*, the dispossessing stepfather is beheaded by Yonec with his father's sword on his mother's death. This decisive event occurs at Caerleon during the feast of St. Aaron. We are told of a castle, *fairer than any other in the world*, inside of which was an abbey. Eliduc, in another lay, makes a voyage from Brittany to land in Totnes and finds himself caught in war-ravaged country around Exeter. Marie's other Arthurian lay, a brief poem of an illicit romantic encounter between Tristan and King Mark's queen, is set on the road to Tintagel, when Mark calls a gathering of his knights at Pentecost.

Lanval was translated into English, perhaps a hundred years later, in a version that was reasonably faithful, but, inevitably, lacked the delicacy of Marie's verse. Its title was *Landeval* and it begins, like *Lanval*, with Arthur holding court in Carlisle, although there is no mention of fighting against the Scots and the Picts.

> *Soothly by Arthur's day*
> *Was Britain in great nobleness,*
> *For in his time a great while*
> *He sojourned at Carlisle.*
> *He had with him a meyne there,*   household
> *As he had elsewhere,*
> *Of the round table the knightes all,*
> *With mirth and joy in his hall.*
> *Of each land in the world wide*
> *There came men on every side,*
> *Young knights and squires*
> *And other bold bachelors,*
> *For to see that nobly*

> *That was with Arthur all way;*
> *For rich gifts and treasure*
> *He gave to each man of honour.*

When the rejected Landeval rides off:

> *Then he taketh toward the west*
> *Between a water and a forest.*

The practical, pedestrian quality of the verse is well illustrated by the depiction of Landeval's despair:

> *"Alas! alas!" was his songe;*
> *Sore wepyng his hondis he wronge.*

After being led to the pavilion by the two maidens, he finds the lady equally enchanting. The poet's description has a certain awkward roughness to it and he blunders through Marie's tantalizing boundary between the real and the faery by telling us that the lady is from Avalon:

> *He found in that pavilion*
> *The king's daughter of Amylione,—*
> *That is an isle of the fairy*
> *In ocean full fair to see.*
> *There was a bead of much price,*
> *Covered with purple byse.*
> *There-on lay that maiden bright,*
> *Almost naked and up-right.*
> *All her clothes beside her lay,*
> *Singly was she wrapped parfay*
> *With a mantle of ermin, . . .*
> *She was white as lily in May*
> *Or snow that falleth on winterday.*
> *Blossom on briar nor no flower*
> *Was not like to her colour.*
> *The red rose when it is new*
> *To her rud is not of hue.*

After they embrace and Landeval prepares to leave, the lady makes her promise and utters her warning:

> *Spend largely on every man,*
> *I will find you enough then.*
> *And when ye will, gentle knight,*
> *Speak with me any night, . . .*
> *And think on me so and so.*

41

> *Anon to you shall I tee.*
> *Nor make ye never boast of me;*
> *And if thou doest, beware be-forn,*
> *For thou hast my love forlorn."*

As Landeval returns to become a success at court, and dances on the castle green, he finds himself the object of the queen's admiration:

> *"Yonder," she said, "is Landeval.*
> *Of all the knights that be here*
> *There is none so fair a bachelor.*
> *And he has neither leman nor wife,*
> *I would he loved me as his life.*
> *Tide me good or tide me ill,*
> *I will assay the knight's will."*

The queen is venomous in responding to Landeval's gentle rejection:

> *"Fie," said she, "thou foule coward,*
> *An harlot ribald I wot thou art.*
> *That thou livest it is pity.*
> *Thou lovest no woman nor no woman thee."*

The queen's false declaration to Arthur is dramatically portrayed:

> *The king came from hunting,*
> *Glad and blithe in all thing,*
> *And to the queen can he tee.*
> *Anon she fell upon her knee;*
> *Wonder loud can she cry:*
> *"A! help me, lord, or I die!*
> *I spake to Landeval on a game,*
> *And he be-shought me of shame,*
> *As a foul viced traitor;*
> *He would have done me dishonour.*
> *And of a leman boast he made,*
> *That worst maid that she had*
> *Might be a queen over me,—*
> *And all, lord, in despite of thee."*

The court proceedings are somewhat changed from Marie's more formal trial, which offers useful clues to court procedure during the reign of Henry II. Perhaps the anonymous author has adapted the story to the practice of his day. As the Duke of Cornwall and other knights were discussing how they might have Landeval's sentence reduced to banishment, they saw the maidens approaching.

> *While they stood thus speaking,*
> *They saw in fear come riding*
> *Two maidens white as flower,*
> *On white palfreys with honour;*

The knights continued to discuss the case when the next two maidens appeared:

> *These maidens rode in to the palace*
> *Right a-fore the king's dais*

And told him to prepare the hall to honour their lady. The queen was fearful that Landeval would be helped when his lady came, and in her guile:

> *She cried and said, "Lord and king,*
> *And thou lovest thine honour,*
> *I were a-venged on that traitor;*
> *To slay Landeval thou wouldest not spare.*
> *Thy barons do thee besmear."*
> *While she spake thus to the king,*
> *They saw where came riding*
> *A lady herself all alone,*
> *On earth fairer was never none,*
> *On a white palfrey comely.*

Her dress is precisely described:

> *Clothed she was in purple pall,*
> *Her body gentle and middle small.*
> *The pane of her mantle in-ward*
> *On her arms she folded outward,*
> *Which well became that lady.*
> *Through the city rode she,*
> *For every man should her see.*
> *Wife and child, young and old,*
> *All came her to behold.*
> *Also soon as Landeval her see,*
> *To all the lords he cried on he:*
> *"Now commeth my love, now commeth my sweet;*
> *Now commeth she my bail shall beat:*
> *Now I have her seen with mine eye,*
> *I nay reck when that I die."*
> *The damsel come riding stout*
> *Alone in the city throughout,*
> *Through the palace in to the hall,*

There was the king, the queen all.
Her four maidens with great honour
Against her came out of the bower,
And held her stirrups so;
The lady did a-light though,
And they gently can her greet,
And she him with words sweet. . . .
Than said the lady to the king:
"Sir, I come for such a thing,—
My true leman, Sir Landeval,
Is accused amongst you all
That he should with traitory
Beseech the queen of villainy.
That is false, by Saint James;
He bad her not, but she bad him.
And of that other that he said,
That my holiest maid
Was fairer than the queen,—
Look anon if it so bene."
The king beheld and saw the sooth,
Also earls and barons both,
Every lord said than
Landeval was a true man.
When the judgement given was,
At the king her leave she takes
And leapt upon hir palfrey . . .
Landeval saw his love would gone,
Upon her horse he leapt anon
And said, "Lady, my leman bright,
I will with thee, my sweet wight,
Whether ye ride or go,
Nor will I never part you from."
"Landeval," she said, "with-out let,
When we first together met . . .
I charged you in all your life
That ye of me never speak should;
How dare you now be so bold
With me to ride with-out leave? . .

"Lady," he said, "fair and good,
For his love that shed his blood,
For-give me that trespass
And put me whole in your grace."
Then that lady to him can speak,
And said to him with words meek:
"Landeval, leman, I you forgive.
That trespass while ye live.
Welcome to me, gentle knight;
We will never twyn day nor night."
So they rode even right,
The lady, the maidens, and the knight. . . .
And thus was Landeval brought from Carlisle,
With his fairy into a jolly isle,
That is clepped Amylyone,   *called Avalon*
That knoweth every Briton.
Of him since heard never man;
No further of Landeval tell I can.

Landeval appeals to a popular audience. The story remains the same, but is given a coarser texture. The verse is not as refined or delicate. The transmission of Arthurian Romances from the French speaking courts of the twelfth century to the rougher English castles and halls of the fourteenth century coarsened the subject matter and expression. The language of high culture among the aristocracy continued to be French.

Landeval had at least two successors. One, *Sir Launfal*, by Thoams le Chestre and in a Kentish dialect, was largely set in Karlyoun. *Sir Lambewell*, an even less successful version, was found in the Percy folio. It opens:

Doughty in King Arthures dayes
When Britain was holden in nobleness,
And in his time a long while
He sojourned in merry Carlisle.

And, having limped along following Marie's original fairly closely, but without her facility, the poem concludes with Lambewell and the lady riding to Avalon:

And she brought Sir Lambwell from Carlisle
Far into a jolly island
That clipped was Amilion,
Which knoweth well every Briton;

Chretien de Troyes
and the Origin of Romance

If Geoffrey of Monmouth is the fount and perhaps the origin of all chronicle or historical accounts of Arthur, Chretien de Troyes is the fount of the romantic tradition.

Chretien wrote four complete or near-complete stories: *Erec and Enide*, *Cliges*, *The Knight of the Cart*, also known as *Lancelot*, and *The Knight with the Lion* or *Ywain*.

Eric and Enide is the tale of a knight who became so besotted with his young wife that he abandoned armour for amour. There is one passing reference to Carduel / Carlisle as the location of Arthur's court, but the story is set in a geographically vague Wales.

Cliges draws on Classical rather than Breton legend and is an elaborate love story, a counter to the adulterous love of Tristan and Isolde. It is set partly in the Mediterranean and partly in southern England.

The Knight of the Cart tells of Lancelot's idolatrous and adulterous love for Guenevere. For her he will undergo all dangers and humiliations. The story elaborates a number of Celtic legends. Its setting is partly in England and partly in a fictional world that lies on the borderland of dreams.

The Knight with the Lion begins in a very real court in Carlisle but moves into a mythical geography as Ywain pursues his adventures.

Each of these romances consists of about 7000 rhyming octosyllabic lines. Chretien handled this potentially repetitive form with unsurpassed flexibility and fluency. The poetry was written to be read aloud, probably not in one sitting which might have lasted up to eight hours, but in several shorter sittings. Some of the tales are presented as triptychs, with a distinct central section framed by an opening and conclusion. Chretien's mastery lies in the presentation of a tightly-structured story - so many other tales were merely conglomerations of adventures - his delight in the detail of person and scene, his insight into character and emotion and a sense of mystery that left these romantic tales poised on the border-line between reality and dream.

His last work was *Perceval, or The Story of the Grail* which he began, but never completed. It seems to have been a more ambitious work than his other romances. The poem stops in mid-sentence at line 9182, leaving many questions unanswered and the story very far from complete.

As ever, we know little about the man, except what can be gleaned from scattered references in his writing.

We can assume he came from Troyes in the Champagne area of France; that he was probably a clerk who moved in court circles; that he travelled and had probably been to England and probably to Winchester and to Wallingford, near Oxford, where he may have been a spectator at a jousting tournament.

Chretien tells us that *The Knight of the Cart*, with its story of adulterous love between Lancelot and Guenevere, was written at the suggestion of Marie de Champagne. Marie was a daughter of Eleanor of Aquitaine by her first marriage to Louis VII of France. This story must have been written sometime after 1159, which is the year of Marie's marriage to Henri the Liberal, Count of Champagne. It is probable that *The Knight of the Cart* was written at about the same time as *The Knight with the Lion* as Chretien makes frequent cross references between the two stories.

Ywain, or The Knight with the Lion, is the one of Chretien's *Romances* that concerns us most. Its opening section, a prologue to the main story, is set in Arthur's Court in Carduel / Carlisle.

Arthur, the good king of Britain whose valour teaches us to be brave and courteous, held a court of truly royal splendour at Pentecost. The king was at Carlisle in Wales. (Cardoel en Galles)

(*Carlisle in Wales* has been the subject of some debate. It might be that Chretien's geography was lacking, although this is unlikely since he had a strong enough sense of southern England for it to be probable that he had been there. On the other hand, Carlisle, or *Carduel*, might be a mis-hearing or mis-reading of Geoffrey's Caerleon or similar. This is also unlikely because of his awareness of place-names elsewhere and Chretien's other references to Carduel in *The Story of the Grail* and to Caerleon in *The Knight of the Cart*. *In Wales* could be used as a wider reference than the present country to indicate the areas of territory that had been occupied by the Britons including Cumbria, Strathclyde and Cornwall. Elsewhere in *The Story of the Grail* Chretien talks of leggings, dress and pavilions being in the Welsh manner and the word might best be glossed as British or of the time and country of Arthur. The form 'Carduel' or 'Karduel' and other variants may have acquired their 'd' by contamination from the Breton town of Kerduel near Lannion)

The knights had dined and they now all gathered in the halls at the invitation of the ladies. The talk was of love, of its sorrows and its anguish and of the joys that came to those who suffered in its cause. In those days, in contrast to the superficiality of today, when love is reduced to lies and mockery, lovers were courtly, valiant, honorable and generous.

Very unusually, and much to the surprise of the knights, Arthur rose early from the great feast and went to his room to rest. And the queen must have detained him for he stayed so long at her side that he forgot himself and fell asleep.

Waiting about, at the entrance to his chamber, were Dodinel, Sagremor, Kay, Gawain and Ywain. They were listening to Calogrenant, who was recounting a tale, which spoke not of his honour, but of his disgrace.

Something that he was saying caught the queen's attention and she slipped quietly from the king's side in order to listen to his story. Calogrenant was the only one that noticed her and immediately he leapt to his feet to show his proper respect. The spiteful Kay felt he had been upstaged by this act of simple courtesy and abused Calogrenant with his sharp tongue. "I see how gallant you are. You think yourself more courteous than the rest of us. But it wasn't laziness that kept us seated. We didn't see my lady until after you had risen."

The queen reprimanded Kay as tiresome and base for this unnecessary outburst. Incredibly Kay responded: "My lady, if we are not improved by your company, make sure we are none the worse for it. It is not courteous or wise to argue over silly things like this. Instead, let's have no more quarreling and get on with the tale."

However, Calogrenant, though he said he was not greatly upset by the quarrel, no longer had any wish to continue with his tale. Kay had wronged him and spoken spitefully, but what could one expect. The dung heap will always smell and a cad will always slander.

Kay, boorishly intervening, said the queen should order him to continue.

The queen was more conciliatory. He must ignore Kay's attack. Kay was always rude and there is no point in punishing him. "If you wish to enjoy my love, pray begin again, at once."

Calogrenant was still smarting from Kay's abuse, but under pressure from the queen, he continued. He asked for a sympathetic hearing: they should listen with their hearts. The ears were merely the channel through which the voice reached the heart. Others had told of dreams, or fables, or lies, but what he would now tell them he had seen with his own eyes.

It happened seven years ago. He was fully armed as a knight should be, but was alone, and riding along through the forest when he found himself on a tangled, treacherous, overgrown path. The forest was named Broceliande.

(The Forest of Broceliande is usually identified as that of Paimpont near Rennes in Brittany. The Forest and a Fountain of Berenton were so named by Wace in his *Brut*. Later Yvain rides from Carduel to Broceliande Forest in Brittany in two days. The journey would be one of four to five hundred miles and would necessitate crossing the English Channel, all of which suggest that Chretien had little regard for the constraints of geography. However, it has been suggested by the distinguished Arthurian scholar, R. S. Loomis, that the name Broceliande was "a blunder" and that Chretien was re-telling a tale that was originally set in Lothian and substituted the famous Breton spring of Berenton for a spring in the Blanche Lande, but still retained the directions for reaching the domain of Duke Laududez in Scotland. However, it may simply be that Chretien, in taking us from the world of the court to one that is somewhat other, a place of adventure and romance, properly chooses not to obey the traveller's usual laws of time and place.)

At the end of the day, Calogrenant emerged into open country. A wooden brattice or fortress lay in front of him. A man stood on the drawbridge with a moulted goshawk on his wrist. He welcomed him and told him, seven times in succession, that the route by which he had travelled was blessed. The vavasour or householder struck a copper gong in the courtyard three times and brought his servants running to take care of the knight's horse and person. A tall, beautiful and proper maiden helped him disarm and clothed him in a peacock-blue mantle. They were left alone together and she led him to sit down in the most beautiful meadow in the world. The knight found her so talented, charming, gifted and comforting that no call of duty would have persuaded him to leave. The vavasour called him away to supper and during the meal, as he sat opposite the beautiful maiden, he urged him to call on their unfrequented lodging on his return.

He left at dawn the following morning. After backing away from some bellicose bulls, he came across a peasant, a giant of a man, a hunchback, like a Moor, ugly and hideous in the extreme, sitting on a stump. He had the eyes of an owl, the nose of a cat and jowls like those of a wolf. He leant on a giant club.

As the knight approached, he leapt on a tree trunk such that he now towered seventeen feet above the timorous knight. Calogrenant had sufficient courage to ask: "Tell me, are you a good creature or not?"

His reply was compliant enough. He was a man who watched over the beasts of the woods and ensured they never left the clearing. They were afraid of his power because he had the confidence to grab hold of the two horns of a beast and reduce the others to fear and trembling by his actions. He was lord over his beasts. In response to the man's question, Calogrenant explained that he was seeking adventure to test his courage and strength.

The man said he knew nothing of adventure, but, if he went to a nearby spring, he would not return untested. He would find a path that would take him to the spring that boils and yet is colder than marble. The spring was shaded by the most beautiful of trees, which never shed its leaves, even in the coldest winter. He would see an iron basin that hung on a chain, and on one side of the spring was an unknown stone and on the other a small and beautiful chapel. If he gathered some water in the basin and cast it upon the stone, he would see such a storm that no creatures would remain in the wood. There would be so much lightning that, if he escaped without trouble, he would be more fortunate than any other knight who had been before him.

Just before noon he found the tree and the spring. The tree was, indeed, the most beautiful in the world, and a basin of the purest gold hung from its thick branches, suspended by a chain. The spring was boiling like hot water. The stone was emerald, hollowed out like a cask and it sat upon four rubies, brighter than the sun at first light. He sprinkled the hollow basin with water from the bowl. Lightning blinded his eyes. The clouds dropped rain, snow and hail. He was terrified that he would be killed by the lightning or the crashing trees.

The storm died as suddenly as it had begun. The fresh clear air filled the knight with joy and every branch and leaf of the tree was covered with birds, whoe were singing softly in perfect harmony, even though each sang a different melody. He had never felt such joy and delight.

As he stood there enraptured, he heard the horrendous clatter of a knight approaching. He rapidly took to his mount. The charging knight flew towards him swifter than an eagle and looking fiercer than a lion.

He shouted the loudest of challenges. He had been shamed. He had not been formally challenged and his woods had been felled and he had been driven from his house by lightning and rain. The knight must receive punishment for the damage he had done.

The assailant was taller and had a stronger horse and the heaviest and thickest of lances. Calogrenant braced himself and dealt his mightiest blow, striking the edge of his opponent's shield and shattering his own lance in the process. The blow from the knight's lance was so forceful as to knock Calogrenant over his horse's crupper and flat upon the ground. The knight rode away with his horse and left him, bewildered and dejected and shamed, lying on the ground.

Calogrenant thought of following the knight, but felt that it was pointless. Having recovered somewhat at the side of the spring, he determined to accept the invitation and return to his host of the previous night. First, however, he removed his armour to make things easier.

He was welcomed just as courteously by the vavasour and the beautiful maiden. Never before had anyone escaped from the spring. All had been killed or captured.

Calogrenant considered himself a fool. To the queen and his fellow knights he confessed, "Now, like a fool I've told you what, until now, I've never wanted to tell anyone."

When Calogrenant had finished his tale, Ywain didn't spare him. He may be his first cousin, but he had been a fool not to tell him for so long, and he would go immediately and avenge the shame Calogrenant has brought.

Kay mocked Ywain's impetuosity. It was the drink talking. Were his greaves polished, his banners unfurled? Will Ywain set out tonight or tomorrow? They would all want to go. He shouldn't go off without their leave.

The queen reprimanded Kay's ill-tempered outburst most severely. He should control his bitter, slanderous tongue. It made him hated everywhere. If he can't learn to control his tongue he should be bound like a lunatic to the choir screen.

Ywain vented his sarcasm on the wise and courteous Lord Kay. He had no wish to quarrel. The man who strikes back is the man who starts the fight.

As this tetchy and unpleasant conversation continued, the king, having just woken, came from his chamber. They all immediately stood up and he asked them to be seated. He sat beside the queen, and in her usual accomplished manner, she repeated Calogrenant's tale, word for word. The king listened most attentively and then swore on the souls of his father, son and mother that within two weeks, on the eve of the Feast of St. John the Baptist, he would go to see the spring, the storm and the marvel. Ywain was put out. He'd intended to go alone. If all went, Kay or Gawain would be given precedence. He determined to go alone and to be in the forest of Broceliande within three days. He would find the narrow path, the pleasing maiden, the nobleman, the clearing and the bulls, the hideous peasant, the stone, the spring and the basin and the birds on the beautiful tree and he would make it rain and storm. But he would win honour or shame before he told of it.

Ywain stole away from the court and went to his lodgings and ordered preparations for his imminent departure. His most trusted squire was told to bring his armour and his horse, well shod, to him when he was outside the city. Meanwhile he rode leisurely through the city gate on a palfrey.

Ywain waited some distance from the city in a secluded spot until his squire came with his horse, armour and other trappings and helped him prepare for his adventure.

And so the scene of the story moves away from Carlisle and, possibly across the sea, to the Forest of Broceliande.

Ywain defeats the knight of the fountain, marries his widow, deserts her in his pursuit of arms, wanders in the forest and is reduced to madness only to be redeemed by the loyal support of a lion. Eventually after much testing and endurance he regains the love of his bride.

An English version of Chretien's poem, *Ywain and Gawain,* composed two centuries later, places the opening scene in Cardiff:

> *He made a feast, the sooth to say,*
> *Upon the Whitsunday*
> *At Kerdyf that is in Wales.*

Ywain is the Owain ap Urien who was a prince of Rheged in the sixth century and is the only Arthurian character that can be claimed as Cumbrian. His is possibly the Castle Hewin near High Hesket and the Giant's Grave in Penrith churchyard. There is a counter claim that one, or both, are connected with a later Owain, who was a prince of Strathclyde.

Chretien also set some of the opening scenes of *Perceval* in Cardoeil, Carduel or Carlisle.

The romance begins in a lonely forest far from civilization, perhaps in North Wales. A young man, we are not told his name, was wandering in the woods, practicing throwing his javelin, when he was awestruck by the sight of a group of knights. At first, seeing their shadowed silhouettes through the boughs of the trees, he thought them devils, but when they emerged in their silver armour into the full glory of the sunlight, he saw them as gods or angels and threw himself on the ground in prayer before them.

The knights were seeking a party of five knights and three ladies, but he ignored the leader's inquiries as he wonderingly asked about his lance, his shield and his hauberk.

The boy told his mother's harrowers about the knights and the party they were seeking. The harrowers were horrified that he had met with the knights because they knew now that he would want to be a knight himself and this would drive his mother out of her mind.

The boy delivered the answer to the knight, but he longed to know where he could find this man who made knights. "Boy," the knight answered, "The king is staying in Cardoeil. (Carlisle) I was there five days ago."

The boy rushed home full of enthusiasm to tell his fearful mother of the glorious angels. She was distraught. Her two elder sons had been knights and were killed in combat as they returned home and her husband, himself a knight of great renown, had died from grief. They had lived a solitary life ever since his father had been wounded in the thigh and the land had been laid waste. All his life she has tried to shield him from the world of chivalry.

His mother was able to restrain him for three days before he left her in search of King Arthur's court, and knighthood. Embracing him and weeping, she told him these things: he should serve and honour ladies, he might kiss them but do no more and if he were offered a purse or a ring he might take it; he should always find out the name of any man he encountered and he should go to church and pray. However, he had been raised in such ignorance and seclusion he did not know what a church was. As he looked back he saw that his anguished mother had fallen into a faint, but, nevertheless he urged his horse forward and rode on through the forest.

The next day he came across the most beautiful pavilion in the world. Inside, on a silken bed, lay a beautiful maiden. The boy, following his mother's instructions, forced his kisses on her seven times and then, even though she resisted, took the golden ring from her finger. The girl was in terror, but the simple boy drank wine and ate one of three venison pies that had been prepared for her lord's return. He left. Her jealous lord extracted the story from her and the beautiful maiden was condemned to misery: her horse would not be fed or shod nor her garments changed and she would follow him, if need be, naked and on foot, until he had cut off the boy's head.

A charcoal burner directed the boy to Carlisle and Arthur's castle: he would find the castle overlooking the sea and he would find the king both joyful and grieving. Arthur had won a great victory, but his knights had departed to their own castles.

The boy heeded him little, but rode on to the strong, elegant castle that stood above the sea. An armed knight was riding out through the gate. He carried a cup of gold in his right hand and held his lance, shield and reins with his left. His armour was all in red and the boy was overcome by its beauty and determined to possess the arms. The knight stopped the impetuous youth and then let him go, saying that if the worthless Arthur will not be his vassal, he should yield to him or send a champion. He had just snatched Arthur's own wine goblet from before his eyes.

The boy heard nothing, but rode directly across the marble flags into the hall and demanded to see Arthur. The king was sitting apart in dejection as his knights drank and made merry.

The boy, in his ignorance, rode up to him and greeted him, but received no response. Exasperated at his second rough greeting being ignored and, feeling that this man could not make anyone a knight, he turned his horse abruptly about. The horse's tail whisking around sent the king's hat flying.

The king shook himself out of his despondency. He apologized to the boy. The Red Knight of Quinqueroy, who demanded his lands, had just snatched his cup and splashed the wine over the queen. She had been furious. She had fled to her chambers and the king feared that she was so distressed she might take her own life.

Not heeding a word, the laughing and handsome but simple youth said, "Make me a knight."

The king told him to dismount. With the arrogance of innocence, he refused, and demanded to be made a knight where he sat on his horse, then and there.

The bemused king did so willingly and the boy asked leave to be a red knight. He wanted to be granted the arms of the wondrous red knight he had met at the castle gate. Sir Kay, in his usual mocking fashion, told him to go and take the arms.

The king reprimanded Kay for his mockery. As the boy turned to leave, he saw a beautiful girl and greeted her. She replied and laughed as she did so, "If you live long, I sense and believe that you will be the world's finest knight."

This girl had not laughed for over six years. Everyone was listening to her. Sir Kay was enraged. He stepped up to her and slapped her face so hard that she fell to the ground. Then he turned and venomously kicked the jester into the roaring fire. It was the jester who had said that the girl would not laugh until she saw the one who would become the greatest knight on earth.

The boy set out after the Red Knight. Yvonet, a page, who knew the short cuts and was always eager to be the bearer of the latest news, ran down across the garden at the back of the hall and through the postern gate, to the path where the Red Knight was waiting. The golden cup had been placed on a block beside him.

The boy rushed towards him, crying out, "Lay down your arms. King Arthur forbids you to carry them."

"Has he sent anyone to challenge me?" demanded the knight.

"How dare you mock me?" shouted the boy. "Take off my arms at once, I command you."

"I asked if he had sent anyone to challenge me."

"Sir knight, I'm telling you, take off those arms or I'll take them off for you. I'll strike you if I have to say it again."

The knight was angry. He swung his lance with all his force and caught the boy across the shoulders and knocked him forward across the neck of his horse. Enraged, the boy let fly with his javelin. It went straight through the knight's eye, through his brain and out at the nape of his neck. Blood and brains gushed out and the knight fell dead from his horse.

The boy laid the knight's lance aside and took his shield from his neck. Then he grabbed and pulled at his helmet and sword. Yvonet laughed at his frustrated efforts and then helped him unbuckle the armour. The boy had thought the armour was welded to the knight's body and that he would have to chop the knight into pieces.

Yvonet dressed the boy in the fine armour, but he absolutely refused to exchange the rough garment and boots his mother had given him for the knight's fine quilted silk and leather. He strapped on the armour. The hauberk and helmet fitted perfectly. The boy was shown how to hang his sword at his side. He was equipped with spurs for the first time and mounted up on the knight's charger with his feet in the unaccustomed stirrups. Finally, Yvonet presented him with the sword and shield.

The boy looked down on Yvonet and offered him his hunting horse. Yvonet was instructed to return the goblet to the king and to tell the girl, who had been struck by Kay, that one day he intended to return to avenge himself on Kay.

They went their separate ways and Yvonet returned to the hall of the castle.

He presented the golden cup to the king and told him that the red knight had been killed. Arthur was incredulous that the Welsh boy, who had caused him such shame, should have been responsible for returning his cup. "Did the Red Knight love him so much that he just gave him the cup?" asked Arthur.

"The boy made him pay dearly for it: he killed him." Then Yvonet told of the Red Knight's fierce blow and of the boy's javelin which thrust through the knight's eye and pushed his blood and brains out on the other side.

Arthur turned on Kay. His uncontrolled offensive tongue had cost him the boy who had served him so well.

At this point, Yvonet mentioned the boy's promise to revenge the girl. The jester leapt about, relishing Kay's discomfort and swearing that, within a fortnight, the boy would take his revenge. Kay's arm would be in a sling and it would not heal for six months.

Kay, looking at the king, suppressed the anger that was bursting within him.

King Arthur spoke to Kay: "You've earned my wrath today. The boy should have been taught the craft of arms. Now he sits astride a horse unable to handle a sword, a ready target for any knight who should come along. He's so naive and untaught, he won't last long."

The king was deeply disappointed and lamented his loss, but knowing he could gain nothing by it, he fell silent.

(The Red Knight is said to be from Quinqueroy. 'Quinqueroy', scholars suggest, might correspond with 'Kyningesburh' and might be either Conisborough in Yorkshire or Coniston in Cumbria. However, the name means king's town and the first element, found in various forms, Coninges, Koninges, Conynges, in twelfth century documents, is an old Norse word and would not be found in Celtic legend of a time before the Norse settlement.)

The boy rode on, through the forest and across the flatland, until he came to a river wider than a cross-bow shot, which ebbed and flowed but stayed within its banks. The boy rode further on. Alongside a rock was a castle that sloped down to the sea.

And so the romance continues.

Perceval, for that is the name of the boy, now begins a series of adventures in which he is variously tested and learns the values of knighthood. He saves Blancheflour and, most importantly of all, he fails to ask the wounded Fisher King in the Wasteland the two essential questions concerning the three red drops of blood and the grail. He thereby forgoes his chance of personal salvation. During his quest we are able to watch his growing spirituality as the innocent all-conquering knight proceeds towards a deeper understanding of the nature of chivalry and honour.

The account of Perceval's quest is interrupted in Chretien's romance by the narrative of Gawain's quest. Sir Gawain is a far more earthly knight, pursuing sensual pleasures, with great success, it must be added, but eventually finding no higher fulfillment.

Chretien's poem, having constructed a world of unresolved mysteries, does not return to Perceval, but breaks off in the middle of line 9012.

Chretien had written the most intriguingly enigmatic poem of the Middle Ages. The poem's lack of completion only served to deepen its mystery.

Over the next century, there were numerous continuations of the *Story of the Grail,* all seeking to resolve the mystery of the grail and the lance.

Chretien had taken the Matter of Britain, the stories of Arthur and his knights, that Breton musicians had made known in the courts of England and France and more widely throughout western Europe, and had transformed them. No longer were they amusing ethnic folk-tales, pale shadows of an earlier Celtic religion. The court of King Arthur became a venue for the understanding of chivalric values, a romanticized world that reflected the changing concerns of the nobility. Geoffrey of Monmouth's epic Arthur, the heroic warrior who articulated an historical impulse, whose concern was politics, became the quiescent king who enabled his knights to pursue their individual quests for enlightenment. Carduel, Camelot, or wherever the court was held, and the Round Table offered a narrative frame for military, amorous and spiritual adventures.

The Story of the Holy Grail,
and Some More Worldly Romances

For a hundred years or more, throughout the thirteenth century, in the French-speaking world, which included the Norman ruling classes in England, and in Germany, Italy, Spain and the Low Countries and even as far afield as Norway and Iceland, poets and entertainers told tales of King Arthur and his Knights of the Round Table. In many of those stories, Arthur held his court at Carduel or Cardoyle or Karidol, that is, Arthur held his court in Carlisle.

Throughout the thirteenth century many writers sought to extend and imitate Chretien's romances. *The Story of the Grail,* unfinished and enigmatic, demanded completion. It brought together eroticism, religious mysticism and chivalric deeds in an irresistible combination. Marie's *Lais* offered an enticing model for some. Geoffrey of Monmouth's earlier epic portrayal of Arthur, romanticized into Norman French by Robert Wace, lent historical weight to the developing fantasy. And the whole expanding edifice was built on the popularity of Celtic legend constantly evolving in the mouths of Breton jongleurs to mirror and match the tastes of the increasingly sophisticated and chivalric courts in France and western Europe. Events in the real world contributed to the mythic excitement of the time. The reputed remains of King Arthur were conveniently exhumed at Glastonbury in 1191. It was an exciting time in which the literary expression and sentiment of the age found form in a secular, and originally foreign, mythology of rare potency.

At the turn of the twelfth century, Robert de Boron completed and extended *The Story of the Grail* with the stories of *Joseph of Arimathie*, *Merlin* and *Perceval*. The mysterious grail was now the Holy Grail, the cup from which Christ drank at the Last Supper. It had been brought to Britain by Joseph of Arimathea, and in an age when every last vestige of any and every minor saint was presumed to be possessed of miraculous power, the glorious Holy Grail was the ultimate relic, the impossible realization of every knightly quest.

Gawain became the popular hero of many profane stories. While other knights dedicated themselves to purity, Gawain resisted or, more often, succumbed to the pleasures of his host's daughter's bed.

Gawain's exploits were celebrated in verse for they were the matter of public performance, usually for a wider public, whereas the developing story of the Grail was written in prose and often presented in increasingly finely illuminated and illustrated manuscripts. Other Arthurian stories and particularly *The Story of the Grail* were matter for private reading and quiet contemplation. They became a vehicle for religious expression and fell increasingly under the influence of the church.

Perlesvaus is a vast work in which Gawain, Lancelot and Perlesvaus (Perceval) all fail to find the Grail. In *The Didot Perceval*, Perceval is entrusted with the Grail by the Fisher King before he dies.

The crowning achievement is the *Vulgate Cycle,* another enormous prose romance which drew together the evolving narratives into a complex whole. The ever noble Lancelot becomes the dominating hero, although it is his son, the pure and dedicated Galahad, who will secure the Grail. It is this composite romance which is the main source of Thomas Malory's *Morte D'Arthur*.

In the *Vulgate Merlin,* Merlin tells Uther Pendragon of the table of the Last Supper and the table of the Grail and proposes that he should establish a third table, a Round Table. Uther agrees to this and the Round Table is founded in Carduel on the day of Pentecost. Fifty knights are selected to sit around the table, but one seat is left empty. This seat will be occupied by that pure knight who eventually achieves the Grail.

Later, at a great Christmas feast in Carduel, Uther sees Ygerne, the wife of the Duke of Tintaiol (Tintagel) and falls in love with her. He attempts to seduce her through the intermediary of one of his knights, but Ygerne reports the matter to her husband and they leave for their own lands. Uther wages war and succeeds with Ygerne when he is transformed to appear like her husband. Her husband is killed, Uther begets Arthur, and marries Ygerne.

The *Perlesvaus* opens in Arthur's palace in Carduel on Ascension Day. Guinevere is in tears at the decline in the splendour of the royal court. There are few knights and the spirit of adventure has long gone. Arthur blames himself. He has lost his largesse and fallen into a feebleness of heart. He proposes to go to the chapel of St Augustine in the forest and pray for his reformation. The night before his departure, a knight dreams of following Arthur to the chapel, of taking a candlestick and being stabbed by a monstrous black man. In the morning he tells his dream to Arthur. However, the knight really has been stabbed and he dies when the dagger is removed. Arthur makes his journey to the chapel, where he has a vision of a hermit and the cross and his spirits are restored. A girl tells him he must reawaken the spirit of romance, and returning, after many adventures to Carduel, he resolves to hold a new court in Pennenoisance (Penzance) on St John's Day. The biggest part of the work is concerned with Perceval's recovery of the Grail.

In *The High Book of the Holy Grail* the following incident occurs:

Perceval descended a deep valley and found himself in a wasteland. He recognized the country around Carlisle. The people he met were uneasy and fearful. Perceval couldn't understand this. "Is not King Arthur still alive?" he asked.

He was alive and in his castle, but he was deeply troubled and afraid for a knight was waging war on him whom no man could endure.

At the foot of the steps leading to the Great Hall, Perceval was met by Lancelot and Sir Gawain and then by the king and the queen and all the court who greeted him with the greatest joy.

Perceval was disarmed and clothed in a splendid gown and made welcome. All were pleased to see that he bore the shield that had once hung on the pillar in the hall.

As the king was seated at dinner that day, four armed knights burst into the hall. Each knight bore a dead knight before him. Their arms and their feet had been cut off, but they remained in full armour. Their armour was black as if they had been struck by lightening.

"Sire," they said, "the disgrace being done to you goes unchecked. The Knight of the Dragon is destroying your land and killing your men and getting ever closer and he boasts that you will never find a knight with the courage to face him in combat."

The four knights departed. The mutilated bodies were left in the middle of the hall. The king ordered the bodies to be taken away and buried with the others. The king was ashamed, as were Lancelot and Gawain. No knight could be expected to face such a man who could throw fire and flame from his shield at will.

A maiden entered into the uneasy hall. Behind was a litter bearing the dead body of a knight. She begged justice of Arthur. "Sitting beside you is the son of the widowed lady. He should not refuse me. The dead knight that I have borne so long in this litter is the son of his uncle, Elinant of Escavalon."

Perceval questioned her. He knew of his uncle, but not of a son.

The damsel replied: "His name was Alain of Escavalon. He was loved for his beauty by the Queen of the Circle of Gold. She had him embalmed after he was slain by the Knight of the Dragon, who is destroying all the land. She would give the Circle of Gold to whoever killed that knight. Kill him and save King Arthur's land."

"Where is the Knight of the Dragon?" asked Perceval.

He is told that the knight is in the beautiful Isle of Elephants below the queen's castle. All was now destroyed and every day she saw him bear knights unharmed from the forest and then kill them and dis-member them.

Perceval took his leave and Lancelot and Gawain went with him to show him the way. The king and queen were so afraid for his safety that they sent to all the holy men and hermits of Carlisle Forest telling them to pray for Perceval and protect him from this demon knight.

The knights journey on through a wasteland until they see the Forbidden Castle.

In addition to the works of Chretien and Marie de France, twenty or more French verse romances survive. In the majority of these, Arhur's court is held in Carlisle. Only occasionally is the court held in Caerleon.

One or two examples will suffice.

La Mule sans Frein, The Mule without a Bridle, by Paion des Maisieres, that is the Pagan of Maisieres as distinct from the Christian of Troyes - the name may be a pun or even a pseudonym for Chretien himself - was written sometime around 1200 in a Champagne dialect.

The story begins on a day of Pentecost with Arthur, according to custom, holding court in Carlisle. Many knights and their beautiful ladies were gathered together, and, after dining, they went to an upper room to amuse themselves. From the upper windows they looked across the meadows and saw a very graceful lady, riding rapidly towards the castle on a mule. There was no bridle on the mule, only a halter. Gawain sent Kay immediately to find the queen and the king and urge them to come and see this strange event.

The girl dismounted before the hall and Gawain and other knights rushed to meet her and serve her, but she appeared to have had great trouble.

The king sent for her. "Sir," she said, "I am angry and sad and I will never be happy until my bridle is restored to me. There must be a knight who has the courage to undertake this task. If he returns my bridle to me, I will be completely his without question. I will give him my mule to find his way to my castle."

Kay stepped forward. He would go, but he demanded that she should kiss him first. She refused him. "When the bridle is mine again, then the castle will be given to you, and you shall have kisses and 'l'autre chose' ".

Kay left quickly, by himself, trusting the mule, with only his sword to protect him. He found himself in a vast, dark forest. The beasts of the forest, lions, tigers and leopards, gathered around him. Kay was terrified, but the savage beasts, because they knew the mule and honoured the lady, knelt down before him. Nevertheless, Kay rapidly went on his way and found himself in a deep and dark and perilous valley. This bitterly cold valley was filled with snakes and serpents and scorpions, who breathed out fire and gave off the most nauseating smell.

Beyond the valley was a meadow, where he watered his mule at a clear spring, and then his way was blocked by a great stretch of water. The only crossing was by a narrow, iron plank. Kay was fearful of the dark, turbulent waters, felt it was pointless to risk his life for such a worthless matter, and turned to make his journey back to Carlisle.

He did not stop and was exhausted and in great distress. In the forest the beasts ran furiously towards him, but held back because of the mule.

When he reached Carlisle, Arthur and Gawain welcomed him because they thought he had the bridle. The girl knew he had failed and tore at her hair and was ready to kill herself. Gawain offered himself. The lady embraced him and he rode away on the mule. He rode through the forest as the beasts knelt down to him and he laughed, thinking how Kay would have been afraid. He braved the stinking valley and eventually came to the dark, turbulent stream. He crossed the narrow, bending plank with some trepidation and then, travelling along a narrow path, he looked up to see a strong and beautiful castle.

The castle was surrounded by a great moat and around the moat were great stakes, each, except for one, bearing the head of a knight. The castle was turning rapidly like a windmill or a spinning top.

He spurred the mule to make one decisive leap through the moving door. He entered the deserted castle. When he dismounted, he was welcomed by a dwarf, who then disappeared.

Gawain explored the vast cellars of the castle. A giant, hairy churl came towards him. He was carrying a broad, heavy axe. The churl wished him good luck, but warned him that his brave journey had been wasted. He would never retrieve the bridle.

The churl showed Gawain to his lodging, stabled his mule, served his food and showed him to his bed. Then, before he lay down, the churl proposed a test. Willingly, Gawain accepted whatever the test should be. "Cut off my head with this sharp axe," the churl said. "Tomorrow, as you have beheaded me, so I will cut off your head."

Gawain was ready. The churl placed his neck on the block and, immediately, with one blow of the axe, Gawain cut off the churl's head. The churl jumped up, took his head and returned to the cellar. Gawain lay down and slept soundly till the morning.

The churl returned with his head restored. In accordance with the agreement, Gawain placed his neck on the block. The giant churl lifted the axe. He relented, impressed by Gawain's loyalty and the way he had kept his promise without flinching.

The churl told him that the bridle was defended by two fierce lions. Gawain was equipped with fine armour, a war-horse and seven shields and made ready to face the first, snarling, raging lion.

On the fourth assault, Gawain pierced the lion to its entrails. The second lion, more ferocious than the first, struck away Gawain's shield with its first blow. With its second blow, the lion ripped open Gawain's chain mail. The churl handed him the seventh and last shield. With one stroke of his sword, Gawain cleft the lion's skull in twain.

The bridle was not yet his. The churl led him through the castle to where a wounded knight lay. The knight claimed he was healed and said that now Gawain must do battle with him. He was the knight who had vanquished the other adventurers and placed their heads on the stakes around the castle.

They clashed on horses and then fought with swords until the knight fell back in exhaustion and Gawain cut his helmet in two. This knight, who would have placed Gawain's head on the pointed stake, pleaded for his own life and Gawain let him go.

The bridle was still not his. He must face two dragons who squirted blood and breathed fire. The churl equipped him in new armour and, placing his shield before him, he fought with the two dragons and decapitated them both.

The dwarf came, helped him disarm and invited him to eat with his lady.

The lady was in her gilded bed. Gawain sat beside her. The dwarf and the churl waited on them. The lady would have it that they ate from the one dish. She admired and praised him greatly. The lady delayed him, but Gawain wanted the bridle he felt he had earned. He had undertaken the adventure for her sister. Now she would have him remain with her and, if he would be her lord, she would give him her thirty-nine castles.

Graciously, Gawain declined. His honour required that he return with the bridle. Gawain took the bridle from its silver nail, placed it on the mule and took his leave. The churl caused the rotating castle to stand still. When Gawain looked back he saw the streets full of people. They were rejoicing because Gawain had freed them from the tyranny of the beasts.

Gawain passed safely across the iron plank and through the stinking valley and through the forest of wild beasts, who knelt down and kissed his feet.

The king and queen saw him as he returned to Carlisle and the girl came to meet him and kissed him more than a hundred times. "It is right that I should place my body at your service. All the knights I have sent have been beheaded. Only you have retrieved the bridle."

The queen and the king and the knights begged her to stay, but she was not free and could not remain. She rode off on her mule without an escort.

In *The Knight with the Sword, Li Chevalier a l'Epee,* the forest and castle are more probable, but Gawain finds himself even more erotically tested. He leaves the court in Carlisle, and in a deep reverie, loses his way in the forest. He is invited to his castle by a knight and responds courteously. He is entertained graciously and is offered the knight's daughter. Even Gawain acknowledges her to be the most beautiful lady in the world. Her father tells her that she must not oppose Gawain in any of his wishes.

That night, her father insists she lie naked beside Gawain in a luxurious bed, surrounded by burning candles. Above them in the bed hangs a sword. Other knights, who have lain beside the lady, have lost their lives when they sought to make love to her. As Gawain nears the lady the sword descends, but merely cuts his side. A second time, it glances against his shoulder. He lies still beside the knight's beautiful daughter throughout the night. In the morning, his virtue, as the best knight in the world, is rewarded with the daughter's hand.

Riding away with the daughter and her greyhounds he encounters a fully-armed knight, who claims the lady as his own. Gawain, unarmed, is unable to fight, and his bride chooses his challenger. He is left with the greyhounds and subsequently he is challenged for those and wins the fight, but loses the girl.

The romance known as *Li Chevalier as Deus Epees, The Knight with Two Swords*, begins in Cardueil. Arthur is holding court at Pentecost in grand style. Ten kings and 366 knights of the Round Table are present when a messenger from King Ris d'Outre-Ombre enters and makes an outrageous demand. His master wants Arthur's beard. He will add it to his mantle which is woven from the beards of conquered kings. Arthur, of course, is indignant and prepares to go immediately to Cardigan, which Ris is about to capture.

The story returns to Cardueil when the lady of Cardigan comes to Arthur's court to beg a boon. She wants him to give her, as a husband, the knight who can free her from the sword she has acquired at the Waste Chapel. Merideuc, the Knight of the Two Swords, turns up, is admitted to the Round Table and frees her on the third day.

Li Atres Perillox, The Perilous Churchyard, is a late fourteenth century tale, probably written in Normandy, that tells of further amatory adventures of Sir Gawain. One is in a perilous graveyard where a girl issues from a tomb. her step mother has taken away her reason, but a devil has restored it, provided she will give herself to him. She is shut in the tomb during the day, and the devil visits her at night. Gawain cuts off the devil's head. There are several other adventures, all set in a fictitious Carduel and the forest thereabouts.

The truth is that the legends of Arthur, Lancelot, Merlin, Tristan and the Holy Grail were told and retold throughout western Europe and that one of several courts where Arthur was to be found was Carlisle.

Thus in Hartmann van Aue's *Erek* and *Ywein*, foundation works of German literature, Arthur's court is in Carlisle. The one reference to Arthur in Gottfried van Strasburg's *Tristan*, talks of Tristan going to Arthur's court in Carlisle. Wolfgang van Eschenbach's *Parzival* makes a passing reference to Carlisle. In the Italian *Vita di Merlino* Merlin tells Uther Pendragon the story of the Holy Grail and bids him found the Round Table in Carduel with fifty knights chosen by imself. There is a Dutch version of *Fergus of Galloway*, *Ferguut*, that retains the locations of the original in Cumberland and the Scottish Borders. There is even a mention of Carlisle in *Povest Trychane*, a sixteenth century version of the Tristan story in Belorussian.

A different connection with Carlisle is found in the early German-Swiss version of Lanzelet by Ulrich von Zanzikhoven. Ulrich claimed to have taken his original story from a Norman French manuscript he received from Hugh de Morville in 1194. Hugh de Morville was one of several knights who gave themselves as substitutes for Richard the Lionheart, when he was being held for ransom in his journey back from the Holy Land. This Hugh de Morville may well have been the notorious Hugh de Morville who was present at the murder of Thomas a Becket. He held the barony of Burgh by Sands. The manuscript might have been based on stories that were of Celtic origin and found in the area.

The one tangible connection Carlisle has with Arthurian romance is the Tristan Fragment, a portion of an old manuscript from the late thirteenth century, that was found in the Carlisle Record Office in 1995. The two leaves contained 154 previously unknown lines from Thomas's *Tristan,* which was written in 1173. They supply an essential part of the story from the moment Tristan and Ysolt drink the love potion to the conclusiion of Ysolt's bridal night with King Mark, when she intentionally has her maid take her place in her husband's bed.

The corpus of thirteenth century Arthurian literature is of enormous extent. Many versions are among the first extant works in their native literatures. The mythical Carlisle, in one of its many forms, Cardeuil, Cardeuyle, Cardoel, Cardoeil, Carduel, Caridoel, Kardeuyle, Karduel, Karidoel is the most frequently found location for Arthur's court.

Fergus of Galloway:
a Border Burlesque

Of all medieval Arthurian poets the author of *Fergus of Galloway* has the surest command of geography. His poem is clearly localized in Carlisle, Galloway, the Borders and Lothian, and, apart from one or two anomalies, most places are identifiable and the details he offers make topographical sense. One exception is the supposed possibility of seeing Cornwall from the top of a high mountain in the Borders.

However, the poem starts in Cardigan. Arthur was holding his royal court on the feast of St John. The usual picture of courtly love seems inverted. Gawain took Ywain's hand and they sat apart talking devotedly to each other much as Achilles and Patroclus might have done. Suddenly Arthur disturbed their companionship. He wanted to go hunting immediately for the white stag in the Forest of Gorriende, near Carlisle.

Some scholars have suggested that the Forest of Gorriende is the wide tract of fell-side above Castle Carrock that is referred to as the King's Forest of Geltsdale, indicating one of the many vast expanses of northern countryside that were reserved exclusively for the royal amusement of the chase.

The white stag was sighted. The chase followed tumultuously over fells and dales, across the swiftest flowing narrow stream in the world and through woodland to Jedburgh Forest, where, not surprisingly, after a run of thirty miles, the stag collapsed against an oak tree. Just as Sir Perceval was about to spear it in a thicket, the stag was away again, with the speed of the wind, across the hills of Lammermuir, through the Forest of Glasgow and then onto Ayr and so, almost coming full circle, to the richly endowed lands of Galloway, which were inhabited by ignorant, stupid and bestial people. There, Perceval cornered the stag and cut its hamstring. As the stag tried to escape through the water, its stomach became so distended that its heart failed and the hounds swam after it and retrieved it from the stream.

The king and his entourage responded to Sir Perceval's horn. Their pavilions were pitched and Arthur presented Perceval with a gilded cup, which he then re-presented to Sir Gawain.

In the morning, having completed their ablutions, they packed up rapidly and, with the prize of the stag, sped post-haste to Carlisle. On their way they passed

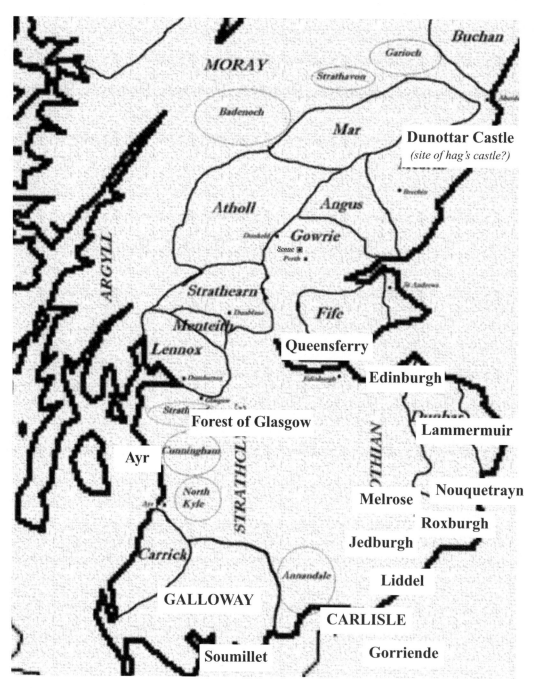

Map of Southern Scotland and the Borders in Medieval times, showing the probable locations of places mentioned in Fergus of Galloway

the wattle and daub fortress of Soumillet, which was perched on an impregnable rock overlooking the sea. A little further on Soumillet's sons were ploughing the fields.

Attracted by the glittering armour, the eldest son waylaid the laggard baggage attendant and politely, with his threatening club, demanded and learned of Arthur and the Round Table. He determined to go to court, to serve Arthur and be his counsellor. He rushed home, begged his father for a suit of armour and was presented with a a short broad sword and a hauberk and helmet that were corroded with thirty-two years of rust. On a stolid horse he rode away from his sorrowing mother.

In the forest he encountered four robbers who demanded his armour and charger. One stroke of his axe felled one robber and a thrust of his javelin pierced another. The other two fled. The young man removed their heads and hung the two of them from his saddle by their beards.

Arthur was holding court in Carlisle with a thousand battle-worn knights in attendance. Our young man rode down the street on his chestnut horse worth a thousand pounds. He went straight to Arthur. After greeting him, he disclosed his name, Fergus, and explained to Arthur that he had come to join his knights and advise him as his counsellor. Sarcastically, Kay suggested that Arthur was in desperate need of a counsellor. Then he complimented Fergus on his strength and physique and his fine armour. He explained that the jester had forecast that a fine knight would arrive and go to Nouquetran, and there he would take the horn and the wimple hanging about the neck of the gentle lion, and then fight with the knight who was as dark as a blackberry and return with him vanquished to Carlisle. Gawain rebuked Kay's offensive behaviour. Fergus suppressed his anger and Arthur calmed the situation by asking him to explain how he came by the two bearded heads.

Fergus had understood that he must find the lion and vanquish the black knight if he was to join the Round Table. Arthur suggested there was no such strenuous requirement. Nevertheless, he, good-naturedly, let the naive Fergus depart on his dangerous quest.

Fergus searched the deserted, drizzling streets of Carlisle for lodgings and in despair ended up dozing off, leaning against his lance, under a laurel tree. The Chamberlain's daughter saw him there, took him in, cared for him and was most impressed by the two heads and the story of his adventures.

After they had dined well, the chamberlain returned and, over wine, it became clear to him that he was dealing with a monstrously foolish simpleton. He persuaded a reluctant Fergus to accept a new suit of armour and to be dubbed a knight the following morning. In the castle, appearing now in his new knightly attire, as the strong handsome super-hero he really was, Fergus was told to prostrate himself before the best king in the world. He pleaded for equipment and swore that he would get his revenge on Sir Kay. The other knights would stop him going against the black knight.

Fergus was dubbed by Arthur and then handsomely armed by the finest of his knights. Mounted, with a huge quartered shield and the strongest of lances, he might have burst the horse on which he sat in the fierceness of his pride. He left the court. Arthur was concerned that such a fine figure of a knight was riding to his death. Kay was ready to give the jester a drubbing for predicting Fergus's success.

He rode for a day without incident and, just before evening, he found himself before a fine castle, that stood beside a river that might have accommodated a small fleet. The castle was called Liddel.

The site of the castle that the author seems to have in mind is at Castleton, above Newcastleton, in Liddlesdale. Fine as the castle site is, standing above a broadening of the valley, it does not command a river that could support a ship, never mind a small fleet. The geography of the area may well have been noticeably different in the thirteenth century and the author might have chosen to fuse two places. Leland, writing three hundred years later talks of visiting Netherby, which is several miles down stream and observing *men alyve have sene rynges and staples yn the walles, as it had bene stayes or holdes for shyppes.*

A worthy man, with a white falcon, and, surprisingly, the most beautiful maiden in the world with ivory teeth and apple breasts, stood on the bridge that led to the castle. Her name was Galiene. Fergus greeted them with awkward courtesy. They looked into each other's eyes and Love, winding up his crossbow, sent his bolt right between the maiden's eyes.

In the castle, Galiene sat next to Fergus in adoring silence. The old man pleaded with Fergus not to pursue the black knight, but he was resolute. During the night Galiene turned her lonely bed upside down in the joustings of love-longing. Driven by her passion, she knelt besides Fergus's bed and placed her hand on his sleeping chest and asked him to return her heart. Fergus claimed he had never seen it. He was life and death to her, but Fergus said that his quest was for something other than love and its pleasures. However, he would be happy enough to call in on his way back from vanquishing the knight. Galiene determined to renounce her love and intended to leave so she might be with her father in Lothian.

Journeying on, Fergus arrived at the mountain of Nouquetran which reaches up into the sky. The castle on its summit would have been inaccessible if it had not been for a footpath built by a giant. Pursuing his quest, Fergus discovered a marble chapel. It was guarded by a giant bronze figure of a churl that was so realistic that all men were terrified and did not dare to approach for fear of the huge steel hammer that he brandished. Fearless Fergus asked repeatedly if the churl knew the whereabouts of the lion. His politeness was met with stony contempt, and he grew increasingly angry. From a safe distance, he hurled a rock at the churl. His arms fell off, and he was left hammerless. Fergus attacked manfully with his sword, and afterwards was ashamed to have struck where he received no response.

He ventured into the chapel. There, in front of him, was the stone lion bearing the horn and the wimple. Escaping with his prizes, Fergus sounded the horn so it was heard over all the countryside. He descended the mountain.

In the forest, he saw the black knight approaching faster than a flash of lightning. There was nothing white about him except his teeth. They clashed with much piercing of hauberks and letting of blood. Fergus triumphed and the black knight was obliged, on pain of death, to ride to Arthur bearing the horn and the wimple.

Fergus went in search of adventures, but, finding none, returned to Liddel. Galiene had disappeared without trace and her father was in despair. Love crept up on Fergus and he was vanquished by Love's anguish for the first time. He bewailed his loss at great length. He would not take lodging even with her uncle. He would not rest until he had found her. He set off immediately on his quest, his shield at his neck and his lance held firmly in his hand.

In a forest glade he was shaken out of his reverie by a challenge when a cat-nosed dwarf clubbed the eye of his horse. Beaten and trampled under the horse's hooves, the dwarf screamed for help. His master emerged from the pavilion, angrily pulling on his breeches. Fergus suggested that if he had any complaint, they should consult a magistrate, or else he should dress himself in his armour and prepare to fight. His dishevelled mistress appeared from the pavilion, clutching a mantle about her. She was immediately ordered to help him arm.

The big-hearted horses charged. Fergus unseated the knight and mocked him as he sat on the ground: "Get up quickly. You're too slow. If your backside had teeth, it would have given you a nasty nip." The knight remounted and the fray was rejoined with their polished sharp-pointed swords. Fergus's keen sword sliced the scalp from the back of his head, and, bleeding profusely in front of his sweetheart, he begged for mercy. The knight, who was turning pale with pain, was told to ride to Arthur's court in Carlisle.

Next, a bold robber, who villainously demanded a toll for crossing a bridge over a chasm, was flung ignominiously in the mud and dispatched to Arthur's court in Carlisle.

Fergus had not so much as tasted bread or spring water for two whole days. Thoughts of food now drove thoughts of his beloved from the mind of this gallant knight. He snatched and gulped down a sizzling capon from the camp-fire made by fifteen robber knights. Challenged for extortionate payment, Fergus seized the burning spit and struck one robber dead and then, with his sharp sword, he slew another dozen. The two that were left were sent on their way to Arthur's court in Carlisle.

Back in Carlisle, Arthur had called his knights together. Kay, the seneschal, suggested the new young knight was bound to keep his promise and return with their enemy, the Black Knight. Gawain told him he'd be more entertaining if he carried a fiddle. Just as Arthur sardonically rebuked Gawain, the Black Knight came riding through the gate bearing the horn and the silk wimple.

The Black Knight mounted the steps to the hall in his shattered armour and prostrated himself at Arthur's feet. His knights advised Arthur to show mercy and allow the Black Knight to join the Round Table. The other vanquished knights appeared and acknowledged that Fergus was the greatest knight in the world. Arthur was dejected for, through Kay's foolishness, he had lost a fine knight.

Weary and exhausted and almost bereft of hope, Fergus arrived at a chapel beside crystal waters. He tasted the water and his spirits were restored. A dwarf spoke of the suffering he had endured for the fair Galiene, whom he had first rejected. "If you are gallant and clever enough and have sufficient valour to be prepared to go to Dunottar to obtain the shining shield guarded by the hairy hag, then you may still have your beloved." The shield would ensure that his blood would never be spilled and that he would never be unseated even though he were to face the whole English army single-handed. To obtain the shield he would have to overcome the fierce hag who was capable of slicing a knight in two with one sweep of her scythe.

Over the ensuing weeks, he searched endlessly for the shining shield. He left Lothian, and, passing through Maiden Castle (Edinburgh), he took a barge across the Forth at Queensferry. When the wind was in the rigging and the barge far from shore, the ten boatmen demanded their payment with menaces. Fergus behind his trusty shield, cleaved nine of them with his sharp sword and the tenth, the captain, leapt into the hungry waters.

After two months fruitless wandering, Fergus sighted the miraculous shining shield. Its radiance was second only to that of the sun.

He saw the hag on the narrow bridge. She had long plaited whiskers and her eyes were two feet apart. He must fight on foot. He pierced her flank with his spear. Her blood gushed out and she roared like an elephant. One sweep of her scythe sliced off his helmet down to his skull cap. She sliced through his shield as he dodged, but her scythe became embedded in the marble pillar. Fergus wasted no time, and, with his keen sword, he sliced through both her wrists and the scythe fell to the ground. As she fled, one sharp blow of his sword caught the giantess below the breast: he cleaved through flesh, bone and guts; and down she fell.

Fergus climbed to the castle and entered a hall filled with the radiant light of the shield. The shield was supported by a pillar which stood at the head of nine steps. An eighteen foot serpent lurked in the recesses beneath the shield. Mesmerized by the light, he unstrapped the shield and then, going down, he stepped on the dragon's step. One swish of the dragon's tail threw him against a pillar, but, with one blow of his trusty sword, he sliced through the dragon's head and half its neck. He left it to a writhing death.

He started on his return journey with the shining shield. Back in Lothian he was told that the country was ruled by a lady of the noblest character and that her name was Galiene. However, she was being besieged in the castle of Roxburgh by a powerful king.

Fergus wandered from his way and found himself at Melrose Mountain facing the husband of the hag, a giant with a massive club. He demanded the shining shield as a right and brought his club down on Fergus's trusty horse. Fergus lost his helmet and his hauberk was torn to shreds as though it were Syrian cloth and he was in great peril. However, that sharp sword of his cut through the giant again and again, severing his wrist and his arm from the shoulder. As the giant lifted him up and squeezed him, Fergus thrust that keenest of swords beneath the giant's breast and cut his heart into slices. The giant fell to the ground with a great clatter.

In the castle's cellar Fergus found the world's most magnificent horse. He broke it to his use and then he returned to the upper rooms, where his inner wounds were tended by two most thankful maidens, now newly rescued from the fearful clutches of the giant's foul son.

He was well placed in this castle to make a fair bid to rescue his sweetheart. From the upper floor, he saw the thirty thousand besieging tents about his beloved's stronghold and all the land about laid waste. The maidens armed him in the finest steel and he mounted that wonderful, obedient horse and, with his fine-honed enamelled lance, our super-hero rode forth alone to rescue his beloved.

He swooped down, striking, shattering and toppling all in his way. The attackers turned to face Fergus and the defenders surged out of the castle. The fighting was fierce as Fergus carved his fearless, forceful way through to face the seneschal. With one stroke he sliced through him down to the horse. When he pulled out his sword, the seneschal dropped down dead. But our Fergus did not stop. He renewed his attack like a lion.

His lady Galiene watched from a tower not knowing him, but she saw the shining shield and thought it was divine intervention. With a new, fresh, ashen lance Fergus charged again and unseated the king's nephew from his chestnut charger. The fallen knight must deliver the valuable horse to his lady with the compliments of the Knight of the Shining Shield. And so, the fighting that day came to an end.

The lady learnt that all had been done for love of her. The fighting had stopped and the Knight of the Shining Shield had disappeared along a forest track.

Fergus returned to the adroit and devoted care of his two ministering maidens. He slept and resumed his attack at the crack of the following dawn. The besieging king sensed defeat. His nephew, Arthofilaus, counselled a duel. If her champion was defeated, the maiden would yield Lothian and herself to the rightful king: if victorious, the siege would be lifted.

Arthofilaus issued a distorted, impetuous and insulting challenge to the maiden. Angrily she responded and taunted him that her champion would readily fight one against his two. A week was fixed for Galiene to find a champion and then all would be decided.

How she regretted her rashness. Her hero was nowhere to be found. A gracious maid, Arondele, offered to find him or to go and seek help from Arthur and his knights.

Within three days she found a dejected Arthur in his deserted court in Carlisle. His knights had left in all directions in search of Fergus. He could offer no help. Arondele was distraught. A kindly, ineffectual Arthur assured her they would all return on Ascension Day in twelve days time and that then all would be well. That was no use to Arondele who rode off in the direction taken by Gawain.

Having ridden through Galloway in all of three days, Arondele, fortuitously, stopped to gaze on the body of the giant that lay outside Melrose Castle. By chance, Fergus, who was amusing himself on the top of a tower, espied her. She told him of her failed promise of aid to her mistress and, innocently, of his own story and her continuing love for the knight that preferred fighting to her love on the banks of the Liddel.

With dramatic irony Fergus assured Arondele that: "As for me, I swear to you that, if she loved me like that, I'd give her real assistance." The giant had been killed by the Knight with the Shining Shield who fought so wonderfully outside Roxburgh castle and, suggests Fergus, he might yet be Galiene's knight in shining armour.

When Arondele returned, she found her mistress weeping, swooning, hysterical, suicidal and she could offer little in the way of hope. Galiene called her ministers "stinking slanderers" for suggesting that marriage to the king would not be so bad. She would have him burn in hell before she would be abandoned in his clutches. Why hadn't she waited in Liddel for the handsome Fergus? She will not have her love in her hour of need and at twelve noon she will throw herself from the tower.

Next morning, king and nephew came and issued their arrogant, taunting challenge. Galiene had climbed to the top of the uppermost turret, 180 feet above the earth. Wrapping her cloak tightly about her, she prepared to leap to her death. "Fergus," she called, "my sweet love, my life has run its course!"

She edged forward. She crossed herself. Someone shouted: "Look at the woods". The forest glowed as though it were aflame. The morning dew having silvered its paintwork, the wonderful shield shone with dazzling effulgence.

Fergus, his shield on his arm, afire with furious prowess, galloped forward and challenged king and nephew. Their arrogant, insolent taunts are turned aside and the knights proceeded to charge. Fergus held his seat rock steady as both lances simultaneously struck his stalwart shield. The tip of his lance pierced and shattered and sliced the heart of Arthofilaus. Fergus would have galloped away with Galiene on his charger, but the saddened king wanted to retrieve his nephew's body. "Leave him there to guard my crops," commanded Fergus as he charged and split his shield and rended his hauberk and cast him asprawl on the earth.

Humiliated, the king begged for mercy. He was told to restore everything to Galiene and to ride and pay due homage to Arthur at his court in Carlisle and to remind the mocking Kay that his day would come.

Sweating with shame, the king made grudging restitution to Galiene and told her that the unknown knight had said that he was responsible for angering her as never before. She sensed it must be Fergus and Love confused her and tormented her and tortured her yet more as the mysterious knight had disappeared into the Roxburgh forest.

Without waiting, the king made his way directly to Cumberland and asked the way to Carlisle.

Arthur was celebrating Ascension in the grandest style. His knights had all returned. However, amidst the bustle and the merry-making, Arthur sat apart, at the end of a beechwood table, thoughtfully whittling at a stick. He neither ate nor drank as he brooded on the loss of Fergus.

The defeated king in his full and vanquished armour entered and, standing before Arthur, recounted his full story. The Knight of the Shining Shield is the champion of the world and his name is Fergus. And he told Sir Kay that he has not been forgotten. The jester mockingly said that one day they would see Sir Kay fishing head down. The jester just escaped as a two-foot-long knife skimmed past his head. Arthur, with restrained anger, rebuked Kay's intemperance and bewailed his silly prattlings that had cost him such a noble knight.

Arthur longed to find Fergus and would have searched all lands this side of the Danube. The defeated king said that he had ridden off into Roxburgh Forest and Gawain proposed a great tournament on Jedburgh plain with a beautiful maiden and the crown of some kingdom for a prize. Fergus was bound to come. All was settled.

Galiene heard of the tourney, and being advised that the victor would be the Knight of the Shining Shield, she prepared to place her future happiness in Arthur's hands.

Knights came from all parts of the country to the immense and magnificent tourney and took up their positions among the trees of the desolate Jedburgh Forest.

With some reluctance, Arthur had felt obliged to grant the importunate Kay the opening joust. Immediately, out of the woods, sprang Fergus on a light coloured horse that ran faster than a small bird flies. The two knights dug their spurs into their steeds and they clashed. Fergus struck dead centre. Kay flew backwards over his saddle and landed head first in a stream. Fergus laughed at Kay fishing in his river without permission. He could catch plenty of fish for the king's supper. He'd made an eel-trap with his byrnie.

Fergus jousted with all and felled even Sir Lancelot. Then he rode away into another part of the forest, leaving others to recoup the booty on the field. The talk afterwards was of a super-human knight.

The following day the opening joust was a fearsome full tilt with Sir Sagremor. The force of the impact plumb on the boss of his shield burst all his straps and his girths and Sir Sagremor was sent ignominiously flying. In the midst of the general jousting that followed, Perceval called for a fight, but Fergus fended him off because of the honour he owed him. But he faced the Black Knight and dispatched him with one violent stroke.

And so the week proceeded happily.

On the Friday, the exquisite Galiene came and placed herself in Arthur's care. She had been Queen of Lothian for a year since her father's death and in that time her country had been laid waste until The Knight with the Shining Shield proved her champion. She would have Arthur find her a husband, find her the knight with the splendid shield, to rule her land.

Gawain proposed to be the first to fight the following day; he would speak with the mysterious knight. He waited and waited for an opponent. Then Fergus emerged from the forest. They talked. Gawain revealed his name. The Knight of the Shining Shield dismounted and flung his arms about Gawain's leg. He was Fergus and he had sent the wimple and horn to Arthur. Overjoyed, Gawain dismounted and they both unlaced their ventails and fell to kissing each other for as long as it takes for a man to walk slowly the length of four good bow-shots.

Gawain took his hand and led him to Arthur, who kissed him on the lips and face and bade him a heart-felt welcome. Fergus, Arthur, Gawain and Galiene took counsel apart. Arthur proposed that their victor should take the Queen of Lothian to wife. Fergus would do as he commanded but wanted to hear from the lady herself that this was what she wanted too. Galiene spoke: "Dear, very good sir, I place at your disposal my mind, my heart, all my sentiments and my entire person."

The celebrations of the wedding that Sunday, the Feast of Saint John, lasted another twenty joyous days. As they parted, Gawain urged him not to abandon knightly deeds for his wife, for fear of becoming a laughing stock.

Fergus and Galiene returned to Roxburgh. He loved her as his tender sweetheart and she him as her noble lover.

And so, just as it should, the romance ends.

William the Clerk, the name must be a nom de plume, ends his work with a flourish:

Guillaume le Clerc comes to the end of his subject and his composition. For in no land does he find any man who has lived long enough to be able to tell anything further of the knight with the splendid shield. Here he plants the boundary-stone and post: this is the end of the romance.

If William the Clerk has borrowed from other authors, notably Chretien de Troyes and those who continued his Perceval, he is not going to have others extrapolate his extended jeux d'espirit further.

And the poem is extended, intelligent, intellectual play. Our author has responded to one of the most beautiful sensitive poets of the previous generation, a man whose work had shaped the way people - the people at court at least - thought and felt, or might have thought they thought and felt - a work that had a seminal, fulcral influence on sentiment and morality for centuries to come, and he has played with the characters and the actions and the sentiment and the form, teasing and testing them, believing them and ridiculing them, making us accept them and then laughing at our response. *Fergus*, once dismissed as the second-rate work of a hack, is a coherent comic masterpiece, well structured to satirize the form of its original and delighting in the play of language and meaning.

Its precise geography is no accident. Behind the flamboyance of the action lies a committed realist. The borderlands of England and Scotland were backward, impoverished countries. Their economies were wasted by the lack of political stability that had seen Carlisle change hands between England and Scotland several times in the previous century. There was probably little trade between the countries and the castle at Carlisle was a military outpost set in a buffer zone between two restless countries.

Attempts have been made to identify the author and particularize the poem. Early editors saw it as dedicated to Alan of Galloway, the great grandson of the historical Fergus, who had been a ruler of that country. However, any author who portrays his patron's subjects as being "stupid and bestial" and his ancestor as a rough countryman living in a wattle and daub castle, is playing a dangerous game.

The politics of the poem suggest an Arthur who is given feudal authority over the south of Scotland. He grants Lothian and Tweedale to Fergus and Galiene. However, we are not offered a picture of Arthur's wider realm and so can not be clear whether the context suggests English authority over Scotland or whether Arthur's Carlisle is itself in a greater Strathclyde and part of Scotland as it had been in the days of William the Lion.

It would be difficult to see Fergus having serious political implications, although it might have strong elements of political satire. A lethargic king in a deserted court or a disconsolate majesty, who whittles away at a stick and can't eat or drink for the loss of a fine figure of a knight, is hardly the epitome of gracious authority.

It is possible that Artholifaus, (Arthur the false?) is a caricature of Arthur of Brittany. In 1202, this Arthur besieged his grandmother, Eleanor of Aquitaine, in the castle of Mirebeau. King John of England, her son and Arthur's uncle, sent William de Braose to intervene and Arthur was defeated and led away in chains. If this idea does apply, the correspondence only appertains to one aspect of the situation and merely caricatures the character and situation of Arthur and has no wider application in the work. But it is exactly such correspondences which would tease and amuse the work's audience.

There was a strong French presence at the Scottish court of the time and it may be that the poem was heard by people who knew the geography of the area. The one surviving manuscript of the poem is in a Picardie dialect from north west France. Anyone hearing the poem in France or England would have a sense of a mythical geography, a geography of the imagination which, despite its precision, could be pictured as the listener wished.

The Alliterative Morte Arthure: Arthur moves from Caerleon to Carlisle

Something like sixteen Arthurian romances in English survive from the two centuries after the reign of Edward I. All drew on French originals and continued the tradition, established in the French language, of building on and developing the stories that were already popular. Rarely, if ever, were they simply translations. These redactions would place their own stamp on the story. Marie's *Lanval* became *Landeval*, and, in the course of mutation, lost its delicacy and grace and took on coarser qualities, which might be more readily appreciated by its wider audiences far removed from the elegant courtly circles. Chretien's *Ywain* became *Ywain and Gawain* and focussed on the practical action rather than the subtle suggestion of refined and ambivalent values.

The finest of these works, *Sir Gawain and the Green Knight* and the alliterative *Morte Arthure* and the tale Chaucer puts in the mouth of the Wife of Bath, are among the greatest poems in the language. Others are essentially good entertainment, lively verse, which, in the hands of a practiced performer, would offer ready amusement for a convivial evening.

The so-called alliterative *Morte Arthure* is one of the masterpieces of the alliterative revival. Anglo-Saxon poetry, such as *Beowulf* and *The Seafarer* had employed alliteration, rather than rhyme and our modern metrical forms, to give form and music to the verse. It was a form of writing that appears to have largely disappeared after the Norman Conquest, when the predominant language became Norman French and there was no longer an English speaking court or nobility to encourage English language poetry.

In the middle of the fourteenth century, and for about a hundred years after that, alliterative poetry experienced a renaissance. The crowning masterpieces of this period were the anonymous *Sir Gawain and the Green Knight* and two other poems probably by the same poet, *The Pearl* and *Cleanness*, and *Piers Plowman* by William Langland. Langland probably lived and wrote in the Malvern Hills and the poet of *Sir Gawain*, on the evidence of his dialect and knowledge of topography, probably came from further north, possibly from Cheshire. The alliterative revival seems to have been confined to that area from the west Midlands northwards and was also very popular in Scotland.

The alliterative *Morte Arthure* is not so well known, but is of a quality and craftsmanship to sit alongside the other poems mentioned.

King Arthur was at the height of his power. He ruled all of the British Isles, was lord of France and conqueror of Germany. Austria and Denmark, Sweden and Norway acknowledged the authority of his sharp sword. He had been hunting the hart in the highlands of South Wales

> *And there a city he set, by assent of his lords*
> *That Caerleon was called, with its curious walls*

These curious walls were massive structures built by the Romans and not by Arthur as the poet implies. Caerleon was to be used as a naval port to enable his followers to go to sea when they liked. However, Arthur chose to spend his Christmas in Carlisle:

> *Then after at Carlisle a Christenmass he holds,*

with all the dukes and overlords of his diverse realms, his earls and archbishops, bishops and all that bowed to his banner. When they were assembled on Christmas Day, he commanded that they should all remain with him for ten days while they celebrated the season:

> *Thus in royal array he held his Round Table . . .*
> *But on the New-Year day, at the noon even,*
> *As the bold at the board was of bread served,*
> *So came in suddenly a senator of Rome,*

The senator saluted the King and all those others present and then made his announcement that Lucius demanded tribute from Arthur:

> *"Sir Lucius Iberius, the Emperor of Rome,*
> *Salutes thee as subject, . . .*
> *I make thee summons in salle to sue for thy lands,*
> *That on Lamass Day there be no let found*
> *That thou be ready at Rome with all thy Round Table*
> *Appear in his presence with thy prize knights*
> *At prime of the day, on pain of your lives, . . .*
> *There shall thou give reckoning for all thy Round Table,*
> *Why thou art rebel to Rome and rents them with-holds!*

If Arthur resisted this summons, he would be *fetched with force and overset forever*. Lucius Iberius demanded the tribute that Julius Caesar won.

The King:

> *Looked as a lion and on his lip bites.*

The Romans were terrified at his look and crouched on the ground like hounds. One asked:

> *"Misdo no messenger . . . and mercy thee beseech; . . .*

78

We come at his commaundment; have us excused."

Arthur determined to take counsel of his knights there assembled. In the meantime, he said:

"Forth shall thou long here and lodge with these lords
This seven-night in solace to sojourn your horses,
To see what life that we lead in these low lands."

Arthur commanded Kay to see that these uninvited guests lacked for nothing.

And then the chancellor them fetched with chivalry noble;
Soon the senator was set as him well seemed,
At the kings own board; two knights him served,
Singley, soothly, as Arthur himself,
Richly on the right hand at the Round Table.
By reason that the Romans were so rich holden,
As of the royalist blood that reigned in earth.

The boastful senator and his knights were then served a feast that mocked their proud and audacious claims.

There come in at the first course, before the king's self,
Boarheads that were bright, burnisht with silver . . .
Peacocks and plovers in platters of gold
Pigs of porcupines that pastured never; . . .
Great swans full swithe on silver chargers,
Tarts of Turkey, taste whom them likes;
Gumbaldes graithly, full gracious to taste;
Then bows of wild boars with the brawn leached,
Barnacles and bitterns in battered dishes,
Thereby braunchers in bread, better was never,
With breasts of barrowes that bright were to show;
Then came there stews several with solace thereafter,
Ondes of azure all over and ardent them seemed;
Of each slice the light launched full high,
That all lads might like that looked them upon;
Then cranes and curlews craftily roasted,
Connies in cretone coloured full fair,
Pheasants enflourished in flame and silver, . . .
Then Claret and Crete skilfully running
Through conduits full curious all of clean silver,
Alsatian and Algarve and other enough
Rhenish wine and Rochelle, richer was never,

Vintage of Venice, virtuous, and Crete,
In faucets of fine gold, fonde whoso likes;
The kings cupboard was closed in silver,
In great goblets overgilt, glorious of hue
There was a chief butler, a chevalier noble
Sir Kay the courteous, that of the cup served;
Sixty cups of a suit for the king himself,
Crafty and curious, carven full fair,
In everyone a part pitted with precious stones,
That no poison should go privily there-under
But the bright gold for breath should burst all to pieces,
Or else the venom should void through virtue of the stones;
And the conquerour himself, so cleanly arrayed,
In colours of clean gold clad, with his knights,
Dressed with his diadem on his dais rich,
For he was deemed the doughtiest that dwelled in earth.

With this enormous feast of such magnificence and splendour laid before the senator and knights, who had so demeaned his country and person and demanded tribute, Arthur addressed them with regal irony:

"Sirs, be knightly of countenance and comfort yourselves;
We know nought in this country of curious meats;
In these barren lands breeds none other;
Therefore, without feigning, force you the more
To feed you with such feeble (food) as ye before find."

The senator was forced to confess that:

There reigned never such royalty within Rome walls!

After feasting Gawain and Gaynor (Guinevere) led the party into a chamber where they drank:

Malmesy and Muscatel, those marvelous drinks.

The evening continued:

With mirth and with melody of minstrelsy noble.

Arthur retired to the Giant's Tower in order to take counsel with his knights. Sir Cador of Cornwall spoke with gusto. They have become losels or wastrels with the delights of peace. He longed for deeds of arms:

"Now wakens the war! Worshipped be Christ!
And we shall win it again by wightness and strength!"

Arthur was rational and moderate in his response. The enthusiastic Sir Cador was a marvellous man, but as King he must consider a truce and take account of the Emperor's anger. The senator had insulted him and grieved him in his own hall and demanded tyrantly tribute for Rome. In the past Rome had taken tribute forcefully from commoners when knights had not been there to defend them. However, Arthur's predecessors:

Belin and Bremin and Bawdewyne the third;

had conquered Rome and claimed tribute and

Then Constantine, our kinsman, conquered it after,
That heir was of England and emperor of Rome.
Thus have we evidence to ask the emperor the same,
That thus reigns at Rome, what right that he claims."

Arthur's sober, reasoned response evoked admiration for its worthiness and knightliness. King Aungers of Scotland recalled how his country suffered under the Romans:

"When the Romans reigned they ransomed our elders
And rode in their riot and ravished our wives."

He vowed vengeance. He will provide twenty thousand men.

The powerful lord of Brittany beseeched Arthur to answer the Romans with bold words. He feared their sharp swords no more:

"Than the dew that is dank when that it down falls;"

He will supply thirty thousand well-armed knights within a month.

The Welsh king was next, speaking with an accent and soldierly prowess as brave and as proud as Llewellyn in Henry V:

"A! A!" says the Welsh king; "worshipped be Christ!
Now shall we wreak full well the wrath of our elders!"

He had been done a villainy once in Viterbo and was now ready to deal dints of death. He will provide two thousand well-horsed men, the strongest that ever came out of the West lands.

Sir Ewain fitz Urien, i.e. Owain ap Urien or Ywain, was eager for the fight;

"To ride on yon Romans and riot their lanes,
We would shape us therefore, to ship when you likes."

Arthur was ready, he vowed to take leave at Lammas, August 1st, and roam through Lorraine or Lombardy, march to Milan and mine the walls of Saint Peters and Pisa and Pont Tremble and then, after resting his forces in Viterbo, he would plant his siege before the prize town until they sued for peace.

Sir Ewain can barely be restrained. He will seize the Emperor's standard with its eagle and *rive it in sonder*. He promised fifty thousand of the finest men.

Lancelot spoke. He was ready to be there to joust with the emperor himself and:

  "Strike him stiffly from his steed with strength of mine hands."
The knights were now brimful of confidence. Sir Lot laughed and said:
  "Me likes that Sir Lucius longs after sorrow;"
He would avenge his elders and carve his way through the rout,
  "Running on red blood, as my steed rushes!"
Whoever followed in his fareway would find the field full of the dead. Arthur praised their enthusiasm and cooled their impetuosity. He would take account of no king while he had such men around him.

  The trumpet sounded to conclude the meeting.

  After seven days the senator asked for Arthur's answer.
  The king in his counsel, courteous and noble,
Made his response: *"Greet well Lucius, thy lord,"* and let him know soon
  "I shall at Lamas take leave and lodge at my large
  In delight in his lands with lords enough, . . .
  By the river of Rhone hold my Round Table,"
He will ride through Lorraine and Lombardy, Milan and Tuscany. Arthur laid down the challenge:
  "And meet me for his manhood in those main lands!
  I shall be found in France, fraist when him likes!
  The first day of February in those fair marches!
  Ere I be fetched with force or forfeit my lands,
  The flower of his fair folk full fey shall be laid!
  I shall him certainly ensure under my seal rich
  To siege the city of Rome within seven winter . . .
  That many a senator shall sigh for sake of my one!"
Having spoken with regal authority, Arthur, in no uncertain terms, made clear the conditions for the messengers' departure:
  "Seven days to Sandwich I set thee at large;
  Sixty mile on a day, the sum is but little!
  Thou must speed at the spurs and spare not thy foals;
  Thou wends by Watling Street and by no way else;"
At night they must fasten their horses and rest under the trees. They must not depart from these rules on pain of their lives.
  "For be thou found a foot without the flood marches
  After the eighth day when undern is rung,
  Thou shall be heaved on high and with horse drawn,
  And then highly be hanged, hounds to gnawn!
  The rent and red gold that unto Rome belongs

Shall not readily, renk, ransom thine one!"

The proud senator was shaken by Arthur's words. Were he once away, he would never return for any emperor. He asked for safe conduct.

"Care not," quoth the king; "thy conduct is known
From Carlisle to the coast there thy cogge lies;
Though thy coffers were full, crammed with silver,
Thou might be surer of my seal sixty mile further."

They bowed to the King and asked to be conducted out of Carlisle. They inclined to the king.

Sir Cador the courteous kend them the ways,
To Catterick them conveyed and to Christ them bekenned.
So they sped at the spurs they pranged their horses,
Hired them hackneys hastily thereafter.
So for terror they rode and rested them never, . . .
By the seventh day was gone the city they reached.
Of all the glee under God so glad were they never
As of the sound of the sea and Sandwich bells.
Without more stunting they shipped their horses;
Weary to the wan sea they went all at once.
With the men of the gunwale they weighted up their anchors
And fled at the fore flood;

They fled through Flanders to Aachen in Germany and then over the St Gothard Pass into Lombardy and on to Tuscany and so to Rome. The Emperor Lucius eagerly awaited Arthur's response. Because the senator was his very own messenger, Arthur, himself, should have waited upon him. The senator had been so deeply impressed by Arthur's majesty and demeanour, he answered Lucius directly:

"I say thee, sir, Arthur is thine enemy forever,
And ettles to be overling of the empire of Rome,"

Arthur was:

"The comeliest of knighthood that under Christ lives!
For if he reaches unto Rome, he ransoms it forever."

The senator had obviously got the message from Arthur.

Geoffrey of Monmouth sets this scene in Caerleon. His Caerleon is richer than other townships, with a river that could readily accommodate the vessels that brought kings from distant realms. The city was adorned with royal palaces, with golden rooves, that made it the equal of Rome. It was a place of religion, music and learning. Geoffrey claims his descriptive powers cannot match the size and magnificence of the procession of kings who waited upon the generous Arthur. In fact, even though he alludes to the coronation of Arthur and Guinevere and suggests the magnificence of robes and music, he does not describe the event itself.

In the succeeding days, the members of this most affluent and sophisticated and fortunate kingdom take part in knightly and other war-like games and are rewarded from Arthur's largesse. The fine ladies scorned to give their love to any man who had not proved himself in battle three times. Geoffrey concludes that this ambition caused the ladies to remain virtuous and chaste and the knights to become ever more daring.

The envoy from Rome enters, twelve men of mature years bearing olive branches, and hand Lucius's letter to Arthur. The letter talks of damage to Rome, outrage and criminal behaviour. Arthur must appear in Rome by the middle of August to receive the punishment the Senate deem meet.

Arthur withdraws to the gigantic tower near the palace entrance with the kings and the leaders and, as they climb the stairs, Cador merrily talks of the sloth of peace and the manly courage of war. Arthur's long and reasoned speech argues that Rome owes him tribute, that Brennius and Constantine, with their conquests set the precedent. Hoel, King of the Armorican Britons, praises Arthur's Ciceronian eloquence, and, with a fine bit of rabble-rousing, promises ten thousand men. King Auguselus of Albany, thirsts for blood, talks of the sweetness of death and wills them to attack these emasculated creatures. King follows king with enthusiastic promises until Arthur finds himself at the head of a putative army of 273,200. This immense force may be the result of scribal error, as Roman numerals were copied and re-copied from manuscript to manuscript, but the excitability of Arthur's kings seems to promise no less.

Arthur orders them to return home and rendezvous at the port of Barfleur. The Roman envoy receives a message that Arthur is coming to Rome to demand tribute and they are ordered to leave.

The Norman-French Wace, elaborates the same scene delightfully from Geoffrey's account. His Caerleon is a bustling medieval city. On the day of the feast, it is more like a fair, with the jousting and sports, gambling and gaming. Men will sit down at the chess or draughts board in furs, wage their all on the outcome of the game and rise and depart in their bare skins. The Romans appear at the feast, twelve grey-bearded men bearing olive branches, but their long and stern message from Lucius is far from peaceful. Arthur's knights are angry, even riotous, until Arthur urges a proper respect for Rome's envoy. Arthur retires with his privy council to the Giant's Tower. Sir Cador, as they climb the stairs, enthusiastically blusters about the manly virtues of war, but Gawain feels that merry tales and songs and ladies' love are delectable to youth. Arthur makes a similar reasoned speech based on historical evidence, though at far greater length. Hoel is the first to respond, praising Arthur's victories and claiming that Arthur is the third of those British kings who will conquer Rome. Aguisel, King of Scotland, speaks of Rome's depravity and depredations and concludes with a triumphal cry for Arthur to rule the whole world. A missive is prepared and Rome's envoy is sent on its way.

Wace has added circumstantial detail to Geoffrey's boastful patriotism, turned the proud propaganda into a courteous romance with character and personal interaction.

Layamon celebrates a rich and splendid Caerleon. Kings and ecclesiasts have assembled from the far reaches of Arthur's realm to be present at his coronation. After three days of festivities and merry-making, twelve knights come from Rome, hail Arthur, but demand his tribute to Lucius. If he fails to comply the emperor will take Arthur with strength and lead him bound to Rome. Arthur's knights are riotous, ready to kill the ambassadors, but Arthur commands that they be shown due respect. Arthur takes counsel with favoured lords in a house of old stone work. Sir Cador speaks first, pleased that the Roman threat has stirred them from the lethargy of peace. Gawain urges the virtues of peace. Arthur addresses the meeting. He talks of Rome's iniquities. He has equal claims through Belin and Brenne, through Maximian and through Constantine. Lucius and Arthur both desire all. God will decide.

Howel of Brittany pledges to sell his silver and raise ten thousand knights. King Angel of Scotland will provide ten thousand foot-soldiers and three thousand mounted knights. He is determined that the Romans will pay for it with their bare lives. There is such an angry clamour from the knights in the hall that Arthur is angered and has to call for silence. He will not send a tribute but will bind and hang the emperor and then destroy all the land and put to the sword all that stand against him.

Arthur gives his message to the envoy and then clothes them in gold and silver and the finest of garments and sends them on their way. In Rome they speak of Arthur's keenness and power and of the boldness of his knights.

The *Alliterative Morte Arthure* has transformed the novelistic material of Wace and Layamon into a symbolically dramatic scene, where characterful speeches are strongly counterpoised and actions, from the feast to the promise of safe conduct, are given a significance that reveals Arthur's qualities and serves to point the moral argument of the poem. The device of the sumptuous feast is introduced to demonstrate Arthur's power, wealth, magnificence and largesse and possibly draws on Layamon's hint of Arthur impressing the envoy with fine clothes.

All earlier texts merely hint at the promise of a safe passage and do not specify it or use it to show Arthur's fine sense of justice and proper conduct. There is no parallel in the earlier texts to Arthur's attractive brand of self-deprecating irony in the face of the wealth of Rome. Neither is there the attractive nuancing of character to be found in the Alliterative *Morte Arthur*. The sequence of transition from Geoffrey through Wace and Layamon to our anonymous poet over a period of more than two centuries shows a significant shift in sensibility. We have moved from Latin into Norman French and then into the English of a re-emergent conquered people and finally to the assured language of a renascent regional poetry. The shift in sensibility has been one from jingoistic propaganda to a finely tuned moral tale that judiciously weighs the worth of Arthur's actions and sees his fall as consequent upon his actions.

The alliterative *Morte Arthure* is very clear in designating Carlisle Arthur's capital. The passing reference to Caerleon, its identity clearly established by reference to the hunting in South Wales and its riverine location and its massive walls, serves to dismiss it as a newly-founded city and as a port for the embarkation of troops.

The geographical details indicate that the poet is definitely thinking of Carlisle. Unlike other poets, whose geography owed much to the imagination, our poet is very knowledgeable and accurate about his geography. He has a sense of distant lands. His awareness of France suggests he has at least an approximate awareness of the country's topography. His knowledge of English geography is detailed and precise. Arthur gives the senator and his knights seven days safe passage to accomplish their journey from Carlisle to Sandwich travelling at sixty miles a day. The distance from Carlisle to Sandwich is 360 modern miles, which are about a tenth longer than the medieval mile. The Romans are to travel via Catterick on Watling Street. Catterick is near Scotch Corner and the journey would take the route of the present A66 across the Pennines and then follow the A1 south. Watling Street is usually thought of as being the line of the the Roman road from London to Wroxeter, but the name, which is *Waecelinga* in Anglo-Saxon, possibly meaning the street of the *Waecel* or Welsh or stranger, was used to designate any of the roads leading to British territories and was so used to describe the road north to Cumbria. Geoffery of Monmouth talked of Watling Street running from Canterbury to Cardigan. One route ran from Canterbury to Wroxeter and then turned south and almost back on itself to Caerleon. Leland, in his *Itinery*, writes of *"The way on Watlyngstrete from Borow Bridge to Carlil. Watlingstrete lyeth about a mile from Gillinge and 3m from Richemount. From Borow Bridge to Caterike"*

The poet is clearly referring to Carlisle, rather than a mis-heard or mistranscribed Caerleon.

Why did he make such a significant, if pointless, change in an established tradition which still carried some slight weight as historical truth? Geoffrey had clearly identified Caerleon with circumstantial detail that accorded with the mythical importance of a city with such imposing Roman ruins in the medieval mind. Wace had followed Geoffrey's lead, and Layamon, who, because of his living in Worcestershire, could be expected of having some cognizance of the city, chose to follow suit. The poet of the alliterative *Morte Arthure* must have had good reason to make such a change.

Aesthetically, the location in Carlisle and not Caerleon makes little difference. The poet has retained the gigantic or giant's tower which has a physical counterpart in Caerleon. The one change that could not fit a Caerleon location is the envoy's return journey through Catterick, but a similar route might have been prescribed from Caerleon. Such a route might have taken a similar time and even followed Watling Street for part of its length.

There may have been a feeling that Carlisle, fought over for centuries and a distant, troubled city on the very edge of the kingdom, was a more appropriate setting for a mythical king than a wealthy river port that was closely tied in with the nation's economy, but our poet is writing a poem that balances on the edge of historical documentation and literary invention. Even so, fourteenth century Carlisle was still primarily a military base, responsible for the policing of the unruly Scottish border, and not a place to be associated with pomp and ceremony and, equally, not a place where a diner, no matter how distinguished, might expect to be presented with such a show of gastronomic magnificence.

There seems little aesthetic argument to be made for the change.

It is possible the poet had some authority for the change. Froissart, who had completed his *Chronicles* by 1369, casually mentions an association of Arthur with Carlisle:

Just in the same manner as the English conducted themselves in Scotland, did the French and Scots in Cumberland, and on the borders of England, where they burnt and destroyed large tracts of country. They entered Westmoreland, passing through the lands of Greystock, and of the baron Clifford, and burnt on their march several large villages where no men at arms had before been. They met with no opposition, as the country was drained, for all men at arms were with the king in his expedition. They came at length before Carlisle, which is well inclosed with walls, towers, gates and ditches: king Arthur formerly resided here more than elsewhere, on account of the fine woods which surround it, and for the grand adventures of arms which had happened near it.

It is suggested that Froissart may have confused Carlisle with Caerleon. This would seem unlikely. Froissart would probably be aware of Geoffrey's *History* and he knew the country well. He had travelled in the north and in Scotland and his *Chronicles* demonstrate that he had a precise conception of Carlisle from his discussion of other historical matters that he connects with the city. In addition, he is generally regarded as one of the most reliable of the chroniclers. There are also the very clear reasons that he offers for Arthur making it not one of his residences, but his most favoured residence. The fine woods are something Froissart would have known both from his experience and, evidently, by reputation. Cumberland retained its forests at a time when southerly areas of England were being more widely farmed.

It is difficult to know what Froissart is referring to by *the grand adventures of arms which had happened near it.* He cannot be referring to the warfare of recent years or centuries, the recurrent Border Wars between England and Scotland since, knowing Geoffrey and the prevailing medieval sense of Arthur, he would conceive of Arthur belonging to a distant past. Yet he does seem to imply an acceptance of the existence of an historical Arthur and the suggestion is that he is aware of specific *grand adventures of arms.* Nennius might provide a sort of answer with his references to the battles of Coed Celadon and the Dubglas and even the battle of Camlann, if Froissart was aware of Nennius. It is equally possible that Froissart is referring to other histories which are now lost or to a view he may have heard expressed by others.

Equally interesting is the concept of the Carlisle of that day which he offers: *Carlisle, which is well inclosed with walls, towers, gates and ditches:* that is of a city sufficient in its defensive and military arrangements to have been a fit city for Arthur.

Froissart's reference to Carlisle, as Arthur's favourite residence, and our alliterative poet's purposed selection of Carlisle, as the city for Arthur to conduct his most significant political and regal action, at least points to a prevailing sense that Carlisle was held to be a city associated with Arthur, if not the principle place of his residence.

The feast in Carlisle is the prologue to a magnificent poem. Arthur convenes a court at York, sails from Sandwich and dreams of a mortal struggle between a bear and a dragon. He wrestles with and vanquishes the villainous giant of Mont St Michel, defeats Lucius in battle and sends his corpse as tribute to Rome. He lays siege to Metz. Before he marches on Rome, he dreams of the turning wheel of fortune and then learns that Mordred has seized his kingdom and married Guinevere. He returns to England. Gawain is slain, and then Arthur kills Mordred and is himself borne away mortally wounded.

It is a wonderfully orchestrated work. The alliterative verse becomes superbly flexible, capable of virtuosic set pieces such as the seven lines all alliterating on *f* that depict the English bowmen firing off their volleys of arrows, just as they would have done at the Battle of Crecy. Battle scenes are described with the verve and precision of a military tactician and the wrestle with the giant is presented in cinematic close-up. The poem is story telling at its finest by a master practitioner. There is a deep awareness of the tragedy of war and a sense of the glory and vainglory of military prowess and earthly ambition.

The alliterative *Morte Arthure* is a powerful war poem that has few, if any, parallels in English.

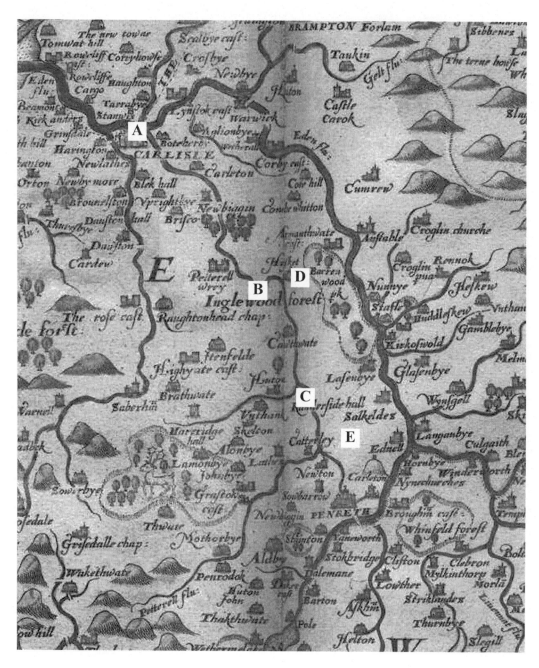

*A detail of Saxton's map of Cumberland and Westmorland from 1576
showing Carlisle, **A**, Inglewood Forest, **B**, and Randerside Hall, **C**, which may be
the same as Rondeshalle. Tarn Wadling is at **D**, and Plumpton Wall at **E***

The Awntyrs off Arthur at the Terne Wathelin: a Ghost and a Joust in Inglewood Forest

The Awntyrs off Arthur at the Terne Wathelin is the other poem in the alliterative tradition that is set in the Carlisle area. It was written in the early fifteenth century, sometime after the alliterative *Morte Arthure*. One version is found in the Thornton manuscript alongside *Morte Arthure* and there are three other versions in existence. The poem is written in a northern dialect, possibly, in so far as an informed guess can be made when a work has been transcribed possibly several times into other dialects, in the dialect of the area around Richmond in North Yorkshire.

Certainly, its precise depiction of the geography of the Carlisle area and the use of many Norse-derived words of a northern provenance, indicate a northerly composition.

The poem is set in Inglewood Forest. Inglewood was the largest royal forest in the country. As a royal forest it was reserved exclusively for the king and was under the jurisdiction of forest law, which considerably limited settlement and development. In practice the large royal reserves of the Border, Inglewood Forest and the King's Forest of Geltsdale, served as buffer zones between the troubled areas on the Scottish border and the rest of England. Most of Cumberland had not been included in the Domesday Book, because it was then part of the Kingdom of Strathclyde. For two centuries, until the reign of Edward I, the area had been subject to military incursions and, in succeeding years, it was still prey to Scottish outlawry, the celebrated reivers, and remained so until the kingdoms were united under James VI of Scotland and I of England.

Tarn Wadling has a very particular place in mythology. The lake no longer exists. It was drained to create agricultural land in the nineteenth century and drained again by Italian prisoners of war during the Second World War.

The tarn, covering an area of a hundred acres or so, lay in the slight glacial depression to the east of High Hesket church, just off the present A6, about half way between Carlisle and Penrith. High Hesket is on a ridge that separates the valleys of the Petteril and the Eden.

However, in the Middle Ages the tarn acquired a reputation out of all proportion to its size. The celebrated Gough Map of 1360, which is one of the earliest detailed maps we have of the country, shows three lakes: two, Loch

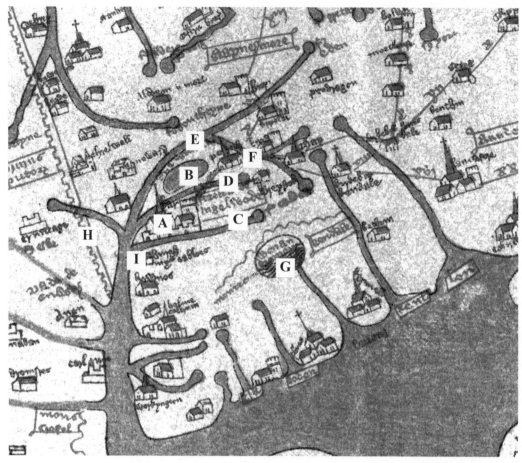

Detail of the Gough map of 1360 showing Tarn Wadling (Terne Wathelan) between the rivers Eden and Petteril. A is Carlisle; B is Tarn Wadling; C is Inglewood Forest; D is the River Petteril and E is the Eden; F is Penrith; G is Windermere; H is Hadrian's Wall and I is Burgh by Sands. North is to the left.

Lomond and Windermere, merit inclusion, but the third, Tarn Wadling, can make no such geographical claim. However, it is correctly positioned between the Eden and the Petteril, even though it is hugely out of scale. This small, shallow puddle appears to be larger than Windermere. Its reputation must have been considerable.

Several legends attach to the tarn. One early one, Laikibrait, talks of a lake that cries and refers to a drowned village. Another story speaks of a witch being mocked by villagers and wreaking her revenge by drowning the village. Tarn Wadling also appears as a major location in several Arthurian poems.

It is hard to account for this mythical importance. The tarn area seems to have

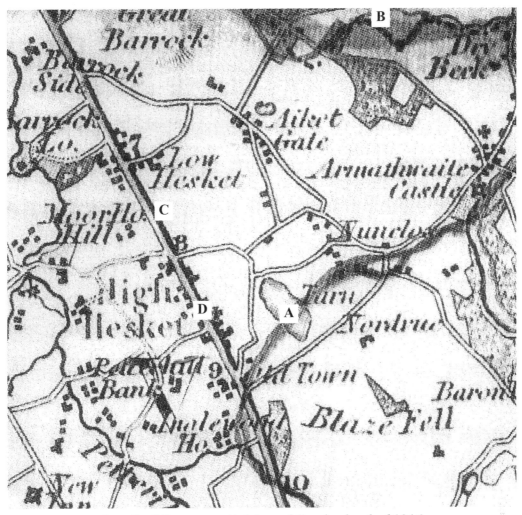

Detail of Greenwood's Map of Cumberland of 1816,
showing Tarn Wadling, A, before it was drained.
B is Castle Hewin, C the Court Thorn and D High Hesket.

had a benign history. The land thereabouts was owned by the Nunnery at Armathwaite. The area was famous for its bilberries and the tarn itself for the size and quality of its carp.

Its legendary reputation may have been prompted by its early history. The name means the lake of the little Irishman. *Tarn* is a Norse word and *Wadling* a Celtic word. It seems odd that a Celtic place name referring to an alien settlement should have survived and been combined with a Norse name in an area where the Norse settlers replaced the British.

Above Tarn Wadling, to the north-east is Castle Hewin. In the eighteenth century, this low hill was surmounted by the remains of a fortress. These have now largely disappeared, but it is possible they were the remains of a Roman fortress commanding the major route south from Lugovallium to Old Penrith and Brovacum (Brougham). Even though the hill is comparatively low, it offers good views north and south along the Petteril Valley.

The name Castle Hewin may recall the name of Owain, Prince of Rheged. There was a later Owain of Strathclyde. This Owain is the same Owain whose name mutated as his legend travelled south through Wales and Brittany to become the Ywain of Chretien de Troyes's romance of *The Knight with the Lion*.

It is possible that, during the Dark Ages, Castle Hewin became the centre of Celtic resistance to Anglo-Saxon settlement, although the pattern of names in the area suggests a low level of relatively peaceful incursion.

The reason for the tarn's reputation may also be indicated by its position between a Thiefside Hill and Wragmire Moss, that is that it was a place of refuge and recuperation in the middle of a dangerous road.

Tarn Wadling is the setting for one of the most dramatic of Arthurian stories.

Arthur, *that conquerour kydde*, with his queen and all his knights had left the court at Carlisle to go hunting in Inglewood Forest, by Tarn Wadling. Gawain escorted Queen Gaynour (Guinevere). She was splendidly dressed in a glittering gown, *Railed with rubies of royal array*, with a blue rain cloak set with sapphires and celedonies, and she rode upon a milk white mule saddled with sambles of silk. Arthur assigned his men to their hunting stations, placing each lord by an oak *with bowe and with barselette* hound. They waited, steadying their hounds in the frosty air. The deer cowered in the dark woods, *for dread of the death droops the doe*. The hunters hallooed, the hounds set on the deer in the thickets. They gave no quarter. The king blew rechase.

All took pleasure in the delights of the chase except Gawain and Gaynour, who walked through the groves and rested under the arbour of a laurel. At mid-morning a marvel occurred:

> *The day waxed also dark*
> *As it were midnight mirk;*

The king and the knights dismounted and ran for the shelter of the rocks:

> *For the sneetering snow smartly them snelles.*

There came a light on the lake

> *In the likeness of Lucifer, loathliest in Hell,*

And glided to Sir Gawayn.

It yammers and yowls with many a loud yell, cursing *"the body me bare!"*

Gaynor yells and weeps and Gawain tries to comfort the queen, saying it is just an eclipse of the sun. The other knights

> *"have me left on my deathday*
> *With the grissliest ghost that ever heard I greet."*

Gawain nobly offered to speak with the ghost, and discover how to relieve its torments.

> *Bare was the body and black to the bone,*
> *All beclagged in clay uncomely clad . . . .*
> *It stammered, it stunned, it stood as a stone,*

Gawain went towards the grissly ghost. He was not afraid.

> *All glowed as a glede the ghost there she glides,*
> *Unbeclipped in a cloud of clothing unclear,*
> *Circled with serpents all about the sides.*

He drew his sword. The ghost stood still. Gawain did not flinch. The hounds hid their heads in the holes. The birds shrieked. Gawain spoke:

> *"As thou was crucified on Cross to cleanse us of sin:*
> *That thou say me the sooth whether thou shall,*
> *And why thou walkest these ways the woods within."*

She replied:

> *"I was of figure and face fairest of all,*
> *Christened and known with kings in my kin; . . . .*
> *God has me given of his grace*
> *To dree my pains in this place.*

She would speak with the queen. She had been greater than Gaynour in wealth and power, but now:

> *"Into care am I caught and couched in clay.*
> *Lo, sir courteouss knight,*
> *How doleful death has me dight!*
> *Let me once have a sight*
> *Of Gaynour the gay."*

> *After Gaynour the gay Sir Gawain is gone,*
> *And to the body he her brought, the bride bright.*

The ghost welcomed her.

> *Lo, how doleful death has thy dam dight! . . .*
> *Now am I a graceless ghost, and grisly I groan; . . .*
> *Thus am I like to Lucifer: take witness by me!*
> *For all thy fresh furs,*

Muse on my mirror;
For, king and emperor,
Thus dight shall you be.

Gaynour should take heed when richest arrayed. She has power to have pity on the poor. When her body is embalmed the prayers of the poor may purchase her peace. But the ghost, her mother, was in torment:

It were full tore any tongue my torment to tell;

She was warned to mend her ways:

Be ware by my woe.

She saw:

"That all thy burly body is brought to be so bare!"

Gaynour will offer anything, bishop's prayers, the consecration of a cloister, priests singing, to bring her mother to bliss.

"But the baleful beasts that on thy body bites
All blenches my ble - thy bones are so black!"
"That is love paramour, lusts and delights
That has me lit and left low in a lake."

If thirty times thirty masses were sung *"My soul were . . . brought to the bliss"*.

Gaynour called on Christ and Mary to bring her mother to bliss and send her grace to perform the masses to save her mother's soul. She wanted to know: "What wrathed God most?" Pride before the people, that causes them to break with his bidding.

Gaynour would know:

"What beads might me best to the bliss bring?"

The ghost answered:

"Meekness and mercy, these are the most;
And then have pity on the poor, that pleases Heaven's king.
Then charity is chief, and then is chastity,"

The ghost told Gaynour to hold these words to her heart for she would live just a short time.

Gawain asked how knights shall fare that are fond of fighting and foul the lands of the folk. He was told directly:

"Your King is too covetous, I warn thee sir knight.
No man may destroy him with strength while his wheel stands

that is, while his wheel is at its height, but Fortune, that wonderful wheelwright, will cause the wheel to come full circle. Arthur had conquered France, the tribune Frollo and his folk,

Brittany and Burgundy all to you bow,
and rich Rome will be over-run, but the Tiber will prove untrue timber.
For you shall lose Brittany
With a knight keen.
and this keen knight will seize the crown
And at Carlisle shall that comly be crowned as king.

Tidings of this treason will reach Tuscany and the Round Table shall lose its renown. *At Romsey/ in Dorsetshire shall die the doughtiest of all, Arthur.* You, Gawain, will die in a valley, and Arthur will be fatally wounded and the royal company of the Round Table shall be routed. The ghost had had her say:

"Have a good day, Gaynour, and Gawain the good;
I have no longer time tidings to tell.
I must walk on my way through this wild wood. . . .
Fore Him that righteously rose and rested on the Rood,
Think on the danger and the dole that I in dwell.
Feed folk for my sake that fail for food
And remember me with matins and Masses in melle.
Masses are medicines to us that bale bides;
Us think a Mass as sweet
As any spice that ever ye eat."
With a grisly greeting
The ghost away glides.

The weather cleared, the clouds parted and the sun shone. The king blew his bugle and all rode to the queen who told of the wonders she had seen. Then they all rode to Rondeshalle.

They had supper, sitting under a canopy of silk. A lovely lady appeared and rode up to the king. She spoke:

"Here comes an errant knight.
Do him reason and right."

The king sat in state in his household and welcomed the lady and promised her knight reason and right. Her grass-green gown was glorious and gay, her woollen cloak was embroidered in gold with birds. Her hair was finely dressed in jewels and gold. They all looked on her and the knight. His helmet was well burnished with a border of gold. His coat of mail was milk-white and his horse was similarly clad.

His shield on his shoulder of silver so shone,
With bear heads of black browed ful bold;
The horse was dressed in fine silk trappings down to its heels:

And, in his cheveron before,
Stood as a unicorn,
As sharp as a thorn,
An anlas of steel.

The knight's steel armour was decorated with gold stars. His gloves and garments glowed like coals with grains of rubies. His shining shinguards were sharp for shredding and he held his lance aloft. His squire followed him. His horse was nervous at all the splendour around him.

Arthur asked: "What wouldst thou . . ? Tell me what thou seekest".

The knight replied that he wanted Arthur to find him a knight to accept his challenge. He was Sir Galeron, the greatest knight in Galway and Lord of Connock, Cunningham, Kyle, Lomond, Losex and Loyan. Arthur had won these lands in war and given them to Sir Gawain. Galeron will fight for his lands and he will rule them unless he is beaten in a fair fight:

"But if he win them in war,
With a shield and a spear,
On a fair field."

Arthur replied: *"We are in our games; . . But yet thou shalt be matched by midday tomorrow."*

Gawain showed the knight and his lady to a rich pavilion hung with purple and pall:

His steed was stabled and led to the stall;
Hay heartily he had in hatches on high.

There Gawain, Galeron and his lady dined on rich dainties
In silver so shine.

The king called his knights to determine who should encounter the knight.

Then said Gawain the good, "Shall it not grieve.
Here my hand I you hight,
I will fight with the knight
In defence of my right."

At dawn the knights heard matins and mass. The lists for the jousting were constructed on level land at Plumpton Wall where no knights had fought before. Gawain was brought three sops of fine bread soaked in wine *for to comfort his brain*. The king commanded the Earl of Kent's son to assist Galeron to prepare. He emerged in his brilliant armour and went to Gaynor to place his lady under her care. The two knights entered the lists.

The King's chair is set
Above on a chacelet;   dais

Many a knight shouted

> *For Gawain the good*
> *Gawain and Galeron gird their steeds;*
> *All in glittering gold, gay was their gear.*

The knights moved rapidly to their places in the lists. They spurred their horses till their sides bled. Their lances were fixed. The shafts shivered their shining shields. And then, with brands bright they struck.

Gawain was gaily dressed in green. His armour was engraved with golden griffons and had other devices with truelove knots between. On his rearing horse he struck astray. Galeron mocked his disarray and struck him on the neck with his keen sword a blow

> *That grieved Sir Gawain to his deathday.*
> *Fifty mails and more*
> *The sword snapped in two,*
> *The collarbone also,*
> *And cleft his shining shield.*
> *He cleft through the cantle that covered the knight,*
> *Through the shining shield a shaftmon and more.*
> *And then the loathly lord laughed upon high,*
> *And Gawain greches therewith and groaned full sore:*
> *"I shall reward thee thy route, if I can read right."*
> *He followed in on the freke with a fresh fare;*
> *Through blazon and brené, that burnished was bright,*
> *With a burly brand through him he bare.*
> *The brand was bloody that burnished was bright.*

Galeron struck back at him standing upright in his stirrups

> *Straight in his stirrups, stoutly he strikes,*
> *And goes at Sir Gawain as if he were mad.*
> *Then his loved one aloud skirls and screeches*
> *When that burly birn blanket in blood.*
> *Lords and ladies of that laike likes*
> *And thanked God of his grace for Gawain the good.*
> *With a swoop of his sword, that swiftly him strikes;*
> *He struck off the steed's head straight where he stood.*
> *The fair foal faultered and fell, by the Rood.*

Gawain leapt out of the stirrups from Grissell the good.

> *"Grissell," quoth Gawain, "gone is, God wote! . . .*
> *I shall venge thee today."*

*He calle*d for his Friesian horse.

> *"No more for the fair foal than for a grassroot.*
> *But for dole of the dumb beast that thus should be dead,*
> *I mourn for no mount, for I may get more."*
> *As he stood by his steed*
> *That was so good in need*
> *Near Gawain waxed wood*
> *So wept he so sore.*

Galeron drew away and dismounted and quickly went towards Gawain with his sword drawn. They battled such that shields were shredded and armour bloodied and many warriors were afraid at how fiercely they fought.

> *Thus they fought on foot on that fair field*
> *Gawain broached him with his brand under the broad shield*
> *Through the waist of the body and wounded him ill.*
> *The sword stent for no stuff - it was so well steeled.*
> *That other starts on back and stands stonestill.*

Even though he was stunned, Galeron strikes Gawain sorely through to his head and neck. He was within a hair's breadth of being slain.

> *Hardily then these hatheless on helms they hew.*
> *They beat down beryls and borders bright;*
> *Shields on shoulders that shone in their show,*
> *Fretted were in fine gold, they failed in the fight.*
> *Stones of iral they scatter and strew;*
> *Stiff staples of steel they strike done straight.*

Their strokes were grievous and terrible. Gaynour grieved for their sake. Gaynour grieved for Gawain, but this knight of courage was cruel and keen, and with a steel brand all the side of Galeron he carved down clean through the rich mails that were strong and round, and, with a hurtful stroke,

> *He strikes Sir Galeron grovelling on ground.*
> *Grisly on ground, he groaned on green.*
> *All wounded as he was,*

he rushed forward and would have slain Gawain, but his sword struck his thigh and slipped on the mail. Gawain held the knight by his collar:

> *Then his lover on loft shrills and shrieks -*
> *She gretes on Gaynour with groaning grylle:*
> *"Lady matchless of might,*
> *Have mercy on yonder knight*
> *That is so doleful dight,*

If it be thy will."

Than willfully Dame Gaynour to the King went;
She caught off her coronal and kneeled to him:
"As thou art Roy royal, richest of rent,
And I thy wife wedded at thy own will -
These birns in the battle so bleed on the bent,
They are weary, iwis, and wounded full ill.
Through their sheen shields, their shoulders are shent;
The groans of Sir Gawain does my heart grill.
The groans of Sir Gawain greives me sore.
Wouldst by thy leave, Lord,,
Make these knights accord,
It were a great comfort
For all that here were."

Galeron spoke to Gawain: "I make thee release and, before these royals, resign thee my right." He turned towards the king and presented his sword saying:
"Of rents and richess I make the release."

As Galeron knelt before him, the king commanded peace. Gawain and Galeron could scarcely stand upright,
What, for buffets and blode, her blees waxed black;
Their blees were bruised, from beating of brands.

Arthur gave Gawain all the lands of Glamorgan and lordship of Wales and baronies in Brittany and said he would dub him a duke if he would release Galeron his right and grant him his lands. Gawain returned his lands in Scotland to Galeron and would have him join the Round Table. The king and queen and all the host returned to Carlisle.

Surgeons soon soothed the knights. Comforted by king and queen, they were both dubbed dukes. Galeron wedded his lady and was made a knight of the Round Table.

Gaynour wrote to all the religious houses to have masses sung and to have the bells rung throughout Britain.

All this happened in Inglewood Forest during the hunting
In the time of Arthur
This awntyr betide.

My abbreviated, modernized and mutilated version is but a pale, pale shadow of the wonderful original. *Awntyrs* is written with a verve and energy that bursts through the exceptionally disciplined and elaborate form to create a work of art which is formally shaped, exquisite in detailing, precise in observation and deeply passionate in meaning and intention. It is a dramatic and powerfully told narrative that sits alongside the very finest of English poetry.

The verse form is one of the most complex and demanding to be found in English verse. Each stanza consists of thirteen lines. The poet rhymes the first eight lines alternately, usually using just two rhyme words, itself a feat worthy of a Lord Byron, but without Byron's recourse to wit and diversion which makes for a far readier rhyme. Within these eight lines, the four or five beats in the line are marked by words that start with the same sound and this strong, structural alliteration is maintained sometimes over several lines, seldom falters, and is employed with such skilful variation as to control the forward movement of the poem and create an appropriate music for the action. The ninth line has four stressed syllables and rhymes with the last line. The tenth, eleventh and twelfth lines use the same rhyme. The last four lines usually have two stressed syllables and alliterate in a less systematic and structured way. This tail to each verse serves to vary the form and bring the stanza to a tight conclusion, as though the poet stops to draw breath. The poem resumes by taking up some of the last words of the previous stanza and thus the forward musical flow of the narrative is maintained and the whole is knitted together

Throughout the fifty-five stanzas, in all the seven hundred and fifteen lines, the poet rarely falters and only occasionally employs empty phrases. In fact, in contrast to the work of the Victorian Swinburne, a northern poet who is one of the few modern poets to use alliteration in this strong, structural way, the poetry is determined principally by meaning and the author is not intoxicated by the excess of his music.

Scholars argue that many phrases that the poet uses are the stock in trade of the alliterative poets, cliches and stereotyped, portmanteau expressions that can be readily fitted into the complicated jigsaw with little concern for meaning. Even if this is so, and the poem reads with a naturalness and consistency that suggests individual creation, the detail throughout is precise and specific. Much of the description is of a very high order. The account of the hunting, the fine beauties of Gaynor's and the lady's dress and coiffure, the description of the exquisite armour and the account of the fight, as accurate and immediate as the best of football commentaries, and the eerily contrived torment of the ghost seem to be alive in their creation, to consist in freshly thought phrases fitted to the matter in hand. A poet renews language, shaping it to his meaning and taking what might be old and hackneyed and using it such, that because it is pertinent and original in its application, the meaning emerges newly charged.

This is poetic craft of the highest order comparable to the work of the poet of *Sir Gawain and the Green Knight,* who was writing within the same tradition, and to the finest of the Welsh poets, who also sought to work in such tight, disciplined and musical forms.

Awntyrs symbolically comes full circle and ends with the lines with which it began:

> *In the tyme of Arthore*
> *This anter betide.*

The image of the wheel of fortune is at the heart of the poem. It is found in the earlier alliterative *Morte Arthure* expressed in similar terms and the idea of a wheel turning, of a king, Arthur, being at the top of the wheel, flushed with success, and then, inevitably, inexorably, being plunged to the bottom as the wheel continues to turn, was a central concept in medieval man's sense of the human condition. Everybody reading or, more probably hearing, the poem would be aware of the story of Arthur, of his Roman triumph, of his betrayal by Mordred and of his death. They would also know of Guinevere's adultery and the death of Gawain and be aware of the dramatic irony in the ghost's words.

However, the irony works as a counterpoint to the whole poem. Gaynour is richly, beautifully, exquisitely dressed, but she will be reduced to black bone, as will Galeron's lover. Gawain's and Galeron's armour is state-of-the-art, the product of the latest and finest craftsmanship, with jewels set to shred another's flesh and an anlas or dagger placed like a horn on the horse's head. The tournament is formal and gracious, rule-bound, a ceremonial which turns nasty as each, in the increasing viciousness of the fighting, loses control and inflicts horrific injuries on the other until that point where the lady's shrieks and Gaynour's formal request return us to a world of grace and decorum, of honour and largesse, where lands are restored and the Round Table is at one again. The poem has shown us that such amity cannot last, that the wheel will turn, that madness, death and hell are constantly threatening.

The overt didacticism of the poem points to moral and political ideas. The moral is carried by the ghost's injunctions to good behaviour, meekness and mercy, pity on the poor, charity, chastity and deeds of arms.

We do not know who wrote *Awntyrs*. It has the vigour to be the product of an oral tradition, constantly changed and honed by successive performances until committed to writing, but the complexity of the exacting structure and the symmetry of the whole makes that seem very unlikely.

The four manuscripts that we have are in various dialects, Yorkshire, West Midlands and Southern, but the dialects are not those of the author, but those of the copyist. Rhyme-words and other features suggest an original in a northern dialect and the detailed use of Carlisle, Inglewood, Tarn Wadling and Plumpton Wall would indicate someone familiar with the immediate area. Some aspects of the content might suggest a cleric, but he would be a cleric with considerable worldly awareness of fashion, jousting and hunting.

The poem was certainly written before 1430. It is found in the Thornton manuscript, which was written in Yorkshire at that time. The differences between the various extant texts suggest that they are each several copies distant from the original. The details of fashion and the development of the armour indicate a date in the latter half of the fourteenth century, but, as *Awntyrs* makes direct references to the alliterative Morte Arthure, it must have been written after that poem, sometime in the years after 1400.

The setting is of considerable interest. Not only does it continue a tradition in the area of Arthurian associations, but it also sees Carlisle, placed almost aside the turbulent Anglo-Scottish border, as a place for the arbitration of disputes.

The finest of all poems about Sir Gawain, and one of the most beautiful poems in the language, *Sir Gawaine and the Grene Knight*, may have a Cumbrian setting. After beheading the green knight at Arthur's court in Camelot, Gawain travels through the wintry landscape to keep his reciprocal pledge and submit his head to the green knight's axe. He journeys northwards through a landscape on a very specific route through North Wales and the Wirral and then on further, to Bertillak's Castle and then the green chapel. The actual route was not indicated and most modern editors have chosen to imagine the green chapel being in the south Pennines, perhaps in Derbyshire. The poem's first editor, Sir Frederick Madden, included the poem in a Bannatyne Club edition which was only published in 150 copies and contained the first printing of many of the Gawain poems and the alliterative Morte Arthure. In a footnote he suggested that Gawain's journey finally went through Inglewood Forest and that Bertillak's castle was Wolsty castle, north of Allonby, and that the green chapel was to be found on the extreme north-west point of England, at Grune Point. The argument carries some mythical weight. It seems aesthetically appropriate that the mysterious castle and chapel should be situated in the furthest extreme of the kingdom. Wolsty Castle had had magical associations since the days of Michael Scotus, who has the rare distinction of being the only person from Britain damned in Dante's *Inferno*. Michael Scotus hailed from the Borders, possibly from Melrose. He was first minister in the Kingdom of the Two Sicilies and acquired a reputation for learning and black magic. He is reputed to have spent his last years at Holm Cultram Abbey and his library of occult books is said to be buried beneath the ruins of Wolsty Castle. The grune of Grune Point refers to the groin or sea wall. The name might, nevertheless, have been

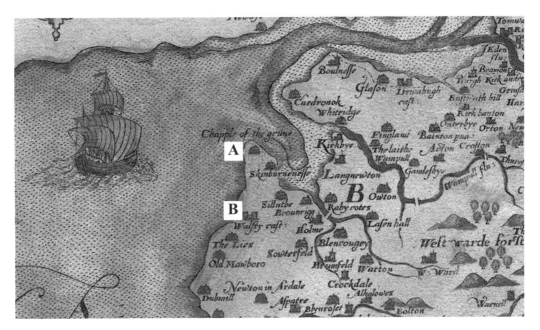

Saxton's map of 1576 showing Chapple of the Grune at A
and Wolsty Castle at B.

thought to mean green. John Saxton's map of 1576, marks a Chapelle of the Grune on the head of the promontory, and its isolated position may well have been the site chosen for a chapel. The area to the west of Skinburness was flooded and laid waste in a storm sometime between 1301 and 1304 and a chapel may have been destroyed in the floods. Hutchinson mentions that a grant was given to the monks of Holm Cultram to build a church at Skinburness, but the later building of the church at Newton Arlosh, suggests that it wasn't built. J.R.R.Tolkien, in his edition of the poem, repeated Madden's argument in his early editions, but changed his view in later editions.

The Wedding of Sir Gawain and Dame Ragnelle: What Women Most Desire

The poet of *The Wedding of Sir Gawain and Dame Ragnelle* is a true story-teller, button-holing his audience, settling them down to listen to a tale of times long past, *In the time of Arthur*, in a country where there was *nothing but chivalry*.

> *I shall you tell of Arthur the King,*
> *How once him befell.*
> *On hunting he was in Inglewood.*

The king and his lords, as they hunted in the king's forest of Inglewood, became aware of a great hart standing silently in the bracken:

> *"Hold you still, every man,*
> *And I will go myself, if I can,*
> *With craft of stalking."*

whispered Arthur. The deer leapt away into the bracken and Arthur followed it for half a mile or so:

> *And at the last to the deer he let fly*
> *And smote him sore and severely -*
> *Such grace God him sent.*

The deer fell in a great brake of fern. Arthur was upon it, fiercely and eagerly, butchering the deer with great skill, and, finally, as the custom was, tasting the fat, *the grease he tasted*.

Suddenly a knight appeared. He was fully armed, strong and of great might. Arthur had wronged him. He had given his lands to Sir Gawain. He threatened Arthur with death:

> *Thou hast me done wrong many a year*
> *And woefully I shall quit thee here;*

His name was Gromer Somer Joure. (Perhaps, simply, the man, groom, of summer's day. The name has folkloric associations with the idea of midsummer night's revelries and mysteries, but may also have echoes, as in *Fergus of Galloway*, of a twelfth century ruler of western Scotland, Somerlied, and the dis-possession of his lands. Malory includes a Sir Gromer Somer Joure among the knights who besieges Guinevere's bedroom in Carlisle Castle.)

Arthur argued for his life. The knight would be disgraced if, fully-armed, he slew a man dressed in his hunting clothes, his *veneré*,

> *"Now," said the King, "so God me save,*
> *Save my life, and what thou most crave,*
> *I shall now grant it thee;*
> *Shame thou shalt have to slew me in veneré,*
> *Thou armed and I clothed but in green, perdé."*

Sir Gromer Somer Joure agreed to spare Arthur's life, but required him to meet him again in twelve months time, in the same place, by himself, dressed as he was then, and that, upon pain of death, he should answer the question:

> *"To show me at thy coming what women love best in field and town"*

If he should fail, he would lose his head.

Arthur agreed to meet him as a matter of honour:

> *"Untrue knight shalt thou never find me - . . .*
> *Farewell, Sir Knight, and evil met.*
> *I will come, if I be alive at the day set,*
> *Though I should 'scape never."*

Arthur blew his bugle. His knights joined him, but he was sad and of heavy cheer. He urged them:

> *"Go we home now to Carlisle;*
> *This hunting likes me not well,"*

Back in Carlisle, Arthur remained depressed. After much questioning, he told his trusted nephew, Gawain, what had happened, of Sir Gromer and the pledge, and the answer he needed to make to save his life, to say *"What women desire most"* and the consequences of failing:

> *"And if I fail of my answer,*
> *I wot I shall be slain right there.*
> *Blame me not though I be a woeful man;*
> *All this is my dread and fear."*

Gawain spurred Arthur to make good cheer and they resolved to scour the country in their search for an answer:

> *The King rode one way and Gawain another*
> *And ever enquired of man, woman, and other,*
> *What women desired most dear.*
> *Some said they loved to be well arrayed,*
> *Some said they loved to be fair prayed,*
> *Some said they loved a lusty man*
> *That in their arms can clip them and kiss them than.*

They each returned with a month to spare. Both had compiled a whole book of answers. Gawain was confident; Arthur still uneasy.

> *"By God," said the King, "I dread me sore;*
> *I cast me to seek a little more*
> *In Inglewood Forest."*

King Arthur rode into Inglewood Forest and there he met the ugliest woman he had ever seen:

> *Her face was red, her nose snotted withall,*
> *Her mouth wide, her teeth yellow overall,*
> *With bleried eyes greater then a ball.*

Her teeth hung over her lips. Her hair was matted. She was hunchbacked. She was a yard broad and made like a barrel and her *pappys*, her breasts, were large enough to be a horse's load. She was the loathly lady.

And yet she rode on a fine palfrey caparisoned with the richest jewels.

She greeted the king and told him to speak to her. She had the answer: his life was in her hands. She wanted to make a bargain with him:

> *"And if my answer save thy life,*
> *Grant me to be Gawain's wife."*

Arthur couldn't make such a promise; that lay with Sir Gawain alone, but he would ride back to Carlisle and ask him. Everyone, even the owl, had a right to a mate, she insisted. She was a lady and her name was Dame Ragnelle. (The name Ragnelle may be an echo of the name of a pagan devil as found elsewhere in medieval plays or it may be connected with Wragmire, a marshy area just north of Hesket and Tarn Wadling.)

When Arthur told Gawain about the loathly lady and her demands, he was sympathetic and very compliant:

> *"Is this all?" then said Gawain;*
> *"I shall wed her and wed her again,*
> *Though she were a fiend;*
> *Though she were as foul as Beelzebub,*
> *Her shall I wed, by the Rood,*
> *Or else were not I your friend."*

Within five or six days King Arthur and Sir Gawain rode out of town together into Inglewood Forest. After a while, Arthur insisted on continuing by himself and rode a mile to the west, where he met Dame Ragnelle.

Arthur promised the loathly lady her wish and, in desperation, asked for his answer:

> *"And your desire now shall ye have,*
> *Both in bower and in bed.*

> *Therefor tell me now all in haste -*
> *What will help now at last?*
> *Have done, I may not tarry."*

She teasingly equivocated with her answer and then spelled out clearly what all women most desire:

> *"Some men say we desire to be fair;*
> *Also we desire to have repair*
> *Of diverse strange men;*
> *Also we love to have lust in bed;*
> *And often we desire to wed."*

Women desire other things too:

> *"To be holden not old, but fresh and young, . . .*
> *But there is one thing is all our fantasy,*
> *And that now shall ye know.*
> *We desire of men above all manner thing*
> *To have the sovreignty, without lessening,*
> *Of all, both high and low.*
> *For where we have sovreignty, all is ours,"*

She warned him that the knight would be angry at being forestalled. Arthur rode through mire, moor and fen to meet his assignation. Sir Gromer greeted him sternly:

> *"Come off, Sir King, now let see*
> *Of thine answer, what it shall be."*

Arthur was firm, brief and clear in his answer:

> *"I say no more, but above all thing*
> *Women desire sovreignty, for that is their liking.*
> *And that is their most desire"*

Sir Gromer was beside himself:

> *"And she that told thee now, Sir Arthur,*
> *I pray to God, I may see her burn on a fire;*
> *For that was my sister, Dame Ragnelle."*

He had lost his chance and would never have Arthur at his mercy again. Arthur rode away, but met with Dame Ragnelle. She insisted on their agreement:

> *"Since I have saved your life, and none other,*
> *Gawain must me wed, Sir Arthur,"*

She would accept no half measures;

> *"Nay, Sir King, now will I not so;*
> *Openly I will be wedded, ere I part thee from*

Else shame will ye have.
Ride before, and I will come after,
Unto thy court, Sir King Arthur."

The loathly lady rode alongside King Arthur through the streets of Carlisle and into the court, even though *it liked him full ill*. Then she demanded:

"Arthur, King, let fetch me Sir Gawain,
Before the knights,"

She wanted to be assured of his promise and would have their troth plighted there and then

" . . . . before all thy chivalry.
Set forth Sir Gawain, my love,"

immediately.

Sir Gawain came forward readily, willing to keep his promise for the king's sake. Dame Ragnelle was moved to say:

"For thy sake I would I were a fair woman,
For thou art of so good will."

Gawain plighted his troth in *weal and in woo*.

"Alas" said Dame Gaynour, (Guinevere), and all the ladies of her bower shed tears for Sir Gawain.

"Alas!" then said both King and knight,
That ever he should wed such a wight,
She was so foul and horrible.
She had two teeth on every side
As boar's tusks, I will not hide,
Of length a large handful.
The one tusk went up and the other down.

Dame Ragnelle would not be married any-old-how. Her wedding was to be proclaimed through shire, town and borough and all the ladies of the land were to come to her bridal.

The wedding day arrived. Gaynour pleaded with her:

"To be married in the morning early,
As privately as ye may."
"Nay!" she said; "By Heaven's King,
That will I never,"

She will be married openly and at the High Mass and afterwards she will dine in the open hall.

The nobles and the ladies made themselves ready, but on her wedding day, Dame Ragnelle was more finely and richly attired than Dame Gaynour herself.

Nevertheless:

> *For all her raiment, she bare the belle*
> *Of foulness, that ever I heard tell -*
> *So foul a sow saw never man.*

After she was wedded, she occupied the place of honour on the high dais. She ate unmannerly, ravenously, gluttonously, tearing at the meat with her three inch nails. She ate and ate, capons and curlews and baked meats, she ate and ate until the tables were cleared and the cloths lifted.

All were horrified, aghast. The knights and squires would have *the devil her bones gnaw*.

Unfortunately there is a page missing at this point from the one and only manuscript of *Dame Ragnelle* (which is kept in the Bodleian Library in Oxford) and the poem makes a dramatic leap from the wedding feast to the bridal chamber and the moment that Dame Ragnelle is demanding her rights as a wife:

> *"A, Sir Gawain, since I have you wed,*
> *Show me your courtesy in bed;*
> *With right it may not be denied."*

If I was fair, she says, you would take another tack:

> *"Yet for Arthur's sake kiss me at the least;"*

Gallantly, the ever-courteous Gawain responds:

> *"I will do more*
> *Then for to kiss, and God before!"*
> *He turned him her until.*
> *He saw her the fairest creature*
> *That ever he saw, without measure.*
> *She said, "What is your will?"*
>
> *"A, Jesu!" he said; "What are ye?"*
> *"Sir, I am your wife, securely.*
> *Why are ye so unkind?"*
> *"Ah, Lady, I am to blame.*
> *I cry you mercy, my fair madame -*
> *It was not in my mind.*
> *Ah! Lady you are fair in my sight,*
> *And today you were the foulest wight*
> *That evere I saw with mine eyes.*
> *Well is me, my Lady, I have you thus."*

He embraced her in his arms and began to kiss her

And made great joy, surely.

She offered him a choice of foul by day and fair by night or fair by day and foul by night. He cannot have both. He must choose.

Gawain knew not which to choose. If she was foul by day, he would lose his self-respect, if, by night, he would lack his pleasure:

> *I no wot in this world what I shall say,*
> *But do as you list now, my Lady gay.*
> *The choice I put in your fist:*

She had been offered the sovereignty. Her response was instantaneous, joyous and gracious:

> *"Gramercy, courteous Knight," said the Lady;*
> *"Of all earthly knights blessed might thou be,*
> *For now am I worshipped.*
> *Thou shall have me fair both day and night*
> *And every while I live as fair and bright;"*

She explained. She had been mis-shapen by her stepmother through necromancy and she would remain a foul hag until the noblest knight in England granted her sovereignty.

> *"Kiss me, Sir Knight, even now here;*
> *I pray thee, be glad and make good cheer,"*
> *There they made joy out of mind,*
> *So was it reason and course of kind,*
> *They two themselves alone.*

They made joy and mirth till break of day and Gawain had them sleep until the king called them to dine.

The king was apprehensive as to Gawain's fate at the hands of the she-fiend and went to his chamber.

> *"Arise," said the King to Sir Gawain;*
> *"Why sleepest thou so long in bed?"*

Gawain protested that he was full well at ease and full loth to rise. Holding his lady by the hand, he opened the door:

> *She stood in her smock all by that fire;*
> *Her hair was to her knees as red as gold wire.*
> *"Lo, this is my repair!*
> *Lo!" said Gawain Arthur unto -*
> *"Sir, this is my wife, Dame Ragnelle,*
> *That saved once your life."*

All was explained: how suddenly she was turned from her shape, her stepmother's dark magic, how she saved Arthur's life and his oath to Sir Gromer Somer Joure in Inglewood, how Gawain gave her sovreignty. Dame Ragnelle turned to Gawain and said:

> *"God thank him of his courtesy;*
> *He saved me from chance and villainy*
> *That was full foul and grim."*

She promised to be obedient and never to disagree with him.

> *"Gramercy, Lady," then said Gawain;*
> *"With you I hold me full well content*
> *And that I trust to find."*
> *He said, "My love shall she have.*
> *Thereafter need she never more crave,*
> *For she hath been to me so kind."*

Gawain was besotted with her. Like a coward, he gave up jousting to be with her day and night and he fathered a son, Gyngolyn, who himself became a knight of the Round Table. Dame Ragnelle was acknowledged the most beautiful lady in the country. She lived with Gawain only five years before she died, but, of his many wives, Sir Gawain loved her the most.

This version of an old story was probably written down some time around 1450. In the last few lines, as he signs off, the author frames a short prayer for Jesu's help that seems more than a conventional coda to the piece. He asks to be helped out of sorrow and talks of being *beset with jailers many*. Thomas Malory was similarly in prison and the case has been made that the great Arthurian is the author of this poem. The version we have is in a West Midland dialect which would not exclude Malory from being the author. It has also been suggested that the plaintive reference to imprisonment might be a satiric reference to Malory by a witty contemporary and that the poem is not in the folk tradition but a teasing parody.

Whatever the case *The Wedding of Sir Gawain and Dame Ragnelle* has a distinguished pedigree. More than half a century earlier Geoffrey Chaucer had placed the essence of the same story in the mouth of the rumbustious, sensuous, coarse and promiscuous *goode wyfe of Bath*. Her tale, set nominally in the time of Arthur, concerns a young knight. He has casually raped a maiden, but his death sentence is forestalled by the queen, who gives him a year and a day to resolve that essential question of what it is that women most desire. His fruitless search is eventually resolved by an old hag - we don't get Ragnelle's enthusiastically extravagant description - who, in return, requires him to grant her first wish, which, inevitably leads to the pair of them lying embarrassingly in bed together. His manhood has deserted him and she lectures him on the nature of true gentility, which lies in deeds and not in birth. He is given a choice: to have her young and faithless or old and faithful. He offers the decision, and thus the *maistrie* or sovereignty, to her, with predictable consequences. Chaucer tells the tale with his customary sophistication, but he is weaving his spell using much earlier material. The undeveloped reference to an Arthurian setting, placing the story in a supposed land of faery, suggests earlier versions that may well have been closer to the later poem of *Dame Ragnelle*.

Chaucer's more moralizing contemporary, John Gower, included a tale of a similar kind in his huge English poem, *Confessio Amantis* or *Tales of the Seven Deadly Sins*. Florent has killed Branchus. His punishment is so contrived that he will be killed in a year's time when he fails to answer the question of women's main desire. On his quest, he encounters an old hag in the forest who reveals the answer in exchange for a promise of marriage. On the wedding night, he turns away, but she pleads with him, tells him not to be so discourteous. In obedience to his oath, he turns towards her, in a room full of light, to clasp a beautiful eighteen-year-old girl in his arms. She is a Sicilian princess. Such is the reward of virtue.

If Chaucer and Gower were familiar with the tale, so was Edward I, a hundred years earlier. In 1299, in, I suspect, a very drunken, regal rehearsal of Arthurian times, when the king and his followers chose to imitate the courtesies of an imagined Round Table, a very loathly lady was the centrepiece of a courtly masque. She had a foot-long nose, ears that would have done a donkey proud, malignant sores on her neck and a gaping mouth stuffed with blackened teeth. She rode in and demanded that Sir Perceval and Sir Gawain, played by two of Edward's more extrovert or obsequious retainers, should recover lost territory and bring peace to an unsettled kingdom.

A fourth version was included by Thomas Percy in his *Reliques of Ancient English Poetry. The Marriage of Sir Gawain* tells a similar story with some interesting variations and is discussed later along with Percy's other poems.

The particular form of the tale may have been in currency for many years. Its main elements - the judgment depending on the question; the question of woman's desire and the answer of sovreignty; the loathly woman and her bedroom transformation - are staples of many folklores. Peculiar to *Dame Ragnelle* and Percy's *Marriage* is the setting in Carlisle and Inglewood Forest.

It would be interesting to know when the story became attached to Gawain, and when and why it came to be localised in the Carlisle area.

In Irish legend Gawain is the sun god, waxing and waning during the day and Dame Ragnelle could be a form of the earth mother. Patterns of Irish and

Norse/Irish settlement are strong in the area. The name Tarn Wadling itself is a mixture of Norse and British and refers to the lake of the little Irishman, so it is not unreasonable to suppose a similar coming together of folkloric elements.

On the other hand, it has been suggested that the version we have is an original composition from about 1450 and that the action is located at Tarn Wadling in response to the *Awntyrs of Arthur*.

The Avowyng of Arthur:
Further Adventures in Inglewood Forest

The Avowyng of Arthur is another poem that begins with Arthur holding court in Carlisle. The setting is largely Inglewood Forest, where Arthur, single-handedly, kills and butchers, in a very professional manner, a satanic boar. Gawain resolves to spend a night's vigil at Tarn Wadling, and the *thrivand thorne,* that is the Court Thorn, is mentioned in passing as a location that would be readily understood.

After the customary acknowledgement of God's creation and the insistence that this is no fable or phantom, despite it being a tale of Arthur, we are launched into our story:

> *The King at Carlisle he lay;*
> *The hunter comes on a day -*
> *Said, "Sir, there walks in my way*
> *A well grim gryse.*
> *He is a baleful boar -*
> *Such a one saw I never ere:*
> *He has wrought me muckle care."*

The boar has killed his hounds. There was none so hardy that they could come near him. The hunter has lost his spear and much of his gear to the boar. No blows seem to hurt or wound him. He destroys everything he meets and he is massive like a bull. He is higher than a horse and he lacks no force when he fights. Faint folk are afraid of him.

> *When he whets his tushes,*
> *Then he beats on the bushes:*
> *All he rives and he rushes,*

He rips up the roots. He's truly fearful. Whoever dares to face up to him is truly a man. The hunter said, *"In Inglewood is he."* Arthur was determined to face this satanic creature. He called on three knights, Sir Gawain, Sir Kay and Sir Baldwin of Brittany. The four of them would go together, no-one else, to kill the boar.

The hunter at the north end blew his bugle and uncoupled the hounds, who headed south. Running as a pack, they picked up the boar's track. The boar went to his den. He struck out at the dogs fiercely, but they held him fast in his hold. He slashed at the bold hounds and gave them no rest. The dogs came running and bayed him full boldly, but there was none so hardy that dared on the fiend fasten. The hunter shouts, *"You there seek him no more . . . I'll set my head on a stake if he doesn't flay you all four, the grisly ghost."* Then the hunter turned home.

Arthur called on Gawain, Baldwin and Kay. He vowed that were he never so hardy, he would try that satan and butcher him without any help by tomorrow morning. He turned and asked for the others' vows. Gawain vowed to go to Tarn Wadling and watch there all night. Kay would ride the forest and if any denied him way, he would fight them to the death. Baldwin, in contrast, made his far less romantic vow:

"I avow by my life	
Never to be jealous of my wife,	
Nor of no bird bright;	woman
Never warn no mon my meat	deny
When I good may get;	
Nor dread my death for no threat	
Neither of king nor knight."	

Having made their vows they rode forth to fulfill them. Gawain went to Tarn Wadling; Kay rode the forest trails looking for adventure, and the matter-of-fact Baldwin rode to town and went to his own bed.

First, to carp of our King, The hounds took their hold; the boar with his shield-like skin followed them and soon wounded them. The king called out and urged them on. He stayed on horseback and as he came near, the boar charged against him. He dreaded the boar that was so fierce and strong

The boar began to roar and groan, and gape and gurn and, bare his teeth. Men could not see his lair for hounds and for slain men that he had drawn to his den and ripped all to bones.

> *Then his tushes gan he whet,*
> *Upon the King for to set;*
> *He lifts up, without let,*
> *Sticks and stones.*
> *With wrath he begins to root:*
> *He rips up many a root*
> *With tusks of three foot,*
> *So grisly he groans.*

Then the King readied his spear, but the great shaft splintered on the boar's hide. His good steed fell and he gave Arthur a hit that he'd feel all his days. The steed was stark dead. Arthur prayed to Jesus to protect him. Arthur steadied himself and leapt nimbly to his feet.

117

Did as a doughty knight -
Brayed out a brand bright
And heaved his shield upon height,
 For spoiled was his spear. . . .
Against the fiend for to fare
 That hideous was of hair.
So they countered in the field:
For all the weapons that he might wield,
The boar tore his shield which protected his breast.
There down kneels he
And prays to Him that was so free:
"Send me the victory!
 This Satan me seeks."
All wroth wax that swine,
Blew, and brayed up his brine;   raised his eyebrows
As kiln or kitchen,
 Thus rudely he reeks.
The King might him not see,
But leant him down by a tree,
So nigh discomforted was he
 For smell or smoke.
And as he neared by an oak,
The King sternly him struck,
That both his brows gone black;
His mastery he makes.

Arthur showed his prowess dealing doughty blows. The king with his noble sword met the boar head on and ran him in at the throat. The boar began to dodder and stagger and sank down in great pain. The king was eager to butcher him. He sundered the broad shoulders. The king was expert in venery. He collared him and set his head on a stake. Then he cut up the beast as venison in the forest and hung the strips and the slices on the oak.

There down kneels he
That loves her that is free;
Said, "This succour thou hast sent me
For thy Son's sake!"
If he were in a dale deep,
He had no knight him to keep.
Forweary, slides he on sleep:

No longer might he wake.
The King has fulfilled his vow.
Of Kay carp we now -
How that he come for his prowess
Ye shall hear more.
As he rode in the night
In the forest he met a knight
Leading a bird bright;
She wept wondrous sore.
She said, "Saint Mary might me speed
And save me my maidenhead,
And give the knight for his deed
Both sorrow and care!"

Kay lingered quietly and listened to her woe and then galloped after the knight and uttered his challenge:

"Recreant knight,
Here I proffer thee to fight
By reason of that bird bright!
I bid thee my gloves."

The other was ready for him. Kay demanded to know who he was. His good father was called Menealfe of the Mountain. He had won the lady at Liddel spilling the blood of her friends. Sir Kay was keen to fight and they rode against each other. Menealfe was the strongest. He struck Kay stiffly with his sharp spear, splintered his shield, and Kay fell out of his saddle, flat on the field, and so, by the laws of war, he was taken. Kay's gear was forfeit and he promised that if the knight went to see Gawain at Tarn Wadling, his ransom would be paid.

He said, *"Sir Kay, thy life I thee promise for a tilt at that knight!"* Yet Menealfe before midnight regretted his haste.

Thus they turned to the Tarn
With the thriving thorn.

Kay told his tale to Gawain. Unless he released him with his courtesy, *"I live never more"*.

"This knight that is of renown
Has taken me to prison,
And thou must pay my ransom,
Gawain, with thy leave."
Gawain asked what he should do.
"When thou art armed in thy gear,

> *Take thy shield and thy spear*
> *And ride to him a course on war;*
> *It shall thee nought grieve."*

The knights prepared to fight. Each gripped a spear as large as a rafter and they ran together so fiercely that neither escaped hurt.

> *If Menealfe was the more mighty,*
> *Yet dints caused him to dodder:*
> *He struck him sad and sore.*

Menealfe was stunned. His horse turned about. He didn't know in which direction. A relieved, enthusiastic and scornful Kay said:

> *"Thou hast that thou hast sought!*
> *My ransom is already bought;"*

And Gawain rode to Menealfe directly, set him upright in his saddle, so he could speak, and took off his helmet to let the wind blow on his face

He spoke in a low voice:

> *"Delivered hast thou Kay.*
> *You have freed him with your sword*
> *And thou was ever courteous*
> *And prince of each play.*

If you would wait a short time I would have an other course and I would pledge this woman by my side."

Then Gawain answered that he was glad to fight for her. The two knights readied their gear and gripped their spears and ran at each other. They clashed with such ferocity that Gawain knocked Menealfe off his steed and caused his brows to bleed as he landed on the ground.

> *Then Kay called on him*
> *And said, "Sir, thou had a fall,*
> *And thy wench lost withal."* . . .
> *Quoth Kay, "Thy love hast thou lost*
> *For all thy brag or thy boast;*
> *Everything you spent on her is lost."*

Gawain rebuked him, reminding him that a man's good fortune is never so sure that he may not come to harm. Then he went and raised up the knight that had been so stunned, but was more deeply hurt by Kay's words. If we were alone, he said to Kay, this strife should I stop

> *"Ye, hardely," quoth Kay;*
> *"But thou hast lost thy fair maiden*
> *And thy life, I dare lay."*

Kay talked on, until Gawain said that he was a doughty knight and should take no ill from Kay's sharp words.

> *"Take thou this damsel sheen;*
> *Lead her to Gaynour the Queen,*
> *This forward to fulfill;*
> *And say that Gawain, her knight,*
> *Sends her this bird bright;*
> *And ransom thee anon right*
> *At her own will."*

This the knight swore to do on his broad sword.

Just at that moment, the king awoke and blew on his bugle and all the knights came to ascertain the king's welfare.

> *To the forest thay take the way -*
> *Both Gawain and Kay,*
> *Menealfe, and the fair maid*
> *Coming to the King.*
> *The boar butchered they find,*
> *Was carved of the King's hand;*
> *If he were lord of that land,*
> *He had no horsing.*
> *Down they take that bird bright,*
> *Set her on behind the knight;*
> *Her horse for the King was dight,*
> *Without letting;*
> *Gave Kay the venison to lead,*
> *And hied homeward, god speed;*
> *Both the bird and the bread*
> *To Carlisle they bring.*

As they rode along, Kay explained to Arthur how he had met and fought with the knight in the forest and how Gawain had redeemed his ransom and won the bride. The king turned to the knight and asked:

> *"What is thy ransom, upon right?"*
> *The other answered him with skill,*
> *"I can not say thee theretil:*
> *It is at the Queen's will;*
> *Why should I lie?*
> *Both my death and my life*
> *Is in the will of thy wife,*

Whether she will stint me of my strife
Or put me to pain."

The king praised Gawain and promised to help Menealfe with his wife in any way that he might.

To Carlisle they took their way, and alighted in the court. Menealfe led the noble lady before the queen, and said:

"Madame, I am hither sent
From Gawain, your knight."

He had brought the lady and his own body for her to do with as she would. The queen gave the knight to the king for he was the master of such things. Gawain spoke of the knight's skill and courage.

Then they fetched forth a book,
All there laws for to look;
The King soon his oath took
 And squithely got him to swear;
And surely, without fable,
Thus dwells he at the Round Table,
As present knight and priveable,
With shield and with spear.
Now good friends are they.

Then Sir Kay reminded Arthur of Baldwin's oath never to be afraid of any man, never to be jealous and always to provide plenteous food for all his guests. He offered to test him out. The king agreed, but warned him that Baldwin was a strong and powerful knight and that he was not to be harmed. Six of them armed themselves and went forth to meet Baldwin. They had sharp weapons, and protected their armour with green cloaks from the rain. Three went on each side to block the wide way. They hid themselves in their cloaks as though they were common men for they did not want to be recognized.

Now as they hovered and they hid,
They saw a shine under shield
Come pricking fast over the field
 On a fair steed;
Well armed, and dight
As freke ready to fight,
Towards Carlisle right
 He hies good speed.
He sees these six in his way;
Then to themselves can they say,

"Now he is feared, I dare lay,
And of his life adread."
Then Kay cries upon height,
All squyth to the knight:
"Either flee or fight":

Then they cast their capes from them. Sir Baldwin saw them, And said, even if you were many more, you would not get me to flee

"I have my ways for to wend
For to speak with a friend;
As ye are herdmen hinds -
Ye mar not me!"
Then the six sembled him in fear
And swore by Him that bought us dear,
"Thou pass never away here
But if thou dead be!"
"Yes, hardly," quoth Kay,
"He may take another way -
And there shall no man do nor say
That shall grieve thee!"

Baldwin stuck to his rights.

"I warn you, frekes, be ye bold,
My right ways will I hold!"

He placed his lance in his fewtre. Kay was next to him and he was toppled off his horse and lay beneath it. Baldwin turned on the other five knights and shattered their shields. Four of them he overcame quickly in the heat of the skirmish. Without delay, the six helped Kay up. Baldwin demanded if they wanted any more.

One answered and
Said, "Thou may wend where thou will,
For thou hast done us nought but skill,
Though we be wounded sore."

Baldwin hastened to the king, who asked if he had heard anything in the woods. Baldwin said that he had heard nothing but good. The king was astonished that he mentioned nothing more.

After mass, Kay returned and told the king
"We are all shent
Of Sir Baldwin, your knight:
He is noble in the fight,

Bold, hardy, and wight
 To bide on a bente.
Flee will he never more:
Him is much lever die there.

I curse the woman that bore him, such hurts have I received at his hands."

The king saw that Baldwin would never flee or fear for his life, but he had also vowed never to refuse food to any man. The king called a minstrel and told him to go and dwell incognito in Baldwin's house in Brittany and observe whether any man went meatless away.

Then the minstrel wends on his way
As fast as he may.
By nones of the third day,
 He found them at the meat,
The Lady and her menage
And guests great plenty.
But porter none found he
 To warn him the gate;
But rayket into the hall
Among the great and the small,
And looked about him over all.
 He heard of no threat,
But royal service and fine:
In bowls birlutte they the wine,
And cooks in the kitchen
 Squythly with sweat.
He bowed to the lady.
 No fault he there found.
Knight, squire, yeoman, nor knave,
They lacked nought that they should have;

They needed only to ask for it to come to their hand.

Then he went to the dais,
before the proudest in the place
The Lady was courteous
And bade him still stand.

He said he was renowned and came from the south and the lady would hear his tales.

A sevennight dwelt he there.
There was no expence for to spare:

Boards they were never bare,
But every cover clean.
Both knight and squire,
Minstrel and messenger,
Pilgrim and palmer
Was welcome, I wene.
There was plenty of food:

Baldwin lingered long at Arthur's court, but when he came home, he brought the king and the queen.

Now there came from the kitchen
Royal service and fine;
There was no wanting of wine
To lesser nor to more.
They had at their supper
Rich meats and deer.
The King, with a blithe cheer,
Bade them slay care.
The king said he had never seen such service.
Then Baldwin smiled and on himself laughed;
Said, "Sir, God has a good plough!
He may send us all enough:
Why should we spare?"

The king commanded Baldwin to go hunting for deer on the following day, while he would stay behind with the ladies. At day's light the following morning, they blew bugles and fared forth into the hunting field.

Then the King called his hunter,
And said, "Fellow, come here! . . .
I command thee to be all night out;
Baldwin, that is stern and stout,
With thee shall he be.
Early in the dawning
Look that ye come from hunting;

whether you've got venison or not. It doesn't matter to me." The king was ready to set the third test.

At even the king called to him a knight and they went to the chamber

Where the Lady of the house
And maidens full beauteous
Were courteous and curious,

125

Forsoothe in bed lay.

The king commanded the chamber door to be opened:

The King bade, "Undo!"
The Lady asked, "Who to?"
He said, "I am coming here, lo,
 In derne for to play."   secret
She said, "Have ye not your own Queen here,
And I my lord to my fere?   mate

Tonight you should not be any nearer to me."

"Undo the door," quoth the King,
"For by Him that made all things,
Thou shall have no harming
 But in thine own will."

A sweet damsel let him in and the king sat on the foot of the Lady's bed. He

Said, "Madame, my knight
Must lie with thee all night
Til tomorrow at day's light"

 She should not come to harm for they are doing it to settle a bet.

Then the King said to his knight, "Get undressed and get into yonder bed. Quickly!".

The knight did as he him bade,
And when she saw him unclad,
Then the Lady wax dread,
He said, "Lie down privily her by,
But neghe not thou that Lady;   touch
For and thou do, thou shall die . . . .
Nor nought so hardy thou stir,
Nor once turn thee to her."
The other said, "Nay, sir!"
 For him had he dread.

Then the king asked for a chessboard and called for a damsel and they sat down together upon the bedside.

Torches was there many light,
And lamps burning full bright;
But not so hardy was that knight
 His head once to hide.
But when they began to play
Till on the morn that it was day,

126

Ever he looked as he lay,
  Baldwin to bide.
And early in the dawning
Come they home from hunting,

They took the fine venison to the kitchen. The king sent for Baldwin and told him to come and see.

He finds the King at his play;
A knight in his bed lay
  With his Lady.

Then said the King, "Tonight missed I my knight and I followed him here and here I hold them still. If you should take it ill, I would not wonder at it."

Then the King asked, "Art thou wroth?"
"Nay, Sir," he said, "without oath,

And I wish the lady no injury. I will tell you why. She did it of her own will else no man would dare come to her. And if I did then take it ill, I would have much dishonour. We have been together for many winters and she has never done me any harm, and each sin should be examined separately and seriously."

The King wanted to know why he was not angry when he found his wife in bed with another man. Baldwin asked the king to sit, while he tried to explain.

"It befell in your father's time,
That was the King of Costantine,
Purveyed a great host and a fine
And went into Spain.
We warred on a sultan
And all his lands we won.

Then we were so glad and I was loved of the king and he gave me the command of a troop of ready and eager lords. He also gave me a castle to hold and all its lordships. I had five hundred and more men at my table, but no women, except for three. One was prettier than the other two. The other two were of one mind. They seized the pretty one and took her to a well, where they told her she should receive the reward for her beauty. There they slew her. We were angry with them and would have put them to death. Then one of them said:

'Let us have our life,
And we shall at your bidding be
As much as we all three;
Is none of you in privacy
Shall have wanting of wife.'

They did as they promised and served us during the day and with their bodies each night.

> *The one was more lovely*
> *That the other had envy:*
> *Her throat in sunder privily*
> *She cut it with a knife.*
> *Much business had we*
> *How that best might be;*
> *They asked counsel of me*
> *To do her to death.*
> *And I answered and said, 'Nay!*
> *Look first what herself will say,*
> *Whether she may serve us all to pay;*
> *That is a better rede.'*
> *There she het us in that hall*
> *To do all that to a woman should fall,*
> *Well for to serve us all*
> *That stood in that stead.*
> *She held us wel that she het,*
> *And dight us on the daylight,*
> *And her body each night*
> *Into our bed bid.*
> *And by this tale I understood,*
> *Woman that is of mild mode*
> *And since gives them to good,*
> *Much may she mend;*
> *And those that gives them to the ill,*
> *And since their follies will fulfill,*
> *I tell you well, by proper skill,*
> *No love will in them linger.*
> *With good will grately home get,*
> *Meek and mild at their meat,*
> *And thrivingly, without threat,*
> *Joy at each end.*
> *Forth jealous shall I never be*
> *For no sight that I see,*
> *Nor no birds bright of ble;*
> *Each earthly thing has end."*

Then the king explained how the lady had agreed and how he had kept guard and assured him that,

> *"He neared never no naked side*
> *Of thy Lady."*

The king said he understood why Baldwin was not jealous, but he didn't understand why he dreaded not his death and why he was always ready to welcome guests unstintingly to his table.

> *Quoth Baldwin, "I shall you tell:*
> *At the same castle*
> *Where this adventure befell,*
> *Besieged we were.*
> *On a day we issued out*
> *And took prisoners stout;*
> *The one of our fellows had doubt,*
> *And durst not further fare.*

The caitiff crept into a tun *That was set thereout in the sun* and there came a missile, flashing like lightning, and landed on the tun that was fastened so fast, and burst it asunder, and there he was slain - his heart was so false - and immediately his head jumped off his neck. Then we came back from the fighting, sound and uninjured, and we thanked God.

Then our fellows could say that no man would die before his day unless he threw himself away through want of wit.

> *And there my avow made I -*
> *So did all that company -*
> *For death never to be dreary:*
> *Welcome is it -*
> *It is a kindly thing."*

"Thou says sooth," quoth the king, and then asked about the third vow:

> *"Tell me why is it,*
> *Why thy meat thou will not warn*　　　　　　　　　　deny
> *To no living bairn?"*
> *Baldwin answers:*
> *"For the siege about us lay still;*
> *We had not all at our will*
> *Meat and drink us to fill:*
> *Us wanted the food.*
> *So came in a messenger,*
> *Bade, 'Yield up all that is here!'*
> *And speak with a stern schere*　　　　　　　　　　manner

129

'I will not, by the Rood!'
I had him bide to nones,   three o'clock
Called the steward soon,
Told him all as he should done, . . .
Had trumpets on the wall,
And covered boards in the hall;
And I myself among them all
As a king stood.

I had them wash; to meat went.
After the steward then I sent:
I bade that he should take intent
That all should well fare -
Bade bring bread plenty,
And wine in bowls of tree,
That no wanting should be
 To less nor to more.
We had no meat but for one day -
It came in a noble array.
The messenger looked ay
 And saw them slay care.
He took his leave at meat.
We had him drink at the gate,
And gave him gifts great,
 And forth did he fare.

But when the messenger was gone,
These officers each one
To me made they great moan,
And drearily con say -
Said, 'In this house is no bread,
No white wine nor red;
You behoves yield up this stead   castle
And for our lives pray.'
Yet God helps aye his man!"

The messenger returned to his captain and said that even though they had been besieging the castle for seven years, they would get nothing there:
 "For they make as merry cheer

As it were Yule Day!"

Then the messenger advised his captain that they should leave the siege for in his army was nothing "But hunger and thirst". The king called his knights to council and they turned their backs on us and rode immediately away. When we saw our enemies were away, everyone said:

> *"He that goods may get*
> *And warns men of his meat,*
> *Good God that is great*
> *Give him sorry care!"*

Then the king said, vehemently, that Baldwin had told the truth and that his vows had been upheld.

> *Then the King and his knights all,*
> *They made mirth in that hall.*

They called for the lady, the fairest on earth, and the King said to Baldwin:

> *"And thou be wise,*
> *Take thou this Lady of prize -*
> *For much love in her lies -*
> *To thine heart hold.*
> *She is a bird full bright,*
> *And thereto seemly to thy sight.*
> *And thou hast held in all that thou hight,*
> *Promised as a knight should!"*

The Avowyng of Arthur is a tale told with a masculine energy and verve, rough at the edges, but in a sound colloquial poetic manner. It maintains a regular pattern of stanzas of three rhyming lines followed by a shorter fourth which links with a later rhyme. The lines are either three or four iambic feet and alliteration, which is found densely throughout, is used to musical and poetic effect, but does not serve a structural purpose.

This is the sort of long poem - it is almost 1200 lines altogether - that could readily be recited or sung by a professional minstrel in a castle hall before or after the feasting.

The dramatically portrayed hunting kills, the decisive combats, the humour, much of it at Kay's expense, and the hard, unsentimental, military anecdotes, that Baldwin recounts, provide material well suited to a garrison mess. One can readily imagine that the soldiers, who found themselves in a distant north country, who knew something of the manners of war and hunting and were well aware in a troublous Border area of the dangers by the wayside, would readily appreciate the content and the moralizing conclusions.

It is a poem at the late and lower end of the courtly tradition. Two to three hundred years after the high ideals of chivalry, subtly and ironically portrayed by Chretien, we find an echo of those same ideals among a rougher class of people living in a far less delicate world.

Baldwin's trust of his wife and freedom from jealousy, pale shadows of the gentility of courtly love, are based not on high sentiment, but on a brutish sexuality where three, two or one woman will serve the turn of five hundred men. His lack of fear in the face of death is justified by a comic anecdote about the coward's fate, and the foundation of his principle of largesse is self-interest and innate cunning.

Medieval Carlisle seems a natural home for such a poem. The references to city and forest are, as nearly always, non-specific, merely givens in the background of the story, and Gawain's vigil at the obviously evil Tarn Wadling is given without any gloss or dramatic enhancement.

However, there is a ready assumption that the audience will appreciate the evil significance of Tarn Wadling at the mere mention of its name.

> *"I avowe, to Tarne Wathelan,*
> *To wake hit all nyghte,"*

says Gawain when he makes his vow and this is sufficient to rank alongside the heroism of the other pledges. The audience must have known the tarn as a fearful place. This suggests that either the poem was read to a north Cumbrian audience or that the evil tarn had a wider, regional or national reputation.

When Kay goes to search for Gawain in order to redeem his forfeit, his journey is briefly described as:

> *Thus they turned to the Tarn*
> *With the thrivand thorn.*

The brevity of the reference again assumes an immediate recognition factor and an audience that was well aware of the significance of the 'flourishing' epithet. The Court Thorn is found between High and Low Hesket on the eastern edge of Inglewood Forest. There is a surgery, Court Surgery, on the site these days, but the *thrivand thorn* has long been a tree of note. A document of 1667 designates Low Hesket as *apud spinum* or 'below the thorn' and another of 1716 identifies the inferior village as *subter spinum*.

William Hutchinson, writing of the Parish of Hesket in his *History of the County of Cumberland* in 1795, states:

The most singular circumstance that relates to this parish is, that yearly, on the day of St Barnabus, the court for the Forest of Inglewood is held there. The suitors are assembled in the open air by the highway side, at the accustomed place, now no otherwise marked than by an ancient thorn; here attend the inhabitants of above twenty mesne manors, from whom, according to the forest court, a jury for the whole jurisdiction is balloted and sworn. Here are paid the annual dues to the lord of the forest, compositions for improvements, purprestures, agistments, and puture of the foresters.

A recent newspaper article of 7th January, 2008, provides a sorry footnote to the story of this thorn tree of historical and mythical significance:

The Court Thorn, the tree under which the Manor Court for the Nether ward of the Forest of Inglewood was held every June for hundreds of years, was bulldozed down. A contractor laying pipes uprooted the tree, despite it being protected by a massive stone fender laid down in the last century.

Sir Gawain and the Carle of Carlisle

The Avowyng of Arthur and *The Wedding of Gawain and Dame Ragnelle* show the independent spirit of the common people at their merry making, ready to make fun of the aspirations and pretensions of their betters. The eponymous Carle of Carlisle is just such a questioner of aristocratic values.

However, the hero of the poem is undoubtedly Sir Gawain. He was both doughty in deed and meek as maid in bower:

> *Certainly, without fable*
> *He was with Arthur at the Round Table,*
> *In romance as we read.*

Arthur sojourned a while in Cardiff, but his lords longed to go to England to hunt. (It has been suggested that the original might have had Arthur in Carlisle and intending to hunt in England, which would make better sense of the geography, but would not take into account a reference to Wales in the previous line.)

Arthur proposed that they should go hunting, for the deer were at their fattest. But first, they had to say mass.

> *King Arthur to his lords gan say*
> *As a lord royal that well may,*
> *"Do us to have a Mass.*
> *Bishop Baldwin shall it do;*
> *Then to the forest will we go,*
> *All that ever here is,*
> *For now is grease-time of the year,*
> *That barons bold should hunt the deer,*
> *And raise them off their rest."*

All the knights of the assembled company were wondrous glad at the proposal, and Gawain who was steward of the hall and master of them all hurried them to get ready. Ironside would ride fully armed in summer, no matter how hot the sun, and in winter too. Giants and he were ever at war. He knew more of venery than all the kings present. Full hardy he was and bold.

> *Knights keen fast they ran;*
> *The King followed with many a man,*
> *Five hundred and more, I wene.*

Folk followed with feathered flights,
Noble archers for the nonce,
  To fell the fallow deer so clean.

Barons gan their horns blow;
The deer came raking in a row,
  Both hart and eke hind.

By mid-morning five hundred lay dead in a row beneath a linden tree.

Then Sir Gawain, Sir Kay and Bishop Baldwin rode after a reindeer until late in the afternoon. A mist arose on the moor. The barons blew their horns and Kay moaned, but the reindeer would not stay:

The reindeer would not dwell.
Hearken what adventure them befell;

Knowing that they would not catch the deer Gawain would have had them stay the night in the forest:

"I reed that we of our horse alight
And bide in this wood all night,
  And lodge under this tree."

Kay was for riding on and finding proper shelter, but Bishop Baldwin had a better idea:

"A Carl here in a castle
A little here near hand.
The Carl of Carlisle is his name:
He may us harbour, by Saint James."

(The concept of a Carl, or common peasant, living in a castle would shock medieval aristocratic sensibilities. We have now left the real, manly world of hunting and slaughter and moved through the screen of forest and mist, into a world in which the established order of things is, at least, unsettled.)

There had never been a knight so bold who had stayed with the carl and escaped with his life. Kay's immediate response was to boastfully suggest:

"Now ride we thither all three."

No matter how stout the Carl was they would beat him all about:

"Such as he breweth, such shall he drink;
He shall be beaten that he shall stink,"

Gawain told Kay to,

"Let be thy boastful fare.
I will pray the good lord, as I you say,
Of harbour till tomorrow day

135

And of meat and meal."

They rode to the castle and at the castle gate they looked for the porter. Kay knocked with a hammer that hung from a chain and Gawain asked politely for hospitality.

The porter warned them not to thank him if they come to harm. The Carl knew no courtesy:

"You 'scapeth not without a villainy."

Gawain was impatient with the porter's joking and told him to take their message to the Carl. But the porter insisted they must be prepared to forfeit their lives or flee full fast.

> *The porter went into the hall;*
> *With his Lord he met withal,*
> *That hardy was and bold.*
> *"Carl of Carlisle, God look thee!*
> *At the gate be barons three,*
> *Seemly arms to wield:*
> *Two knights of Arthurs in,*
> *A bishop, and no more men,*
> *Certain, as they me told."*
> *Then said the Carl, "By Saint Michael,*
> *That tidings liketh me right well.*
> *Saith they this way wolde."*

> *When they came before that sire,*
> *They found four whelps lay about his fire*

and he also had a wild bull and a lethal boar, a lion and a big bear that roamed unloosed. The four whelps would have risen and attacked the knights if the Carl had not bade them to let the knights be. The lion loured, the bear growled and the bull roared and the boar whetted his tusks.

> *Then said the Carl, "Lie still! Hold on!"*
> *They fell adown for fear of him,*
> *and crept under the table.*

The knights beheld the Carl, a dreadful man with his stout and bold visage, his long cheeks, turned-up nose, wide mouth, grey beard and locks that fell across his shoulders, which were two tailor's yards broad.

> *Sir Kay marvelled greatly then.*

He was nine yards tall. His legs were long and his thighs were thicker than any tree trunk and even his fingers were as great as any leg that we bear.

136

Gawain began to kneel, but the Carl stopped him:

> *"Let be thy kneeling, gentle knight;*
> *Thou lodgest with a carl tonight,"* . . .
> *The butler brought a cup of gold -*
> *Nine gallons it could hold -*

The knights drank quickly and then went to look to their horses, which were well supplied with corn and hay. A small foal stood next to the bishop's palfrey, but the bishop pushed it away: the little foal was not going to be the equal of his fine palfrey while he was bishop in the land.

> *The Carl then came with a great speed*
> *And asked, "Who hath done this deed?"*
> *The Bishop said, "That was I."*
> *"Therfore a buffet thou shalt have,"*
> *"I am a clerk of orders high."*
> *"Yet knowest thou nought of curtesy."*
> *He gave the Bishop a buffet though*
> *That to the ground he gan go;*
> *In swooning he gan lie.*

Sir Kay also came to tend to his steed and drove the foal out of the door. Seeing this, the Carl gave Kay such a buffet that it set him smartly on the ground.

> *"Evil-taught knights" the Carl gan say;*
> *"I shall teach thee ere thou wend away*
> *Some of my courtesy."*

When they returned, Sir Gawain very politely asked if he might attend to his horse, but the Carl knew what he was about and a fierce storm arose that made Gawain grateful for such lodging as he had.

Gawain found the foal standing outside in the rain. He covered him with his green mantle, brought him in and fed him and the Carl thanked him full courteously.

By that time their supper was ready *dight*:

> *The Bishop gan the table begin*
> *With a great delight.*
> *Sir Kay was set on the other side*
> *Against the Carl's wife so full of pride,*
> *That was so fair and white:* . . .
> *No lovelier of sight.*
> *She was so glorious and so gay:* . . .
> *"Alas," thought Kay, "thou Lady fair,*
> *That thou shouldest thus perished be*

With such a foul wight!"
"Sit still," quoth the Carl, "and eat thy meat;"
No-one told Gawain to sit. The Carl told him to do his bidding:
"Go take a spear in thy hand
And at the buttery door go take thy pace
And hit me even in the face;
 Do as I thee command.
And if thou bear me against the wall
Thou shall not hurt me withal,
 While I am giant in land."

So Gawain got a spear by the buttery door and came at him with great anger. He gave the stone wall such a rap that the good spear broke, the fire flew out of the flint. The Carl said, *"Gentle knight, thou hast well done,"* and shook Gawain by the hand.

A chair was fetched for Sir Gawain, . . .
 Before the Carl's wife was he set.
So much his love was on her alight,
Of all the supper he might
 Neither drink nor eat.
The Carl said, "Gawain, comfort thee,
For sin is sweet, and that I see. . . .
She is mine thou wouldst were thine.
Leave such thoughts and drink the wine,
 For her thou shalt not get."
Sir Gawain was ashamed in his thought.
The Carl's daughter forth was brought,
 That was so fair and bright.
As gold wire shone her hair. . .
With rich stones her clothes were set,
With rich pearls about her fret,
 So seemly was that sight.

That over all the hall she shone like a sunbeam. Then the Carl said: "Where is the harp thou shouldst have brought with thee? Why hast thou it forgot?" She sat in front of her father with her harp made of the finest maple, with its pins of gold. First she harped and then she sung of love and Arthur's arms.

When they had supped and made them glad, the Bishop and Kay were laid to bed and Gawain was taken to the Carl's bedchamber.

The Carl ordered Gawain to get into the bed and then:

The Carl bad his own Lady go in,
That lovesome was of sight.

A squire unarmed Gawain. The Carl said, "Sir Gawain, go take my wife in thy arms and kiss her in my sight."

Sir Gawain answered him anon,
"Sir, thy bidding shall be done,
 Certainly indeed,
Kill me,slay me, or lay me down."
To the bed he went full soon,
 Fast and that good speed,
For softness of that Lady's side
Made Gawain do his will that tide;
 Thereof Gawain took the Carl good heed.
When Gawain would have done the private far,
Then said the Carl, "Whoa there!
 That game I thee forbid.
But, Gawain, since thou hast done my bidding,
 Some kindness I must show thee in anything,
 As far forth as I may.
Thou shalt have one too so bright
Shall play with thee all this night
 Till tomorrow day."
To his daughter's chamber he went full right,
And bade her arise and go to the knight,
 And warn him not to play.
She durst not against his bidding do,
But to Gawain she came full soon
 And still down by him lay.

"Now, Gawain, are you well paid?" said the Carl. "Right well," said Gawain." "Now," said the Carl, "I'll go to my chamber. My blessing I give you both to play together all this night."

A glad man was Sir Gawain. The lady bright could not recall such a knight.

In the morning, Kay would have gone without Gawain, but the bishop said wait. Mass was said. The lady said, "Wherever shall I find another knight?" Before Gawain went, the Carl asked him first to dine and then he might go with his blessing.

The Carl became confidential. "It is twenty winter gone," said the Carl, that he made a vow that, if any man should lodge in his dwelling, he would be slain unless he did as he was told. "Found I never, Gawain, none but thee." Now all his bale to bliss is turned.

He led Gawain into a desolate dwelling where there were ten cartloads of bones stained with blood. There were many bloody shirts hanging there emblazoned with diverse crests.

> *"These slew I, Gawain, and my helpers,*
> *I, and also my four whelps.*
> *For soothe, as I thee say,*
> *Now will I forsake my wicked ways; . . .*
> *Gawain, for the love of thee*
> *All shall be welcome to me*
> *That cometh here by this way.*
> *And for all these souls, I undertake,*
> *A chantry here will I let make.*
> *Ten priests singing until doomsday."*

By that time dinner was served. The Carl was pleased to see much mirth between Gawain and his daughter. He gave the bishop a cross, a mitre and a ring for a blessing. Then he gave Kay, the angry knight, a blood red steed. He gave Gawain his daughter, a white palfrey and a packhorse charged with gold.

Then they rode, singing, away, Gawain, and the beautiful lady, Kay and the bishop. They told Arthur of the wonders they had seen and delivered the Carl's earnest invitation.

> *In the dawning forth they rode; . . .*
> *Trumpets met them at the gate,*

and harps, fiddles, psautries, lutes, gitterns and minstrelsy welcomed them into the hall.

> *The Carl kneeled down on his knee*
> *And welcomed the King worthily*
> *With words ware and wise.*

The king wanted for nothing. The walls were decorated with gold and azure.

> *The King let say grace and went to meat,*
> *And was served without let.*
> *Swans, pheasants, and cranes,*
> *Partridges, plovers, and curlews*
> *Before the King was set.*
> *Gold bowls were brought in that were too heavy*
> *The King swore, "By Saint Michael,*
> *This dinner liketh me as well*

140

As any that ever I found."

He dubbed the Carl knight on the following morning and made him lord of the country of Carlisle.

"Here I make thee in this stownde
A knight of the Table Round:
Carlisle thy name shall be."
On the morn when it was daylight
Sir Gawain wedded that Lady bright,
That seemly was to see.

The rich feast lasted a whole fortnight with game, mirth and play. Then the lords took their leave and went on their way.

A rich abbey the Carl gan make
To sing and read for God's sake
In worship of Our Lady.
In the town of merry Carlisle
He let it build strong and well;
It is a bishop's see.
And therein monks gray
To read and sing till doomsday,
As men told it me,
For the men that he had slain, iwis.
Jesu Christ, bring us to Thy bliss
Above in heaven, in Thy see.

Such, it appears, is the redemptive power of courtesy and, equally, the sexual rewards that come to those who are polite. The story is told with a rumbustuous looseness that is both amusing and dramatic.

Throughout there are echoes of earlier folk literature. It reads like the fluent production of an able performer, steeped in the stories and phraseology of the itinerant minstrels who probably passed from castle to castle and readily told their tales with that popular mixture of melodramatic terror, prurient sexuality and moral righteousness, which is still the stock in trade of the *News of the World* and its sister journals.

However, in *Sir Gawain and the Carl of Carlisle* there is much that might bear significantly on the history of the Borders. It is a bold egalitarian statement to suggest that carls, no matter how wealthy and physically powerful, might be the equals of knights, nobles, bishops and kings. The poem also implies that the only difference between the boorish treatment the Carl metes out at the beginning and the polite savoir-faire, the noblesse oblige, he displays at the end of the poem, is that he has been treated, by Gawain, at least, with courtesy and respect. The society of the Borders may have been far less hierarchical and immobile than we might imagine.

The story also feels as though it must have an echo of actual events, as though there might have been a powerful, rough-living man, who terrorized the neighbourhood, came to terms with the authorities and became a member of polite society and a politically influential noble and was responsible for founding both a chantry in the area and an abbey in Carlisle, which later became the see of a bishop.

The cathedral in Carlisle was originally an Augustinian Priory. It was founded by Henry I in 1122. Eleven years later the priory church became St Mary's Cathedral and the seat of the bishop of the newly created diocese of Carlisle.

The Augustinian friars were known as the grey friars, which corroborates the poem's *monks gray* and the cathedral is dedicated to St Mary, that is to the Virgin.

John Denton, writing in 1610, speaks thus of the foundation of the cathedral:

K. Hen. Ist founded a college of secular priests in the 2nd year of his reign and made Athelwold his confessor or chaplain (Prior of St. Botolphs) first prior of Carliell, dedicating the church to the honour of the blessed Virgin Mary, and endowing them with the tiths of the churches then founded in the forest of Englewood. But being hindered by the tumults and troubles of his time he could not perfect things before the 33rd year of his reign, and then strucken for grief for the loss of his children that were drowned coming from Normandy, by the council of the prior Athelwald and to please God for his sins (as he thought) he erected a bishop's see at Carliell, and made the said Athelwald first bishop thereof, whom the Archbishop of York named Thurstan did consecrate in the year 1133. And in his stead another chaplain of the said King Henry named Walter was made the second prior of the house who a little before his election had taken upon him a religious habit that of a regular canon there, which order of canons the King and Bishop Athelwold had placed in that house, banishing the secular priests immediately upon his consecration. The said Walter gave to his church of Carliell for ever in pure alms his lands in Lynstock, Richardby, Crosby, Little Crosby, Walby, Brunskewgh, Carleton, Little Carleton and the wood and the churches and the rectories of St Cuthbert in Carlisle, and Staynwiggs (which the King had given him) and the same gift was confirmed onto them both by the King and Bishop Athelwold.

There is, perhaps, enough material here to suggest that the *Carle of Carlisle* is not a complete fabrication.

The Stanzaic Morte Arthur:
Lancelot and Guinevere

The second poem with the title *Morte Arthur* is the only poem in medieval English that tells the story of Lancelot and Guinevere. It is a beautifully paced poem of almost four thousand lines that moves inevitably towards its overwhelmingly tragic conclusion.

The love of Lancelot for Guinevere has torn the kingdom apart. Friend has fought against friend. Lancelot has killed Gawain's brothers and is now his mortal enemy. Lancelot and the king who made him a knight are bitter enemies and the fellowship of the Round Table is no more.

The poem is usually referred to as the stanzaic *Morte Arthur* to distinguish it from the alliterative poem of the same title. It is written in eight line stanzas in a form that corresponds to the octosyllabic lines of the French Romance tradition. The poet handles the form with remarkable facility. It is a form that is difficult to use in English, because of the need for two times four rhymes in each stanza..

The story itself is drawn closely from the French *Mort Artu,* which was probably written in 1230, some hundred and fifty years or so before its English counterpart. The *Mort Artu* is told with all the intelligence and complexity of French chivalric romances, weaving and interlacing together strands of different narratives. *Morte Arthure* tells the same tale with a clarity and directness that makes for a dramatic and moving narrative. The French poem is vague on its geography, mentioning few places and, even then, seeming unaware of their precise location. Salisbury Plain, for instance, is imagined as being near the sea. The geography in *Morte Arthur* is precise. The author has a sense of the country and an awareness of the locations he uses for his story. The *Mort Artu* does not mention Carlisle, but the *Morte Arthur* uses the city as the setting for one of its grandest scenes.

The quest for the Holy Grail has been completed. Arthur's enemies have been defeated. Arthur and Guinevere were lying in bed together:

> *Till on a time that it befell*
> *The king in bed lay by the queen;*
> *Of adventures they began to tell,*
> *Many that in that land had been:*
> *"Sir, if that it were your will,*
> *Of a wonder thing I would you mene,*

> *How that your court beginneth to spill*
> *Of doughty knights all bydene;"*

Knights were deserting the court and Arthur determined to hold a tournament at Winchester. Lancelot would not attend because he was in love with Guinevere.

> *Lancelot left with the queen,*
> *And sick he lay that ilke tide;*
> *For love that was them between,*
> *He made excuses for to abide.*

The queen urged Lancelot to go to the tournament for she was fearful of the deceitful Agravain. Men told:

> *That Lancelot by the queen lay;*
> *For to take them with the deed,*
> *He awaits both night and day.*

Lancelot agreed, but intended to go to the tournament in disguise.

Lancelot left his armour at the Castle of Ascolot where the young Maid of Ascolot (Tennyson's Maid of Shalott) is obsessively in love with him. She begged for his love:

> *"Sir, but if that ye it make,*
> *Save my life no leach may."*

> *"Lady," he said, "thou must let;*
> *For me ne give thee nothing ill;*
> *In another stead mine heart is set;"*

He agreed to wear her sleeve as a token. In the tournament Ector split Lancelot's helm and he was blinded in his own blood. Lancelot retired to a secluded place, where he was nursed by the Maid of Ascolot. Gawain discovered him and Guinevere thereby was led to think that he was in love with the maid. She jealously sent him away when he returned to court.

Guinevere inadvertantly poisoned a knight with an apple and was sentenced to death. She had forty days to find a champion to fight against the victim's fearsome brother, Sir Mador of the Moor. Meanwhile the Maid of Ascolot died of her unrequited love and her funeral barge floated down to Camelot. Guinevere learnt the truth. Lancelot returned at the last minute to be her champion and save her from the stake.

Agravain, a brother to Sir Gawain, told Arthur that Lancelot and the queen were lovers and persuaded the king to leave the castle so that they might entrap the adulterous pair. Lancelot, unarmed, joined the queen in her bedchamber, where he was surprised by a dozen knights. He killed all except Agravain. Then he fled the court with a hundred knights.

Guinevere was sentenced to be burnt to death. As she was about to be tied to the stake, Lancelot and his men rescued her. Gawain's two remaining brothers were killed in the fracas. Gawain, and the King, swore vengeance:

> "Betwix me and Launcelot du Lake,
>> Nis man on earth, for sooth to say,
> Shall truces set and peace make
>> Ere either of us have other slain!"

Lancelot sent a maid as messenger to Gawain. He was prepared to fight to prove his honour.

> Said that lies were said him upon;
>> True they were by day and night;
> To prove it as a knight should don
>> Launcelot proffers him to fight.

Lancelot was grieved when he received Arthur's defiant answer:

> Launcelot sighed wonder sore,
>> Tears from his eyes gan glide.

Arthur laid siege to Joyous Gard for seventeen weeks. Lancelot, greatly troubled, reluctantly prepared to fight.

> "Alas," quoth Launcelot, "Woe is me,
>> That ever should I see with sight
> Again my lord for to be,
>> The noble king that made me knight!
> Sir Gawain, I beseech thee,
>> As thou art man of much might,
> In the field let not my lord be,
>> Nor that thyself with me not fight."

They fought and Arthur was unhorsed:

> "Alas," quoth Launcelot, "Woe is me,
>> That ever should I see with sight
> Before me him unhorsed be,
>> The noble king that made me knight!"
> He was then so courteous and free
>> That down off his steed he light;
> The king there-on then horses he,
>> And bade him flee, if that he might. . . .

> He thought on things that had been ere;

> *The tears from his eyes ran;*
> *He said, "Alas," with sighing sore,*
> *"That ever yet this war began!"*

At the end of this battle, when

> *Steeds that were bold and snell*
> *Among them waded in the blood;*
> *But by the time of even-bell*
> *Launcelot's party the better stood.*

> *Of this battle was no more,*
> *But thus departed they that day;*
> *Folk their friends home led and bore,*
> *That slain in the fields lay.*

The Pope heard of England's grievous troubles:

> *And yet at Rome it was full couth*
> *In England was such sorrow strong;*
> *There-of the Pope had great ruth;*
> *A letter he sealed with his hand:*

The Pope sent the Bishop of Rochester, as his messenger, to Arthur in Carlisle:

> *To England he, the messenger, came,*
> *To Carlisle there the king was;*
> *The Pope's letter out he nome,*
> *In the palace, before the dais,*
> *And bade them do the Pope's doom*
> *And hold England in rest and peace.*

The Pope commanded that the queen be returned to Arthur and that there should be peace between Arthur and Lancelot or the whole of England would be placed under a papal interdict.

> *Read it was before all bydene,*
> *The letter that the Pope did make,*
> *How he must have again the queen*
> *And accord with Lancelot du Lake,*
> *Make a peace them between*
> *For ever more, and truce make,*
> *Or England interdicted should been*
> *And turn to sorrow for their sake.*

Arthur would readily agree to have his Queen again and avoid England being destroyed. Gawain's grievance ran far deeper. Lancelot had killed his three brothers and he will never make peace with him.

> *The king against it would not been,*
> *To do the Pope's commandment,*
> *Blithely again to have the queen;*
> *Would he not that England were shent;*
> *But Gawain was of heart so keen*
> *That to him would he never assent*
> *To make accord them between*
> *While any life were in him lent.*

The bishop next went to Lancelot at Joyous Gard and made his proposal that the queen be returned to Arthur and a truce be made:

> *And asked if he would the queen*
> *Courteously to him betake,*
> *Or England interdite should been*
> *And turn to sorrow for their sake.*

Lancelot was resentful. He had served Arthur well in many battles and had saved many castles and towers and had received little honour in return.

> *Lancelot answered with great favour,*
> *As knight that hardy was and keen:*
> *"Sir, I have stand in many a stour,*
> *Both for the king and for the queen;*
> *Full cold had been his best tower*
> *If that I not had myself been;*
> *He quits me with little honour,*
> *That I have served him all bydene."*

The bishop was Lancelot's equal. Those victories he had won, he had won through the grace of God. He should act on the bishop's advice. He should think of the queen who was weak and he should not let England be destroyed:

> *The bishop spake without fail,*
> *Though he were nothing afrought:*
> *"Sir, think that ye have vanquished many a battle,*
> *Through grace that God hath for you wrought;*
> *Ye shall do now by my counsel;*
> *Think on Him that you dear bought;*
> *Women are frail of their entail;*
> *Sir, let not England go to nought!"*

Lancelot does not care for castles. He has enough in his own country of

Benwick. However, he is afraid that if he were to yield the queen up to Arthur, she would be harmed.

> *"Sir Bishop, castles for to hold,*
> *Wit you well, I have no need;*
> *I might be king, if that I would,*
> *Of all Benwick, that rich thede,*
> *Ride into my lands bold,*
> *With my knights stiff on steed;*
> *The queen, if that I to them yield,*
> *Of her life I have great dread."*

> *"Sir, by Mary, that is maiden flower,*
> *And by God that all shall rede and right,*
> *She nay shall have no dishonour;*
> *There-to my troth I shall you plight,*
> *But boldly brought into her bower,*
> *To ladies and to maidens bright,*
> *And holden in well more honour*
> *Than ever she was by day or night."*

If he is to accept the bishop's assurance of the Queen's safety, can he rely on Gawain to maintain a truce?

> *"Now, if I grant such a thing*
> *That I deliver shall the queen,*
> *Sir Bishop, say my lord, the king,*
> *Sir Gawain and them all bydene,*
> *That they shall make me a securing,*
> *A truce to hold us between."*

The bishop was happy with Lancelot's reply and rode rapidly to Carlisle to secure the truce.

> *Then was the bishop wonder blithe*
> *That Lancelot gave him this answer;*
> *Till his palfrey he went as swithe,*
> *And to Carlisle gan he fare.*

Lancelot's words spread rapidly about the court and Arthur and his knights were well pleased with the truce. But Gawain still felt at daggers-drawn with Lancelot. However, he was prepared to keep the truce until the queen was returned to the court:

> *Though Gawain were of heart keen,*

There-against was he nought,
To hold a truce them between
While Launcelot the queen home brought;
But accord there him never ween
Ere either other heart have sought.

A truce was drawn up and sealed by three bishops,

The wisest that were in all the land

They went first to Joyous Gard and delivered the letters of agreement to Lancelot:

And there-to Lancelot held his hand

The bishops then went on their way,
To Carlisle there the king was;

Lancelot was to follow on the next day with the queen.

The following day he entered the city. Lancelot and the queen rode at the head of a hundred of his finest knights. They were both dressed in the richest robes of samite white, sparkling with silver. They were mounted on white steeds and their saddles were of purest ivory. Their saddle-clothes were of the same white samite that had been woven in the orient. Lancelot held the queen's bridle as they rode forward.

Each one of the hundred knights was dressed in green silk. They wore no armour, but each one carried an olive branch in his hand. They rode on saddles set with jewels such that all around them shone. As the knights rode behind Lancelot and the queen, they were singing.

Lancelot and the queen were clad
In robes of a rich weed,
Of samite white, with silver shred,
Ivory saddle and white steed,
Sambues of the same thread,
That wrought was in the heathen thede;
Launcelot her bridle led,
In the romance as we read.

The other knights everyone,
In samite green of heathen land,
And in their kirtles ride alone,
And each knight a green garland;
Saddles set with rich stone;

149

Each one a branch of olive in hand;
All the field about them shone;
The knights rode full loud singing.

They entered the castle and dismounted before the palace. Lancelot courteously offered his hand to the queen as she alighted from her palfrey.

To the castle when they come
In the palace gonne they alight;
Launcelot the queen off her palfrey nome;
They said it was a seemly sight.

Arthur acknowledged Lancelot as a man of great power. There were few fair words said and many of the knights were in tears at the scene before them:

The king then salutes he full soon,
As man that was of much might;
Fair words were there fone,
But weeping stood there many a knight.

Lancelot spake, as I you mene,
To the king of mickle might:
"Sir, I have thee brought thy queen,
And saved her life with the right,
As lady that is fair and sheen
And true is both day and night;
If any man says she is not clean,
I proffer me therefore to fight."

The king Arthur answers there
Words that were keen and thro:

Arthur's words were bitter and unflinching. He never supposed that Lancelot would have brought this woe. They had been dear friends, yet, even, while they were friends, Lancelot had behaved like his enemy. He is sorely pained that there should be war between the two of them.

"Launcelot, I ne wend never more
That thou would me have wrought this woe;
So dear as we same were,
There-under that thou was my foe;
But nought-for-thy me rues sore
That ever was war betwixt us two."

Lancelot listened in silence. Arthur had blamed him, but Arthur knew he was wrong. He had been at his side in times of trouble and yet he believed the lies about him.

> *Launcelot then answered he,*
>   *When he had listened long:*
> *"Sir, thy woe thou wittest me,*
>   *And well thou wost it is with wrong;*
> *I was never far from thee*
>   *When thou had any sorrow strong;*
> *But liars listened thou to lie,*
>   *Of whom all this word out sprung."*

Gawain spoke. Lancelot cannot deny that he has slain his three brothers. He will not be happy until one of them is slain on the field of battle:

> *Then bespake him Sir Gawain,*
>   *That was hardy knight and free:*
> *"Launcelot, thou may it not withsay*
>   *That thou hast slain my brethren three;*
> *For-thy shall we prove our main*
>   *In field whether shall have the gree.*
> *Ere either of us shall other slay,*
>   *Blithe shall I never be."*

 Lancelot, deeply hurt and with tears running from his eyes, said he was there, but that others were responsible for the death of Gawain's brothers and those others have since paid dearly for their actions.

> *Launcelot answered with heart sore,*
>   *Though he were nothing afrought:*
> *"Gawain," he said, "Though I were there,*
>   *Myself thy brethren slew I nought;*
> *Other knights fell there were*
>   *That since this war dear have bought."*
> *Lancelot sighed wondrous sore;*
>   *The tears of his eyes sought.*

Lancelot would have peace, accord, between them:

> *"Sir, shall I never of cordement ween,*
>   *That we might friends be again?"*

But Gawain will not be appeased:

> *"Nay, accordement there thee never ween*
>   *Till one of us have other slain!"*

Lancelot asked leave of Arthur to ride away to his own lands and never set foot in England again.

> *"Since it never may betide*
> *That peace may be us between,*
> *May I into my lands ride,*
> *Safely with my knights keen?*
> *Then will I here no longer bide,*
> *But take leave of you all bydene;*
> *Where I wend in world wide,*
> *England will I never see."*

Arthur, passionate in his grief, swore that no living man would stop him:

> *The king Arthur answered there -*
> *The tears from his eyes ran -*
> *"By Jesu Christ," he there swore,*
> *"That all this world wrought and won,*
> *Into thy lands when thou wilt fare,*
> *Thee shall let no living man."*
> *He said, "Alas!" with sighing sore,*
> *"That ever yet this war began!"*

Lancelot asked that he be allowed to live in peace in his own country and that Arthur would not pursue him and make war afresh. Gawain angrily intervened:

> *"Nay,*
> *By Him that made sun and moon,*
> *Dight thee well as ever thou may,*
> *For we shall after come full soon.*
> *Lancelot his leave hath taken there;"*
> *It was no longer for to bide;*
> *His palfrey found he ready yare,*
> *Made him ready for to ride;*
> *Out of the castle gone they fare;*
> *Grimly tears let they glide;*
> *There was dole and weeping sore;*
> *At the parting was little pride.*

Lancelot and his knights rode out of Carlisle Castle. The bitterness was not resolved. The civil war would continue until the Fellowship of the Round Table was totally destroyed. Lancelot and his men returned to Joyous Gard and then made their way without stopping to Caerleon, where they took ship for France and Lancelot's own country of Benwick.

Mordred was left in charge of the country and Arthur sailed to France to besiege Lancelot in his fortress at Benwick. Lancelot still longed for peace, but battles were fought. Lancelot wounded Gawain in several battles, but each time he spared his life.

In the meantime Mordred had usurped the throne. Arthur and Gawain returned immediately. As they disembarked at Dover, Gawain was killed by being struck on an old head wound inflicted by Lancelot. Mordred fled to Salisbury Plain. Arthur was prepared to make peace, when a knight drew his sword to kill an adder and so the last battle began.

Arthur killed Mordred, but in so doing was himself fatally wounded. Sir Bedivere carried him to the sea shore and there the dying king asked him to cast Excalibur into the waters:

> *"Have Excaliber, my sword good,*
> *A better brand was never seen;*
> *Go cast it in the salt flood,*
> *And thou shalt see wonder, as I ween;*
> *Hie thee fast, for Cross on Rood,*
> *And tell me what thou hast there seen."*

Bedivere could not part with the wondrous sword and twice returned to Arthur without having done his bidding. The third time:

> *Sir Bedivere saw that boot was best,*
> *And to the good sword he went;*
> *Into the sea he it cast;*
> *Then might he see what that it meant.*
> *There came an hand withouten rest,*
> *Out of the water, and fair it hent,*
> *And braundished as it should brast,*
> *And sithe, as glem, away it glent.*
>
> *To the king again went he there*
> *And said: "Leve sir, I saw an hand;*
> *Out of the water it came all bare*
> *And thrice brandished that rich brand."*
> *"Help me, soon that I were there."*
> *He led his lord unto that strand;*
> *A rich ship, with mast and oar,*
> *Full of ladies there they found.*

The ladies tended to Arthur's wounds as the ship moved away:

> *The king spake with sorry sound:*

> *"I will wend a little stound*
> *Into the vale of Aveloun,*
> *A while to heal me of my wound."*

Bedivere departed and wandered in the woods until he found a small chapel. A hermit told him that:

> *"About midnight were ladies here,*
> *In world ne wiste I what they were;*
> *This body they brought upon a bier*
> *And buried it with woundes sore."*

Guinevere became a nun and Lancelot returned to England to search for her.

> *As he came through a cloister clere -*
> *Almost for weeping he was mad -*
> *He saw a lady bright of lere,*
> *In nunnes clothing was she clad;*

She fainted at the sight of Lancelot. She acknowledged to her abbess that their love had brought so much destruction and so many worthy men had died because of it.

> *"Abbess, to you I knowledge here*
> *That through this ilke man and me,*
> *For we together have loved us dear,*
> *All this sorrowful war hath be;*
> *My lord is slain, that hath no peer,*
> *And many a doughty knight and free;*
> *Therefore for sorrow I died ner,*
> *As soon as I ever gan him see.*

Her life is now dedicated to God and finding forgiveness:

> *"Yset I am in such a place*
> *My soul heal I will abide,*
> *Till God send me some grace,*
> *Through mercy of his wounds wide,*
> *That I may do so in this place,*
> *My sins to amend this ilke tide,*
> *After to have a sight of His face,*
> *At Doomsday on His right side."*

> *"Therefore, Sir Launcelot du Lake,*
> *For my love now I thee pray,*
> *My company thou aye forsake,*

And to thy kingdom thou take thy way,
And keep thy realm from war and wrack,
And take a wife with her to play,
And love well then thy world's mate;
God give you joy together, I pray!"

She tells Lancelot:
"That never in thy life after this
Ne come to me for no succouring."

However, Lancelot could never desert her:
"Now, sweet madam, that would I not do
To have all the world unto my meed;
So untrue find ye me never more;
It for to do Christ me forbid!"

He would follow the same destiny as Guinevere:
"To please God all that I may
I shall hereafter do mine intent,
And ever for you specially pray,
While God will me life lend."

Both will live in penance. Lancelot cannot bear to part:
The sorrow that the the one to the other gan make
Might none earthly man see it.
"Madam," then said Launcelot du Lake,
"Kiss me, and I shall wend as-tite."

"Nay,"said the queen, "that will I not;
Launcelot, think on that no more;
To abstain us we most have thought
From such we have delighted in ere.
Let us think on Him that us hath bought,
And we shall please God therefore.
Think on this world, how there is nought
But war and strife and battle sore."

What helpeth longer for to spell?
With that they gan depart in twain;
But none earthly man could tell
The sorrow that there began to ben;
Wringing their hands and loud they yell,

As they never more should blinne,
And sith in swoon both down they fell;
Who saw that sorrow ever might it mean.

Guinevere is borne away by the nuns. Lancelot becomes a monk and serves at the tomb of King Arthur in Glastonbury. Lancelot dies and goes to heaven and Guinevere is buried beside Arthur.

Morte Arthur was dismissed for many years as a rather poor and shoddy work. It seemed to be repetitive, full of stock phrases and burdened by poor rhymes. Malory, however, was aware of the story's poignancy since he borrowed readily from the poem, in many places echoing its very words. Tennyson, who may only have known the story through Malory, although an edition was available in his time, must also have found the story deeply moving as it prompted two of his finest and most popular poems: *The Lady of Shalott* and his own *Morte D'Arthur.*

Morte Arthur was written to be performed. Repetition is part of its structure, as is a certain slackness in the content. It would be performed before a wide audience in a castle hall. The gallantry and chivalry, the conflict of values between love and loyalty, the destructive effects of civil war and the final hope of religion would have a wide appeal. The pacing of the poem, the way it moves forward rapidly with the action and then can slow to accommodate the moment of spectacle or the tense dialogue, shows the hand of a master at work. *Morte Arthur* would have been a magnificent evening's entertainment. If the poem is measured by its finest moments, then it is a powerful work that deserves to be better known.

We do not know when it was written. There is only one surviving copy in a manuscript compilation made by John Collyns, a bookseller, in the early sixteenth century. This is now in the British Museum. However, the handwriting indicates that the section containing the *Morte Arthur* was probably written fifty years earlier, sometime between 1460 and 1480. The poem, itself, may have been composed at any time in the previous hundred years. The dialect and the style, which takes such pleasure in alliteration, indicate that it was written in the Midlands or the North.

The scene at Carlisle, when Lancelot and Guinevere with their hundred knights clad in white samite and bearing olive branches ride in procession towards the castle to make peace with King Arthur, is one of the most memorable in the poem. The French *Mort Artu* presents the story differently. The night before Guinevere must return to Arthur, she and Lancelot exchanged rings. They prepared themselves splendidly. They rode with five hundred knights on horses all covered in silk. As they went along they jousted and showed the greatest possible joy.

Arthur came to meet them with a large body of knights. Lancelot dismounted and, taking the reins of the queen's horse, he presented her to Arthur, saying that she would have died if he had not risked his life to save her from the disloyalty of those in his castle. She was the worthiest lady in the world and it would have been too great a shame for her to have been burnt at the stake.

The king received her, and thought long and sadly on Lancelot's words.

Lancelot stated, "My Lord, if the love between the queen and me had been adulterous as you have been told, I would not have handed her back and you would never have regained her through force."

The king, somewhat meekly, says he is very grateful for what Lancelot has done, but an angry Gawain steps forward and demands that Lancelot leave the country and never set foot in it again. There can be no peace between them. Gawain will not exchange the whole world for the chance to cut off Lancelot's head.

The author of the stanzaic *Morte Arthur* has chosen to set his scene in Carlisle and not taken the setting from his French model. It is possible that he was prompted by another French version. However, it seems more probable that he was drawing on an English tradition. The alliterative *Morte Arthure* sets Arthur's court in Carlisle and refers to Caerleon as a port newly founded by Arthur. The stanzaic *Mort Arthur* has Lancelot depart by sea from Caerleon en route to his lands in Benwick. Froissart had written of Carlisle being Arthur's city.

From an aesthetic point of view there is no reason why the encounter should not have been set in Camelot or Winchester. The tournaments have been held in Winchester and Camelot and contemporary royal tournaments and celebrations, including Edward III's construction of a round table, may have prompted the location in Winchester. Carlisle's association in the poem is with war and military activity, which would correspond to its position in the public imagination.

Thomas Malory and Morte Darthur

One work above all others created the Arthur we know today. It drew together the vast growth of medieval story and romance in French and English and shaped it into a book that many regard as the starting point of the modern novel. The fantasy and sentiment of the Middle Ages was given a pragmatic and realistic turn. The high ideals of chivalry were retained, but the knights and their ladies stepped forward as real people torn by human conflicts.

Yet *Morte Darthur* was written by the most unlikely of men. If the bare records we have in legal documents are indicative of the true character of the man, Thomas Malory of Newbould Revel in Warwickshire, was the least chivalrous of knights. He refers to himself as a knight-prisoner and he knew the insides of several jails.

In 1443, when he was in his late twenties, Thomas Malory was charged with an assault on property. Eight years later, on 4th January, 1451, he lay in ambush 'with other malefactors' in the woods of Combe Abbey with the intent of murdering the Duke of Buckingham. On the 25th May, of the same year, he broke into the house of a neighbour, Hugh Smyth of Monks Kirby, and raped his wife, Joan. Just ten weeks later, he repeated the offence. In June and July, he led cattle raids at Cosford and Caludon and, to complete these six months of mayhem, he attempted to extort money by threat. He was arrested on 23rd July and placed in the custody of the Sheriff of Warwickshire at Coleshill. He was only in prison for five days before he escaped by swimming the moat at night. He broke into Combe Abbey and stole money and valuables from the abbot's chests. The following day he broke in again, damaged eighteen doors, stole more money and insulted the abbot.

Thomas Malory was imprisoned in the Tower of London, but for various reasons, he was not brought to trial and, in 1454, he was bailed and chose to settle in Essex. Again he plotted robbery, was jailed at Colchester, escaped and was recaptured and imprisoned in the Marshal prison. Over the next six years he was in and out of prison until, in January, 1460, he was sent to Newgate. He was never tried on any of the charges levelled against him and, in 1462, he was granted a royal pardon.

Malory joined the forces of Warwick the Kingmaker as he journeyed north in support of Edward IV against King Henry VI. He was at the sieges of the castles at Alnwick, Bamburgh and Dunstanburgh in Northumbria and thereby had a special insight into Arthur's exceptionally long siege of Joyous Gard, which, as Malory writes, *Somme men say it was Anwyk, and somme men say it was Bamborow.* However, in June 1468, he was again made a prisoner. He may have been involved with Warwick in a political intrigue against the king.

He spent the next three years, until his death on 14th March, 1471, in the Tower of London. He may have been accommodated in some comfort. He had access to one of the best libraries in the country and it was during these years that he wrote *The Whole Book of King Arthur and his Noble Knights of the Round Table.*

William Caxton printed a copy of the book in 1485 and mistakenly called it *Morte Darthur,* after the title that Malory had given to the last section. Only one complete copy of Caxton's Malory survives. Amazingly, a manuscript copy of Malory's work was found in the warden's bedroom in Winchester College in 1934. This copy was significantly different from Caxton's printed edition, even though marks of printer's ink on the text suggest that Caxton may have used it as a cross reference as he set up his text.

Malory was a compiler and translator of brilliance. His text is mostly a direct translation of the French *Suite du Merlin*, written about 1240, which was itself a development of the *Vulgate Merlin* and the works of Robert du Boron. The two English works he used were the alliterative *Morte Arthure* and the stanzaic *Mort Arthur*.

The language Malory uses is very close to the one we speak today, but the oddity of the spelling makes it appear somewhat alien. By and large, when quoting Malory, I have simply rendered him in modern spelling, except for a few sentences in the original spelling in order to give some feeling of the original.

Morte Darthur centres on the chivalric court of Camelot, which Malory identified with Winchester. Camelot is mentioned in the region of sixty times throughout the book and Winchester thirteen times. The identification is made the first time he mentions Winchester, when he is describing how *Merlion lette make by hys suttelyte that Balynes swerde was put into a marbil stone stondynge upryght as grete as a mylstone, and hovel allwayes above the watir, and dud many yeres. And so by adventure hit swamme downe by the streme unto the cite of Camelot, that ys in Englysh called Wynchester.* He makes a similar comment at other times when he mentions Winchester. The most frequent mention of Winchester occurs when Malory is retelling the story he found in the stanzaic *Morte Arthur*. He copies the original and simply refers to Winchester, although, at one point, he does say that Sir Lancelot and Sir Lavayne *cam to Camelot, that tyme called Wynchester.* The only other mention is when Mordred would take Guinevere to be his wife, but she tricks him and escapes to the tower of London: *And aftirwarde he drew hym unto Wynchester, and there he toke quene Gwenyver, and seyde playnly that he wolde wedde her (which was hys unclys wyff and hys fadirs wyff) And so he made redy for the feste, and a day prefyxte that they shulde be wedded; wherefore quene Gwenyver was passyng hevy. But she durst nat discover her harte, but 'Take fayre, and aggreed to sir Mordredys wylle. And anone she desyred of sir Mordred to go to London to byghe all maner thynges than longed to the brydale. And bycause of her fayre speche sir Mordred trusted her and gaff her lever and so whan she cam to London she toke the Towre of London, and suddeynly in all haste possyble she cuffed hit with all maner of vytayle, and well garnysshed hit with men, and so kepte hit.*

Winchester was a ready choice for Arthur's court. Edward I, in the 1270s, had marked the tradition by building a round table of immense proportions, which still hangs on the wall of the Great Hall in the castle. The table must have presented an exceptional challenge to any carpenter. It was eighteen feet in diameter and made of 121 separate pieces of oak. It weighed one ton four hundred weight and was supported by a massive central column and twelve outer legs. Its political weight was yet more significant. After the periods of baronial unrest, Arthur's great symbol of equality made a clear statement about Edward's position as primus inter pares, as first among equals. He was also keen to use Arthur to stress the legitimacy of his claim to be ruler of the whole of the British Isles.

His grandson, Edward III, also appreciated the prestige that came from an association with Arthur and began to build, in 1344, a house for a round table for three hundred knights in Windsor Great Park. This appears to have been abandoned, for Edward later found political advantage in the smaller exclusive association of the twenty four Knights of the Order of the Garter.

Malory refers to Caerleon (Carlion, Carlyon), Geoffrey of Monmouth's favourite residence for Arthur, on ten occasions all near the beginning of the book in *The Tale of King Arthur*. Malory extracted this section of his book from a thirteenth century French romance usually referred to as the *Suite du Merlin*. Two later passing mentions refer to Arthur holding his court there.

Carlisle is mentioned twelve times in various forms from *Cardolle, Cardoylle, Carlehylle, Carleyle, Carleil, Carleyl*. The city is the location of four separate events.

The first reference to Carlisle is early in the work and tells, to quote Caxton's rubric at the beginning of the chapter, *How fyve kynges came into this londe to warre ayenst kyng Arthur and what counceyl Arthur has ayenst them*. This brief picture shows something of the troubled life of medieval kings: Arthur says, "*Yet had I never rest one month since I was king crowned of this land"*. It also shows a king raising his army, writing to the barons to hie them after him to meet the invading forces. We have a glimpse of the love between Arthur and Guinevere at that time: he would have him with her because he would miss her and her presence will cause him to be more hardy. She, needless to say, replies: *"Sir," she said, "I am at your commandment, and shall be ready at all times."*

The full episode is as follows:

And as king Arthur rode to Camelot and held them a great feast with mirth and joy, and soon after he returned unto Cardolle. And there came unto Arthur new tiding that the king of Denmark and the king of Ireland, that was his brother, and the king of the Vale and the king of Sorleyse and the kyng of the Ile of Longtaynse, all their five kings with a great host was entered into the lands of king Arthur and burnt and slew and destroyed clean before them both the cities and castles, that it was pity to hear. "Alas!" said Arthur, "yet had I never rest oner month since I was king crowned of this land. Now shall I never rest till I meet with those kings in a fair field, that I make mine avow; for my true liege people shall not be destroyed in my default. Therefore go with me who so will, and abide who that will."

Then king Arthur let write unto king Pellinor and prayed him in all haste to make him ready "with such people as we might lightliest rear", and to hie him after in haste. Then all the barons were wrothe privily that the king would depart so suddenly; but the king by no means would abide, but made writing unto them that were not there and bade hie them after him such as were not at that time at that court. Then king came to queen Guinevere and said unto her, "Madame, make your ready, for ye shall go with me, for I may not long miss you. Ye shall cause me to be the more hardy, what adventure so befall me; yet will I not wit my lady to be in no jeopardy."

"Sir," she said, "I am at your commandment, and shall be ready at all times."

So on the morn the king and the queen departed with the fellowship as they had and come into the North, into a forest beside Humber, and there lodged them.

Malory tells the story of the alliterative *Morte Arthure* in Book Five of his *Morte D'Arthur*: *The Tale of the Noble King Arthur that was Emperor Himself Through Dignity of his Hands*. Malory's version is about two thirds the length of the original. He strips away much of the description to concentrate on the action and he tones down some of the graphically brutal descriptions of the fighting. But the trace of the original can be clearly seen through Malory's text. The narrative is much the same and in many places the lines and phrases of the poem are found word for word, Malory readily incorporating the alliterative stresses of the poem into his very fluent and rhythmical prose. Certain of the alliterative phrases that he uses and some of the additional material suggest that he was not using the one copy of the poem which has come down to us, the one found in the Thornton manuscript now in Lincoln Cathedral. It would have been surprising if he had used this version as it was part of a household collection in Yorkshire. Gaps in the manuscript and obvious mis-copyings, as well as the dating of the language, suggest that the manuscript that Malory rewrote in his prison cell was a copy of either a much earlier original or probably a copy of a copy, such was the tenuous and uncertain way that literature was propagated before the age of printing. Each text was so limited in its reproduction, so variable in its copying and so precarious in its substance, that the few texts we have are miraculous survivors from a far larger body of literature.

Malory gets on briskly with his tale: *Hyt befelle whan kyng Arthur had wedded quene Gwenyvere and fulfylled the Rounde Table, and so aftir his mervelous knyghts and he had vanquiyshed the moste party of his enemyes . . . and than kyng Arthur helde a ryal feeste and Table Rounde.*

And then graphically and tersely we are straight into the action itself. *The Emperor Lucius, Procurour of the publyke wele of Rome,* through his messengers, demanded his tribute. *When King Arthur wist what they meant he looked up with his grey eyes and angered at the messengers passing sore. Then were these messengers afeard and kneeled still and durst not arise, they were so afeard of his grim countenance.* If Arthur failed to pay, the terrified messenger was forced to threaten, Lucius would deprive him of all his realms. Arthur will take seven days to consider his answer. Arthur's younger knights would have slain the messengers there and then, but Arthur warns them, *on pain of death not to mis-say them nor do them any harm.*

On Arthur's command, Sir Cleges was to ensure that his Roman guests *were led into chambers and served as richly of dainties that might be got. So the Romans had thereof of great marvel.* There is no mention of the magnificent feast but, with a few deft expressions, Malory has shown us the imperious and imperial effect that Arthur has had on the Roman delegation.

The knights of the Round Table assembled in a tower for their council. Sir Cador of Cornwall was well pleased: *The letters of Lucius the Emperor like me well, for now we shall have war and worship.*

Arthur, even though *their spyteous speche grevyth so my herte,* was more cautious. He adduced the evidence of the conquests by Sir Belin and Sir Bryn and of Constantine our kinsman as his right to holy Rome.

King Angwysshaunce of Scotland promised to send twenty thousand men: *I shall give them my wages for to go and war on the Romans and to destroy them* and the King of Little Britain, of Brittany, promised *thirty thousand men shall ye have at my costs and wages.* A mighty duke of west Wales pledged to *vanquish with victory the viscount of Rome* and at his own cost he would bring a further thirty thousand men. (It is interesting to note that the pragmatic, one-time soldier, Malory, has introduced the practical detail of costs and wages in the midst of the patriotic fervour.) Sir Ewain and his son Ider will bring a further thirty thouand knights *to the walls of Milan and so over to Poynte Tremble (Pontremoli) into the vale of Viterbo, and there to vital my knights.*

Then leapt in young Sir Launcelot du Lake with a light heart. Even though his lands shared a border with the enemy he would bring *twenty thousand helmets with halberks.* Sir Baldwin of Brittany would bring *ten thousand good men's bodies that shall never fail while their lives last.*

Laconically Arthur replied: "Now I thank you with all my true heart. I suppose by the end be done and dealt the Romans had been better to have left (not bothered) with their proud message."

When the seven nights were up, the senators required an answer from Arthur. That answer was impressive in its clarity, firmness and brevity: *"Now say to your Emperor that I shall in all haste me ready make with my keen knights, and by the river of Rome hold my Round Table. And I will bring with me the best people of fifteen realms, and with them ride on the mountains in the mainland and mine down the walls of Milan the proud and then ride onto Rome with my royalist knights. Now ye have your answer. Hie ye that ye were hence and from this place to the port there ye shall pass over; and I shall give you seven days to pass unto Sandwich.*

"Now speed you, I counsel you, and spare not your horses, and look ye go by Watling Street and no way else, and where night falls on you, look you there abide, be it fell or town, I take no keep; for it belongs not to aliens to ride on nights. And may any be found a spear-length out of the way and that ye be in the water by the sevennights' end, there shall be no gold under God pay for your ransome." . . .

Thus they passed from Carlisle unto Sandwich-ward that had but seven days to pass through the land and so Sir Cador brought them on their way. But the Senatotrs spared for no horse, but hired them hackneys from town to town and by the sun was set by the seven days' end they came unto Sandwich; so blithe were they never.

Malory continues the story of the campaign in France and Italy keeping it very much as it is in the *Alliterative Mort Arthur.* The latter part, when Arthur hears of Mordred's usurpation of the throne and returns for the last battle, is not used.

The next episode that is set in Carlisle is the healing of the Hungarian knight, Sir Urry. He has been grievously wounded and wanders the earth in the charge of his mother and sister searching for the greatest knight in the world to search and heal his wounds.

Then, as the French book maketh mention, there was a good knight in the land of Hungary whose name was sir Urre. And he was an adventurous knight, and in all places where he might hear any adventures deeds and of worshp there would he be.

So it happened in Spain there was an earl, and his son's name was called sir Alpheus. And at a great tournament in Spain this sir Urry, knight of Hungary, and sir Alpheus of Spain encountered together for very envy, and either undertook other to the utterance. And by fortune sir Urry slew sir Alpheus, the earl's son of Spain. But this knight that was slain had given sir Urry, or ever he were slain, seven great wounds, three on the head and three on his body, and one up on his left hond. And this sir Alpheus had a mother which was a great sorceress; and she, for the despite of her son's deth, wrought by her utile crafts that sir Urry should never be whole, but ever his wounds should one time fester and another time bleed so that he should never be whole until the best knight of the world had searched his wounds. And thus she made her avaunte, wherethorough it was known that this sir Urry should never be whole.

Then his mother let make an horse-litter and put him herein, with two palfreys carrying him. And then she took with him his sister, a full fair damsel whose name was Fyleloly, and a page with them to keep their horses, and so they led sir Urry thorough many countries. For, as the French book saith, she led him so seven year thorough all lands christened and never could find no knight that might ease her son.

So she came unto Scotland and into the bounds of England. And by fortune she came unto the feast of Pentecost until king Arthur's court that at that time was holden at Carlehylle. And when she came there she made it to be openly known how that she was come into that land for to heal her son. Then king Arthur let call that lady and asked her the cause why she brought that hurt knight into that land.

"My most noble king," said that lady, "wit you well I brought him hither to be healed of his wounds, that of all this seven year might never be whole."

And thus she told the king, and where he was wounded and with whom, and how his mother discovered it in her pride how she had wrought by enchantment that he should never be whole until the best knight of the world had searched his wounds.

"And so I have passed all the lands christened thorough to have him healed except this land, and if I fail here in this land I will never take more pain upon me. And that is great pity, for he was a good knight and of great noblesse." "What is

his name?" said king Arthur.

"My good and gracious lorde," she said, "his name is sir Urre of the Mounte."

"In good time," said the king. "And since ye are come into this land, ye are right welcome. And wit you well, here shall your son be healed and ever any Christian man heal him. And for to give all other men of worship a courage, I myself will assay to handle your son, and so shall all the kings, dukes and earls that be here present at this time, not presuming upon me that I am so worthy to heal your son be my deeds, but I will courage other men of worship to do as I will do."

And then the king commanded all the kings, dukes and earls and all noble knights of the Round Table that were there that time present to come into the meadow of Carlehyll. And so at that time there were but an hundred and ten of the Round Table, for forty knights were away. And so here we must begin at king Arthur, was kindely to begin at him that was that time the most man of worship christened.

Then king Arthur looked upon sir Urre, and he thought he was a full likely man when he was whole. And then the king made to take him down off the litter and laid him upon the earth, and anon there was laid a cushion of gold that he should kneel upon. And then king Arthur said,

"Fair knyght, me rueth of thy hurt, and for to courage all other knights I will pray thee softly to suffer me to handle thy wounds."

"My most noble christian king, do ye as ye list," said sir Urre, "for I am at the mercy of God and at youre commandment."

So then king Arthur softly handled him. And then some of his wounds renewed upon bleeding.

And the king Clarence of Northumberland searched and it would not be.

And then Malory tells us how all one hundred and ten knights searched sir Urry's wounds individually and *it would not be.*

All these hundred knights and ten searched sir Urrye's wounds by the commandment of king Arthur. "Mercy Jesu!" said king Arthur, "where is sir Launcelot du Lake, that he is not here at this time?"

And thus as they stood and spake of many things, one espied sir Launcelot that came riding toward them, and anon they told the king. "Peace," said the king, "let no man say nothing until he be come to us."

So when sir Launcelot had espied king Arthur he descended down from his horse and came to the king and saluted him and them all.

And anon as the damsel, sir Urrye's sister, saw sir Launcelot, she roamed to her brother thereas he lay in his litter and said, "Brother, here is come a knight that my heart giveth greatly unto."

"Fair sister," said sir Urre, "so doth my heart light greatly against him, and my heart giveth me more unto him than to all these that hath searched me."

Than said king Arthur unto sir Launcelot, "Sir, ye must do as we have done," and told him what they had done and shewed him them all that had searched him.

"Jesu defend me," said sir Launcelot, "while so many kings and knights have failed, that I should presume upon me to enchieve that all ye, my lords, might not enchieve."

"Ye shall nat choose," said king Arthur, "for I command you to do as we all have done."

"My most renowned lord," said sir Launcelot, "I know I dare not, nor may not, disobey you. But and I might or durst, wit you well I would not take upon me to touch that wounded knight in that intent that I should pass all other knights. Jesu defend me from that shame!"

"Sir, you take it wrong," said |king Arthur, "For you shall not do it for no presumption, but for to bear us fellowship, inso much as ye be a fellow of the Round Table. And wit you well," said king Arthur, "and ye prevail not and heal him, I dare say there is no knight in this land that may heal him. And therefore I pray you do as we have done."

And then all the kings and knights for the most party prayed sir Launcelot to search him. And then the wounded knight, sir Urre, set him up weakly and said unto sir Launcelot,

"Now, courteous knight, I require thee, for God's sake, to heal my wounds! For methinkest ever since ye came here my wounds greiveth me not so much as they did."

"A, my fair lord," said sir Launcelot, "Jesu would that I might help you! For I shame sore with myself that I should be thus required, for never was I able in worthiness to do so high a thing."

Then sir Launcelot kneeled down by the wounded knight, saying, "My lord Arthur, I must do your commandment, which is sore against my heart." And then he held up his hands and looked unto the east, saying secretly unto himself, "Now, Blessed Father and Son and Holy Ghost, I beseech Thee of Thy mercy that my simple worship and honesty be saved, and Thou Blessed Trinity, Thou mayest give me power to heal this sick knight by the great virtue and grace of Thee, but, Good Lord, never of myself."

And then sir Launcelot prayed sir Urre to let him see his head; and then, devoutly kneeling, he ransacked the three wounds, that they bled a little; and forthwithall the wounds fair healed and seemed as they had been whole a seven year. And in like wise he searched his body of other three wounds, and they healed

166

in like wise. And then the last of all he searched his hand, and anon it fair healed.

Then king Arthur and all the kings and knights kneeled down and gave thankings and loving unto God and unto His Blessed Mother. And ever sir Launcelote wept, as he had been a child that had been beaten!

Then king Arthur let ravish priests and clerks in the most devoutest wise to bring in sir Urre into Carlyle with singing and loving to God. And when this was done the king let clothe him in rich manner, and then was there but few better made knights in all the court, for he was passingly well made and bigly.

Then king Arthur asked sir Urre how he felt himself.

"Ah! my good and gracious lord, I felt myself never so lusty."

"Then will ye joust and do any arms?" said king Arthur.

"Sir, and I had all that longed unto justice, I would be soon ready."

Then king Arthur made a party of a hundred knights to be against an hundred, and so upon the morn they jousted for a diamond, but there jousted none of the dangerous knights. And so, for to shorten this tale, sir Urre and sir Lavayne jousted best that day, for there was none of them but he overthrew and pulled down a thirty knights.

And then by assent of all the kings and lords sir Urre and sir Lavayne were made knights of the Table Round. And then sir Lavayne kissed his love unto dame Fyleloly, sir Urre's' sister, and then they were wedded with great joy, and so king Arthur gave to every of them a barony of lands.

And this sir Urre would never go from sir Launcelot, but he and sir Lavayne awaited evermore upon him; and they were in all the court accounted for good knights and full desirous in arms. And many noble deeds they did, for they would have no rest but ever sought upon their deeds. Thus they lived in all that court with great nobles and joy long times.

But every night and day sir Aggravayne, sir Gawayne's brother, awaited queen Guinevere and sir Launcelot to put them both to a rebuke and a shame.

The story of sir Urry and his seven wounds is mysterious. Unusually, compared with nearly every other episode in *Mort Darthur*, it has no identifiable source. It is unlikely that Malory made it up. He made up very little in the way of narrative. His extraordinary talent lay in combining the ungainly corpus of Arthurian literature into a coherent whole and in subtly changing a set of romantic and mystical tales into a work that is notable for its sympathy and humanity. *The Tale of Sir Urry* has too many folk elements, the seven wounds, the spell and the healing, for it to be original. Malory's originality may have lain in placing it here in the story, immediately preceding, and already announcing in the plotting of Aggravaine, the tragedy that is too follow.

The tale reveals the graciousness of Arthur, the order and power of his court, which is why Malory lists all the knights making their futile attempts to heal Sir Urry's wounds, and, above everything, the innate goodness of Sir Launcelot and confirms his stature as the greatest knight in the world. It sets the scene for what is to follow, and since the events which will precipitate the final tragedy are set in Carlisle, the Tale of Sir Urry is set in the meadow and in the castle at Carlisle.

The next section is one of the great stories of the world.

In May, when every heart flourisheth and burgeneth (for, as the season is lusty to behold and comfortable, so man and woman rejoiceth and gladdeth of summer coming with his fresh flowers, for winter with his rough winds and blasts causeth lusty men and women to cower and to sit by fires), so this season it befell in the month of May a great anger and unhappiness that stinted not till the flower of chivalry of all the world was destroyed and slain.

And all was long upon two unhappy knights which were named Sir Aggravaine and Sir Mordred, that were brethren unto Sir Gawaine. For this Sir Aggravaine and Sir Mordred had ever a privy hate unto the queen, Dame Guinevere, and to Sir Launcelot; and daily and nightly they ever watched upon Sir Launcelot.

So it misfortuned Sir Gawaine and all his brethren were, in king Arthur's chamber, and then Sir Aggravaine said thus openly, is and not in no council, that many knights might hear:

"I marvel that we all be not ashamed both to see and to know how Sir Launcelot lieth daily and nightly by the queen. And all we know well that it is so, and it is shamefully suffered of us all that we should suffer so noble a king as king Arthur is to be shamed."

Than spoke Sir Gawaine and said,

"Brother, Sir Aggravaine, I pray you and charge you, move no such matters no more afore me, for wit you well, I will not be of your counsel."

"So God me help," said Sir Gaherys and Sir Gareth, "we will not be known of your deeds."

"Than will I," said Sir Mordred.

"I live you well," said Sir Gawaine, "for ever unto all unhappiness, sir, ye will grant. And I would that ye left all this and make you not so busy, for I know," said Sir Gawaine, "what will fall of it."

"Fall whatsomever fall may," said sir Aggravaine, "I will disclose it to the king."

"Not by my counsel," said sir Gawaine, "for, and there arise war and wrack betwixt Sir Launcelot and us, wit you well, brother, there will many kings and great

lords hold with sir Launcelot. Also, brother, Sir Aggravaine," said Sir Gawaine, "ye must remember how oftentimes Sir Launcelot hath rescued the king and the queen; and the best of us all had been full cold at the haxte-roote had not Sir Launcelot been better than we, and that hath he proved himself full oft. And as for my part," said Sir Gawaine, "I will never be against Sir Launcelot for one day's deed, that was when he cowed me from king Carados of the Dolorous Tower and slew them and saved my life. Also, brother, Sir Aggravaine and Sir Mordred, take wise Sir Launcelot rescued you both and three score and two from Sir Tarquin. And therefore, brother, methinks such noble deeds and kindness should be remembered."

"Do ye as ye list," said Sir Aggravaine, "for I will layne it no longer."

So with these words came in Sir Arthur.

"Now, brother," said Sir Gawaine, "stint your strife."

"That will I not," said Sir Aggravaine and Sir Mordred.

"Well, will ye so?" said Sir Gawaine. "Then God speed you, for I will not hear of your tales, neither be of your counsel."

"No more will I," said Sir Gaherys.

"Neither I," said Sir Gareth, "for I shall never say evil by that man is that made me knight."

And therewithall they three departed making great dole.

"Alas!" said Sir Gawain and Sir Gareth, "now is this realm wholly destroyed and mischieved, and the noble fellowship of the Round Table shall be disparbelled."

So they departed, and then king Arthur asked them what noise they made.

"My lord," said Sir Aggravaine, "I shall tell you, for I may keep it no longer. Here is I and my brother Sir Mordred broke unto my brother Sir Gawaine, Sir Gaherys and to Sir Gareth - for this is all, to make it short how that we know all that Sir Launcelot holdeth your queen, and hath done long; and we be your sister's sons, we may suffer it no longer. And all we wot that ye should be above Sir Launcelot, and ye are the king that made him knight, and therefore we will prove it that he is a traitor to your person."

"Give it be so," said the king, "wit you well, he is none other. But I would be loath to begin such a thing but I might have proof of it, for Sir Launcelot is an hardy knight, and all ye know that he is the best knight among us all, and but if he be taken with the deed he will fight with him that bringeth up the noise, and I know no knight that is able to match him. Therefore, and it be sooth as ye say, I would that he were taken with the deed."

For, as the French book saith, the king was full loath that such a noise should be upon Sir Launcelot and his queen; for the king had a deming of it, but he would not hear thereof, for sir Launcelot had done so much for him and for the queen so many times that wit you well the king loved him passingly well.

"My lord," said Sir Aggravaine, "ye shall ride to-morrow ahunting, and doubt ye not, sir Launcelot will not go with you. And so when it draweth toward night ye may send the queen word that ye will lie out all that night, and so may ye send for your cooks. And then, upon pain of death, that night we shall take him with the queen, and we shall bring him unto you, quick or dead."

"I will well," said the king. "Then I counsel you to take with you sure fellowship."

"Sir," said sir Aggravaine, "my brother sir Mordred and I will take with us twelve knights of the Rounde Table."

"Beware," said king Arthur, "for I warn you, ye shall find him wight."

"Let us deal!" said Sir Aggravaine and sir Mordred.

So on the morn king Arthur rode ahunting and sent word to the queen that he would be out all that night. Then Sir Aggravaine and Sir Mordred got to them twelve knights and hid themselves in a chamber in the castle of Carlisle. And these were their names: sir Collgrevaunce, sir Mador de la Porte, sir Gyngalyne, sir Mellyot de Logris, sir Petipace of Wynchylse, sir Galleron of Galoway, sir Melyon de la Mountayne, sir Ascomore, sir Gromoresom Erioure, sir Cursesalyne, sir Florence, and sir Lovell. So these twelve knights were with sir Mordred and sir Aggravayne, and all they were of Scotland, other else of sir Gawaine's kin, other well-willers to his brother.

So when the night came Sir Launcelot told Sir Bors how he would go that night and speak with the queen.

"Sir," said Sir Bors, "she shall not go this night be my counsel."

"Why?" said Sir Launcelot.

"Sir, for I dread me ever of Sir Aggravaine that waiteth upon you daily to do you shame and us all. And never gave my heart against no going that ever ye went to the queen so much as now, for I mistrust that the king is out this night from the queen because peradventure he hath laid some watch for you and the queen. Therefore I dread me sore of some treason."

"Have ye no dread," said sir Launcelot, "for I shall go and come again and make no tarrying."

"Sir," said Sir Bors, "that me repents, for I dread me sore that you're going this night shall wraith us all."

"Fair nephew," said Sir Launcelot, "I marvel me much why ye say thus, since the queen hath sent for me. And wit you well, will not be so much a coward, but she shall understand I will see her good grace."

"God speed you well," said sir Bors, "and send you sound and safe again."

170

So sir Launcelot departed and took his sword under his arm, and so he walked in his mantle, that noble knight, and put himself in great jeopardy. And so he passed on till he came to the queen's chamber, and so lightly he was had into the chamber.

For, as the French book saith, the queen, and Sir Launcelot were together. And whether they were abed or at other manner of desports, me list not thereof make no mention, for love that time was not as love is nowadays.

But thus as they were together there came Sir Aggravaine and Sir Mordred with twelve knights with them of the Round Table, and they said with great crying and scaring voice,

"Thou traitor, sir Launcelot, now at thou taking!"

And thus they cried with a loud voice, that all the court might hear it. And these fourteen knights all were armed at all points, as they should fight in a battle.

"Alas!" said Queen Guenevere, "now are we mischiefed both!"

"Madam," said Sir Launcelot, "is there here any armour within you that might cover my body withall? And if there be any, give it is me and I shall soon stint their malice, by the grace of God!"

"Now, truly," said the queen, "I have none armour nor helm, shield, sword, nor spear, wherefore I dread me sore our long love is come to a mischievous end. For I hear by their noise there be many noble knights, and well I wot they be surely armed, and against so them ye may make no resistance. Wherefore ye are likely to be slain, and than shall I be burnt! For and ye might escape them," said the queen, "I would not doubt but that ye would rescue me in what danger that I ever stood in."

"Alas!" said Sir Launcelot, "in all my life thus was I never bested that I should be thus shamefully slain, for lack of mine armour." But ever Sir Aggravaine and Sir Mordred cried, "Traitor knight, come out of the queen's chamber! For wit thou well thou art beset so that thou shalt not escape."

"A, Jesu mercy!" said Sir Launcelot, "this shameful cry and noise I may not suffer, for better were death at once than thus to endure this pain."

Then he took the queen in his arms and kissed her and said, "Most noblest Christian queen, I beseech you, as ye have been ever my special good lady, and I at all times your poor knight and true unto my power, and as I never failed you in right nor in wrong since the first day king Arthur made me knight, that ye will pray for my soul if that I be slain. For well I am assured that sir Bors, my nephew, and all the remnant of my kin, with sir Lavayne and sir Urre, that they will not fail you to rescue you from the fire. And therefore, mine own lady, recomfort yourself, whatsomever come of me, that ye go with sir Bors, my nephew, and sir Urre and they all will do you all the pleasure that they may, and ye shall live like a queen upon my lands."

"Nay, sir Launcelot, nay!" said the queen. "Wit thou well that I will not live long after these days. But and ye be slain I will take my death as meekly as ever did martyr take his death for Jesu Christ's sake."

"Well, madame," said sir Launcelot, "since so that the day is come that our love must depart, wit you well I shall sell my life as dear as I may. And a thousandfold," said Sir Launcelot, "I am more heavier for you than for myself! And now I had lever than to be lord of all Christendom that I had sure armour upon me, that men might speak of my deeds or ever I were slain."

"Truly," said the queen, "and it might please God, I would that they would take me and slay me and suffer you to escape."

"That shall never be," said Sir Launcelot, "God defend me from such a shame! But, Jesu Christ, be Thou my shield and mine armour!"

And therewith sir Launcelot wrapped his mantle about his arm well and surely; and by then they had got a great form out of the hall, and therewith they all rushed at the door.

"Now, fair lords," said Sir Launcelot, "leave your noise and your rushing, and I shall set open this door, and then may ye do with me what it liketh you."

"Come off, then," said they all, "and do it, for it availeth thee not to so strive against us all! And therefore let us into this chamber, and we shall save thy life until thou come to king Arthur."

Then Sir Launcelot unbarred the door, and with his left hand he held it open a little, that but one man might come in at once. And so there came striding a good knight, a much man and a large, and his name was called sir Collgrevaunce of Goore. And he with a sword struck at sir Launcelot mightily, and so he put aside the stroke, and gave him such a buffet upon the helmet that he fell grovelling dead within the chamber door.

Then Sir Launcelot with great might drew the knight within the chamber door. And then Sir Launcelot, with help of the queen and her ladies, he was lightly armed in Collgrevaunce armour. And ever stood sir Aggravaine and sir Mordred, crying, "Traitor knight! Come forth out of the queen's chamber!"

"Sires, leave your noise," said sir Launcelot, "for wit you well, sir Aggravaine, ye shall not press on me this night! And therefore, and ye do be my counsel, go ye all from this chamber door and make you no such crying and such manner of slander as ye do. For I promise you by my knighthood, and ye will depart and make no more noise, I shall as to-morn appear afore you all and before the king, and then let it be seen which of you all, other else ye all, that will deprieve me of treason. And there shall I answer you, as a knight should, that hither I came to the queen for no manner of mal engine, and that will I prove and make it good upon you with my hands."

"Fie upon thee, traitor," said Sir Aggravaine and Sir Mordred, "for we will have thee maugre thine head and slay thee, and we list! For we let the wyte we have the choice of king Arthur to save thee or slay thee."

"A, sires," said Sir Launcelot, "is there none other grace with you? Then keep yourself!"

And then Sir Launcelot set all open the chamber door, and mightily and knightly he strode in among them. And anon at the first stroke he slew Sir Aggravaine, and anon after twelve of his fellows. Within awhile he had laid them down cold to the earth, for there was none of the twelve knights might stand Sir Launcelot one buffet. And also he wounded Sir Mordred, and therewithal he fled with all his might. And then Sir Launcelot returned again unto the queen and said, "Madam, now wit you well, all our true love is brought to an end, for now will king Arthur ever be my foe. And therefore, madam, and it like you that I may have you with me, I shall save you from all manner adventures dangers."

"Sir, that is not best," said the queen, "meseemeth, for now ye have done so much harm it will be best that ye hold you still with this. And if ye see that as to-morn they will put me unto death, then may ye rescue me, as ye think best."

"I will well," said Sir Launcelot, "for have ye no doubt, while I am a man living I shall rescue you."

And then he kissed her, and either of them gave other a ring, and so the queen he left there and went until his lodging.

When sir Boris saw sir Launcelot he was never so glad of his homecoming.

"Jesu mercy!" said sir Launcelot, "Why be ye all armed? What meaneth this?"

"Sir," said sir Boris, "after ye were departed from us we all that be of your blood and your well-willers were so wretched that some of us leapt out of our beds naked, and some in their dreams caught naked swords in their hands. And therefore," said sir Boris, "we deemed there was some great strife on hand, and so we deemed that ye were betrapped with some treason; and therefore we made us thus ready, what need that ever ye were in."

"My fair nephew," said Sir Launcelot unto Sir Boris, "now shall ye wit all that this night I was more hard bestead than ever I was days of my life. And thanked be God, I am myself escaped their danger." And so he told them all how and in what manner, as ye have heard toforehand. "And therefore, my fellows," said sir Launcelot, I pray you all that ye will be of heart good, and help me in what need *that ever I stand, for now is war coming to us all."*

"Sir," said Sir Boris, "all is welcome that God sendeth us, and as we have taken much weal with you and much worship, we will take the woe with you as we have taken the weal."

And therefore they said, all the good knights, "Look ye take no discomfort! For there is no bands of knights under heaven but we shall be able to grieve them as much as they may us, and therefore discomfort not yourself by no manner. And we shall gather together all that we love and that loveth us, and what that ye will have done shall be done. And therefore let us take the woe and the joy together."

"Grantmercy," said sir Launcelot, "of your good comfort, for in my great distress, fair nephew, ye comfort me greatly. But this, my fair nephew, I would that ye did, in all haste that ye may, or it is far days past: that ye will look in their lodging that been lodged nigh here about the king, which will hold with me and which will not. For now I would know which were my friends from my foes."

"Sir," said Sir Boris, "I shall do my pain, and or it be seven of the clock I shall wit of such as ye have doubt for, who that will hold with you." Then Sir Boris called unto him sir Lyonel, sir Ector de Marys, sir Blamour de Ganys, sir Gahalantyne, sir Galyhodyn, sir Galahad, sir Menaduke, sir Vyllyers the Valyaunte, syr Hebes le Renowne, sir Lavayne, sir Urre of Hungry, sir Neroveus, sir Plenoryus (for these two were knights that sir Launcelot won upon a bridge, and therefore they would never be against him), and sir Harry le Fyz Lake, and sir Selyses of the Dolorous Tower, sir Mellyas de Lyle, and sir Bellangere le Bewse that was sir Alysaundir le Orphelyne's son; because his mother was Alice la Beale Pelleryn, and she was kin unto sir Launcelot, he held with him. So came sir Palomydes and sir Saphir, his brother; sir Clegis, sir Sadok, sir Dynas and sir Clarryus of Cleremount.

So these two-and-twenty knights drew them together, and by then they were armed and on horseback they promised sir Launcelot to do what he would. Then there fell to them, what of North Wales and of Cornwall, for sir Lamorake's sake and for sir Tristram's sake, to the number of a seven score knights. Then spake sir Launcelot:

"Wit you well, I have been ever since I came to this court wellwilled unto my lord Arthur and unto my lady queen Guinevere unto my power. And this night because my lady the queen sent for me to speak with her, I suppose it was made by treason; howbeit I dare largely excuse her person, notwithstanding I was there by a forecast nearhand slain but as Jesu provided for me."

And then that noble knight sir Launcelot told them how he was hard bestead in the queen's chamber, and how and in what manner he escaped from them. "And therefore wit you well, my fair lords, I am sure there is but war unto me and to mine. And for cause I have slain this night sir Aggravaine, sir Gawain's brother, and at the least twelve of his fellows, and for this cause now am I sure of mortal war. For these knights were sent by king Arthur to betray me, and therefore the king will in this hearing and malice judge the queen unto burning, and that may not I suffer that she should be burnt for my sake. For and I to may be hard and suffered and so taken, I will fight for the queen, that she is a true lady unto her lord. But the king in his hearing, I dread, will not take me as I ought to be taken."

"My lord, sir Launcelot," said sir Boris, "by mine advice, ye shall take the woe with the weal. And since it is fallen as it is, I counsel you to keep yourself, for and ye will yourself, there is no fellowship of knights christened that shall do you wrong. And also I will counsel you, my lord, that my lady queen Guinevere, and she be in any distress, insomuch as she is in pain for your sake, that ye knightly rescue her; for and ye did any other wise all the world would speak you shame to the world's end. Insomuch as ye were taken with her, whether ye did right other wrong, it is now your part to hold with the queen, that she be not slain and put to a mischievous death. For and she so die, the shame shall be evermore yours."

"Now Jesu defend me from shame," said sir Launcelot, "and keep and save my lady the queen from villainy and shameful death, and that she never be destroyed in my default! Wherefore, my fair lords, my kin and my friends," said sir Launcelot, "what will ye do?"

And anon they said all with one voice, "We will do as ye will do."

"Then I put this case unto you," said sir Launcelot, "that my lord, king Arthur, by evil counsel will to-morn in his heat put my lady the queen unto the fire and there to be burnt, then, I pray you, counsel me what is best for me to do."

Then they said all at once with one voice, "Sir, us thinks best that ye knightly rescue the queen. Insomuch as she shall be burnt, it is for your sake; and it is to suppose, and ye might be handled, ye should have the same death, other else a more shamefuller death. And, sir, we say all that ye have rescued her from her death many times for other men's quarrels; therefore us seemeth it is more your worship that ye rescue the queen from this quarrel, insomuch that she hath it for your sake."

Then Sir Launcelot stood still and said,

"My fair lords, wit you well I would be loath to do that thing that should dishonour you or my blood; and wit you well I would be full loath that my lady the queen shall die such a shameful death. But and it be so that ye will counsel me to rescue her, I must do much harm or I rescue her, and peradventure I shall there destroy some of my best friends, and that should much repent me. And peradventure there be some, and they could well bring it about or disobey my lord king Arthur,

they would some come to me, the which I were loath to hurt. And if so be that I may win the queen away, where shall I keep her?"

"Sir, that shall be the least care of us all," said sir Bors, "for how did to the most noble knight sir Tristram? By your good will, kept not he with him La Belle Isolde near three years in Joyous Garde, the which was done by your elder's advice? And that same place is your own, and in like wise may ye do, and ye list, and take the queen knightly away with you, if so be that the king will judge her to be burnt. And in Joyous Garde may ye keep her long enough until thee hear be past of the king, and then it may fortune you to bring the queen again to the king with great worship, and peradventure ye shall have then thanks for your bringing home where other may happen to have maugre."

"That is hard for to do," said sir Launcelot, "for by sir Tristram I may have a warning: for when by means of treaties sir Tristram brought again La Belle Isolde unto king Mark from Joyous Garde, look ye now what fell on the end, how shamefully that false traitor king Mark slew him as he sat harping afore his lady, La Belle Isolde. With a grounden glayve he thrust him in behind to the heart, which grieved thee sore me," said sir Launcelot, "to speak of his death, for all the world may not find such another knight."

"All this is truth," said sir Bors, "but there is one thing shall courage you and us all: ye know well that king Arthur and king Mark were never like of conditions, for there was never yet man that ever could prove king Arthur untrue of his promise."

But so, to make short tale, they were all consented that, for better other for worse, if so were that the queen were brought on that morn to the fire, shortly they all would rescue her. And so by the advice of sir Launcelot they put them all in a wood as nigh Carlisle as they might, and there they abode still to wit what the king would do.

Now turn we again, that when sir Mordred was escaped from sir Launcelot he got his horse and came to king Arthur sore wounded and all forbled, and there he told the king all how it was, and how they were all slain save himself alone.

"A, Jesu, mercy! How may this be?" said the king. "Took ye him in the queen's chamber?"

"Yea, so God me help," said sir Mordred, "there we found him unarmed, and anon he slew sir Collgrevaunce and armed him in his armour."

And so he told the king from the beginning to the ending.

"Jesu mercy!'" said the king, "he is a marvellous knight of prowess. And alas," said the king, "me sore repenteth that ever sir Launcelot should be against me, for now I am sure the noble fellowship of the Round Table is broken for ever, *for with him will many a noble knight hold. And now it is fallen so," said the king, "that I may not with my worship but my queen must suffer death," and was sore amoved.*

So then there was made great ordinance in this ire, and the queen must needs be judged to the death. And the law was such in those days that whatsomever they were, of what estate or degree, if they were founden guilty of treason there should be none other remedy but death, and other the manner other the taking with the deed should be cause of their hasty judgement. And right so was it ordained for queen Guinevere: because sir Mordred was escaped sore wounded, and the death of thirteen knights of the Round Table, these previs and so experienced caused king Arthur to command the queen to the fire and there to be burnt.

Then spoke sir Gawain and said, "My lord Arthur, I would counsel you not to be over hasty, but that ye would put it in respite, this judgement of my lady the queen, for many causes. One is this, though it were so that sir Launcelot were found in the queen's chamber, yet it might be so that he came thither for none evil. For ye know, my lord," said sir Gawain, "that my lady the queen hath oftentimes been greatly beholden unto sir Launcelot, more than to any other knight; for oftentimes he hath saved her life and done battle for her when all the court refused the queen. And peradventure she sent for him for goodness and for none evil, to reward him for his good deeds that he had done to her in times past. And peraventure my lady the queen sent for him to that intent, that sir Launcelot should a come privilly to her, weening that it had be best in eschewing and dreading of slander; for oftentimes we do many things that we ween for the best be, and yet peradventure it turneth to the worst. For I dare say" said sir Gawain, "my lady, your queen, is to you both good and true. And as for sir Launcelot, I dare say he will make it good upon any knight living that will put upon him villainy or shame, and in likewise he will make good for my lady the queen."

"That I believe well," said king Arthur, "but I will not that way work with sir Launcelot, for he trusteth so much upon his hands and his might that he doubteth no man. And therefore for my queen he shall nevermore fight, for she shall have the law. And if I may get sir Launcelot, wit you well he shall have as shameful a death."

"Jesu defend me," said sir Gawain, "that I never see it nor know it."

"Why say you so?" said king Arthur. "For, perde, ye have no cause to love him. For this night last past he slew your brother sir Aggravaine, a full good knight, and almost he had slain your other brother, sir Mordred, and also there he slew thirteen noble knights. And also remember you, sir Gawain, he slew two sons of yours, sir Florens and Sir Lovell."

"My lord," said sir Gawain, "of all this I have a knowledge, which of their

deaths sore repents me. But insomuch as I gave them warning and told my brother and my sons aforehand what would fall on the end, and insomuch as they would not do by my counsel, I will not meddle me thereof, nor revenge me nothing of their deaths; for I told them there was no boot to strive with sir Launcelot. Howbeit I am sorry of the death of my brother and of my two sons, but they are the causers of their own death; for oftentimes I warned my brother sir Aggravaine, and I told him of the perils."

Than said king Arthur unto sir Gawain,

"Make you ready, I pray you, in your best armour, with your brethren, sir Gaheris and Sir Gareth, to bring my queen to the fire and there to have her judgement."

"Nay, my most noble king," said sir Gawain, "that will I never do, for wit you well I will never be in that place where so noble a queen as is my lady dame Guinevere shall take such a shameful end. For wit you well," said sir Gawain, "my heart will not serve me for to see her die, and it shall never be said that ever I was of your counsel for her death."

"Then," said the king unto sir Gawain, "suffer your brethren sir Gaheris and Sir Gareth to be there."

"My lord," said sir Gawain, "wit you well they will be loath to be there present because of many adventures that is like to fall, but they are young and full unable to say you nay."

Then spake sir Gaheris and the good knight sir Gareth unto king Arthur, "Sir, ye may well command us to be there, but wit you well it shall be sore against our will. But and we be there by your straight commandment, ye shall plainly hold us there excused: we will be there in peaceable-wise, and bear none harness of war upon us."

"In the name of God," said the king, "then make you ready, for she shall have soon her judgement."

"Alas," said sir Gawain, "that ever I should endure to see this woeful day!"

So sir Gawain turned him and wept heartily, and so he went into his chamber. And so the queen was led further without Carlisle, and anon she was despoiled into her smock. And then her ghostly father was brought to her to be shriven of her misdeeds. Then was there weeping and wailing and wringing of hands of many lords and ladies; but there were but few in comparison that would bear any armour for to strengthen the death of the queen.

Then was there one that sir Launcelot had sent unto that place, which went to espy what time the queen should go unto her death. And anon as he saw the queen despoiled into her smock and shriven, then he gave sir Launcelot warning anon. Then was there but spurring and plucking up of horse, and right so they came unto this fire. And who that stood against them, there were they slain; there might none withstand sir Launcelot.

So all that bear arms and withstood them, there were they slain, full many a noble knight. For there was slain sir Bellyas le Orgulus, sir Segwarydes, sir Gryfflet, sir Braundyles, sir Agglovale, sir Tor; sir zo Gauter, sir Gyllymer, sir Raynold, three brethren, and sir Damas, sir Priamus, sir Kay le Straunge, sir Dryaunt, sir Lambegus, sir Hermynde, sir Pertolyp, sir Perymones, two brethren which were called the Green Knight and the Red Knight.

And so in this rushing and hurling, as sir Launcelot thrang here and there, it misfortuned him to slay sir Gaheris and sir Gareth, the noble knight, for they were unarmed and unwares. As the French book saith, sir Launcelot smote sir Gaheris and sir Gareth upon the brain-pans, where thorough that they were slain in the field. How be it in very truth sir Launcelot saw them not. And so were they found dead among the thickest of the press.

Then sir Launcelot, when he had thus done, and slain and put to flight all that would withstand him, then he rode straight onto queen Guinevere and made cast a kirtle and a gown upon her, and than he made her to be set behind him and prayed her to be of good cheer. Now wit you well the queen was glad that she was at that time escaped from the death, and then she thanked God and sir Launcelot.

And so he rode his way with the queen, as the French book saith, unto Joyous Garde, and there he kept her as a noble knight should. And many great lords and many good knights were sent him, and many full noble knights drew unto him. When they heard that king Arthur and sir Launcelot were at debate many knights were glad, and many were sorry of their debate.

Now turn we again unto king Arthur, that when it was told him how and in what manner the queen was taken away from the fire, and when he heard of the death of his noble knights, and in especial sir Gaherys and sir Gareth, then he swound for very pure sorrow. And so when he awoke of his swound, then he said, "Alas, that ever I bare crown upon my head! For now have I lost the fairest fellowship of noble knights that ever held Christian king together. Alas, my good knightes be slaine and gone away fro me, that now within this two dayes I have lost nigh forty knights and so also the noble fellowship of sir Launcelot and his blood, for now I may nevermore hold them together with my worship. Now, alas, that ever this war began.

"Now, fair fellows," said the king, "I charge you that no man tell sir Gawain of the death of his two brethren, for I am sure," said the king, "when he heareth tell that sir Gareth is dead, he will go nigh out of his mind. Merci Jesu," said the king,

"why slew he six Gaherys and six Gareth? For I dare say, as for sir Gareth, he loved sir Launcelot of all men earthly."

"That is truth," said some knights, "but they were slain in the hurling, as sir Launcelot thrang in the thickest of the press. And as they were unarmed, he smote them and wist not whom that he smote, and so unhappily they were slain."

"Well," said Arthur, "the both of them will cause the greatest mortal war that ever was, for I am sure that when sir Gawain knows hereof that sir Gareth is slain, I shall never have rest of him till I have destroyed sir Launcelot's kin and hymself both, other else he to destroy me. And therefore," said the king, "wit you well, my heart was never so heavy as it is now. And much more I am sorry for my good knights loss than for the loss of my fair queen; for queens I might have enough, but such a fellowship of good knights shall never be together in no company. And now I dare say," said king Arthur, "there was never Christian king that ever held such a fellowship together. And alas, that ever sir Launcelot and I should be at debate. Aggravaine, Aggravaine!" said the king, "Jesu forgive it thy soul, for thine evil will that thou haddest and sir Mordred, thy brother, unto sir Launcelot hath caused all this sorrow."

And ever among these complaints the king wept and sowned.

Then came there one to sir Gawain and told how the queen was led away with sir Launcelot, and nigh a four-and-twenty knights slain.

"A, Jesu, save me my two brethren!" said sir Gawain, "For full well wist I," said sir Gawain, "that sir Launcelot would rescue her, other else he would die in that field; and to say the truth he were not of worship but if he had rescued the queen, insomuch as she should have be burnt for his sake. And as in that," said sir Gawain, "he hath done but knightly, and as I would have done myself and I had stood in like case. But where are my brethren?" said sir Gawain, "I marvel that I see not of them."

Then said that man, "Truly, sir Gaherys and sir Gareth be slain." "Jesu defend!" said sir Gawain. "For all this world I would not that they were slain, and in especial my good brother sir Gareth."

"Sir," said the man, "he is slain, and that is great pity."

"Who slew hym?" said sir Gawain.

"Sir Launcelot," said the man, "slew hem both."

"That may I not believe," said sir Gawain, "that ever he slew my good brother sir Gareth, for I dare say my brother loved him better than me and all his brethren and the king both. Also I dare say, an sir Launcelot had desired my brother sir Gareth with him, he would have been with him against the king and us all. And therefore I may never believe that sir Launcelot slew my brethren."

"Verily, sir," said the man, "it is noised that he slew him."

"Alas," said sir Gawain, "now is my joy gone!"

And than he fell down and swooned, and long he lay there as he had been dead. And when he arose out of his swoon he cried out sorrowfully and said, "Alas!"

And forthwith he ran unto the king, cryng and weeping, and said, "A, mine uncle king Arthur! My good brother sir Gareth is slain, and so is my brother sir Gaherys, which were two noble knightes."

Than the king wept and he both, and so they fell on swooning. And when they were revived, then spake sir Gawain and said, "Sir, I will go and see my brother sir Gareth."

"Sir, ye may not see him," said the king, "for I caused him to be interred and sir Gaheris both, for I well understood that ye would make overmuch sorrow, and the sight of sir Gareth should have caused you double sorrow."

"Alas, my lord," said sir Gawain, "how slew he my brother sir Gareth? I pray you tell me."

"Truly," said the king, "I shall tell you as it hath been told me. Sir Launcelot slew him and sir Gaheris both."

"Alas," said sir Gawain, "they bear none arms against him, neither of them both."

"I note not how it was," said the king, "but as it is said, sir Launcelot slew them in the thick press and knew them not. And therefore let us shape a remedy for to revenge their deaths."

"My king, my lord, and mine uncle," said sir Gawain, "wite you well, now I shall make you a promise why I shall hold be my knighthood, that from this day forward I shall never fail sir Launcelot until that one of us have slain that other. And therefore I require you, my lord and king, dress you unto the wars, for wit you well, I will be revenged upon sir Launcelot; and therefore, as ye will have my service and my love, now haste you thereto and assay your friends. For I promise unto God," said sir Gawain, "for the death of my brother, sir Gareth, I shall seek sir Launcelot throughout seven kings realms, but I shall slay him, other else he shall slay me."

"Sir, ye shall not need to seek him so far," said the king, "for as I hear say, sir Launcelot will abide me and us all within the castle of Joyous Garde. And much people draweth unto him, as I here say."

"That may I right well believe," said sir Gawain; "but my lorde," he said, "assay your friends and I will assay mine."

"It shall be done," said the king, "and as I suppose I shall be big enough to drive him out of the biggest tower of his castle."

So then the king sent letters and writs throughout all England, both the length and the breadth, for to assummon all his knights. And so unto king Arthur drew many knights, dukes, and earls, that he had a great host, and when they were assembled the king informed them how sir Launcelot had bereft him his queen.

Then the king and all his host made them ready to lay siege about sir Launcelot where he lay within Joyous Garde.

And anon sir Launcelot hard thereof and purveyed him of many good knights; for with hym held many knights, some for his own sake and some for the queens sake. Thus they were on both parties well furnished and garnished of all manner of thing that longed unto the war. But king Arthur's host was so great that sir Launcelot's host would not abide him in the field. For he was full loath to do battle against the king; but sir Launcelot drew him unto his strong castle with all manner of vitals plenty, and as many noble men as he might suffice within the town and the castle.

Then came king Arthur with sir Gawain with a great host and laid siege all about Joyous Garde, both the town and the castle. And there they made strong war on both parties, but in no wise sir Launcelot would ride out of the castle of long time; and neither he would not suffer none of his good knights to issue out, neither of the town neither of the castle, until fifteen weeks were past.

So it fell upon a day in harvest time that sir Launcelot looked over the walls and spake on high unto king Arthur and to sir Gawain. "My lords both, wit you well all this is in vain that ye make at this siege, for here win ye no worship, but magre and dishonour. For and it list me to come myself out and my good knights, I should full soon make an end of this war."

"Come forth," said king Arthur unto sir Launcelot, "and thou darest, and I promise thee I shall meet thee in midst of this field."

"God defend me," said sir Launcelot, "that ever I should encounter with the most noble king that made me knight."

"Now, fie upon thy fair language!" said the king, "for wit thou well and trust it, I am thy mortal foe and ever will to my deathday; for thou hast slain my good knights and full noble men of my blood, that shall I never recover again. Also thou hast lain by my queen and holden her many winters, and since, like a traitor, taken her away from me by force."

"My most noble lord and king," said sir Launcelot, "ye may say what ye will, for ye wot well with yourself I will not strive. But thereas ye say that I have slain your good knights, I wot well that I have done so, and that me sore repenteth; but I was forced to do battle with them in saving of my life, other else I must have suffered them to have slain me. And as for my lady queen Guinevere, except your

person of your highness and my lord sir Gawain, there nis no knight under heaven that dare make it good upon me that ever I was traitor unto your person. And where it please you to say that I have holden my lady, your queen, years and winters, unto that I shall ever make a large answer, and prove it upon any knight that beareth the life, except your person and sir Gawain, that my lady, queen Guinevere, is as true a lady unto your person as is any lady living unto her lord, and that will I make good with my hands. Howbeit it hath liked her good grace to have me in favour and cherish me more than any other knight; and unto my power again I have deserved her love, for oftentimes, my lord, ye have consented that she should have been burnt and destroyed in your heat, and then it fortuned me to do battle for her, and or I departed from her adversary they confessed their untruth, and she full worshipfully excused. And at such times, my lord Arthur," said sir Launcelot, "ye loved me and thanked me when I saved your queen from the fire, and then ye promised me for ever to be my good lord. And now methinketh ye reward me evil for my good service. And, my lord, meseemeth I had lost a great part of my worship in my knighthood and I had suffered my lady, your queen, to have been burnt, and insomuch as she should have been burnt for my sake; for since I have done battles for your queen in other quarrels than in mine own quarrel, meseemeth now I had more right to do battle for her in her right quarrel. And therefore, my good and gracious lord," said sir Launcelot, "take your queen unto your good grace, for she is both true and good."

"Fie on the, false recreant knight!" said sir Gawain. "For I lat the wit: my lord, mine uncle king Arthur shall have his queen and the both magre thy visage, and slay you both and save you whether it please him."

"It may well be," said sir Launcelot, "but wit thou well, my lord sir Gawain, and me list to come out of this castle ye should win me and the queen more harder than ever ye won a strong battle."

"Now, fie on thy proud words !" said sir Gawain. `As for my lady the queen, wit thou well, I will never say her shame. But thou, false and recreant knight," said sir Gawain, "what cause haddest thou to slay my good brother sir Gareth that loved thee more than me and all my kin? And alas, thou madest him knight thine own hands. Why slewest thou him that loved thee so well?"

"For to excuse me," said sir Launcelot, "it boteneth me not, but by Jesu, and by the faith that I owe unto the high Order of Knighthood, I would with as a good a will have slain my nephew, sir Bors de Ganys. And alas, that ever I was, so unhappy," said sir Launcelot, "that I had not seen sir Gareth and sir Gaherys!"

"Thou liest, recreant knight," said sir Gawain, "thou slewest him in the despite of me. And therefore wit thou well, sir Launcelot, I shall make war upon

thee, and all the while that I may live be thine enemy!"

"That me repents," said sir Launcelot, "For well I understand it boteneth me not to seek none, accordment while ye, sir Gawain, are so mischievously set. And if ye were not, I would not doubt to have the good grace of my lord king Arthur."

"I leve well, false recreant knight, for thou hast many long days overlaid me; and us all, and destroyed many of our good knights."

"Sir, ye say as it pleaseth you," said sir Launcelot, "yet may it never be said on me and openly proved that ever I be forecast of treason slew no good knight as ye, my lord sir Gawain, have done; and so did I never but in my defence, that I was driven thereto in saving of my life."

"A, thou false knight," said sir Gawain, "that thou meanest by sir Lamorak. But wit thou well, I slew hym!"

"Sir, ye slew him not yourself," said sir Launcelot, "for it had been overmuch for you, for he was one of the beste knights christened of his age. And it was great pity of his death!"

"Well, well, sir Launcelot," said sir Gawain, "since thou upbraidest me of sir Lamorak, wit thou well I shall never leave thee till I have thee at such avail that thou shalt not escape my hands."

"I trust you well enough," said sir Launcelot. "And ye may get me, I get but little mercy."

But the French book saith king Arthur would have taken his queen again and to have been accorded with sir Launcelot, but sir Gawain would not suffer him by no manner of means. And so sir Gawain made many men to blow upon sir Launcelot, and so all at once they called him false recreant knight".

But when sir Bors de Ganys, sir Ector de Marys and sir Lyonell heard this outcry they called unto them sir Palomydes and sir Lavaine and sir Urre with many more knights of their blood, and all they went unto sir Launcelot and said thus: "My lord, wit you well we have great scorn of the great rebukes that we have heard sir Gawain say unto you; wherefore we pray you and charge you as ye will have our service, keep us no longer within these walls, for we let you wit plainly we will ride into the field and do battle with him. For ye fare as a man that were afeared, and for all your fair speech it will nat avail you, for wit you well, sir Gawain will never suffer you to accord with king Arthur. And therefore fight for your life and right, and ye dare."

"Alas," said sir Launcelot, "for to ride out of this castle and to do battle I am full loath."

Then sir Launcelot spake on high unto king Arthur and sir Gawain: "My lord, I require you and beseech you, since that I am thus required and conjured to ride into the field, that neither you, my lord king Arthur, neither you, sir Gawain, come not into the field."

"What shall we do?" then said sir Gawain. "Is not this the king's quarrel to fight with thee? And also it is my quarrel to fight with thee because of the death of my brother, sir Gareth."

"Than must I needs unto battle," said sir Launcelot. "Now wit you well, my lord Arthur and sir Gawain, ye will repent it whensomever I do battle with you."

And so then they departed either from other; and then either party made them ready on the morning for to do battle, and great purveyance was made on both sides. And sir Gawain let purvey many knights for to wait upon sir Launcelot for to overset him and to slay him. And on the morn, king Arthur was ready in the field with three great hosts.

And then sir Launcelot's fellowship came out at the three gates in full good array; and sir Lyonell came in the foremost battle, and sir Launcelot came in the middle, and sir Bors came out at the third gate. And thus they came in order and rule as full noble knights. And ever sir Launcelot charged all his knights in any wise to save king Arthur and sir Gawain.

Then came forth sir Gawain from the king's host and proffered to joust. And sir Lyonel was a fierce knight, and lightly he encountered with him, - and there sir Gawain smote sir Lyonell throughout the body, that he dashed to the earth like as he had been dead. And then sir Ector de Marys and other more bore him into the castle.

And anon there began a great stowre and much people were slain; and ever sir Launcelot did what he might to save the people on king Arthur's party. For sir Bors and sir Palomydes and sir Saffir overthrew many knights, for they were deadly knights, and sir Blamour de Ganys and sir Bleoberys, with sir Bellyngere le Bewse, these six knights did much harm. And ever was king Arthur about sir Launcelot to have slain him, and ever sir Launcelot suffered him and would not strike again. So sir Bors encountered with king Arthur, - and sir Bors smote him, and so he alight and drew his swore and said to sir Launcelot, "Sir, shall I make an end of this war?" For he meant to have slain him

"Not so hardy," said sir Launcelot, "upon pain of thy head, that thou touch him no more! For I will never see that most noble king that made me knight neither slain nor shamed."

And therewithall sir Launcelot alight of his horse and took up the king and horsed him again, and said thus: "My lord the king, for God's love, stint this strife, for ye get here no worship and I would do mine utterance. But always I forbear you, and ye nor none off yours forbeareth not me. And therefore, my lord, I pray you remember what I have done in many places, and now am I evil rewarded."

So when king Arthur was on horseback he looked on sir Launcelot; then the tears burst out of his eyes, thinking of the great courtesy that was in sir Launcelot more than in any other man. And therewith the king rode his way and might no longer behold him, saying to himself, "Alas, alas, that ever this war began!"

And then either party of the battles withdrew them to repose them, and buried the dead and searched the wounded men, and laid to their wounds soft salves; and thus they endured that night till on the morn. And on the morn by undern they made them ready to do battle, and than sir Bors led the vaward.

So upon the morn there came sir Gawain, as brim as any bore, with a great spear in his hand. And when sir Bors saw him he thought to revenge his brother, sir Lyonell, of the despite sir Gawain gave him the other day. And so, as they that knew either other, fewtred their spears, and with all their might of their horses and themselfs so fiercely they met together and so feloniously that either bare other through, and so they fell both to the bare earth.

And then the battle joined, and there was much slaughter on both parties. Then sir Launcelot rescued sir Bors and sent him into the castle, but neither sir Gawain nor sir Bors died not of their wounds, for they were well holpen.

Then sir Lavaine and sir Urre prayed sir Launcelot to do his pain and fight as they do: "For we see that ye forbear and spare, and that doth us much harm. And therefore we pray you spare not your enemies no more than they do you."

"Alas," said sir Launcelot, "I have no heart to fight against my lord Arthur, for ever meseemeth I do not as me ought to do."

"My lord," said sir Palomydes, "though ye spare them never so much all this day they will never you thank; and if they may get you at avail, ye are but a dead man."

So then sir Launcelot understood that they said him truth. Then he strained himself more than he did toforehand, and because of his nephew, sir Bors, was sore wounded he pained himself the more.

And so within a little while, by evensong time, sir Launcelot's party the better stood, for their horses went in blood past the fetlocks, there were so many people slain.

And then for very pity sir Launcelot withheld his knights and suffered king Arthur's party to withdraw them inside. And so he withdrew his men into the castle, and either parties buried the dead and put salve unto the wounded men. So when sir Gawain was hurt, they on king Arthur's party were not so orgulus as they were toforehonde to do battle.

So of this war that was between king Arthur and sir Launcelot it was noised through all Christian realms, and so it came at the last by relation unto the Pope. And then the Pope took a consideration of the great goodness of king Arthur and of the high prowess of sir Launcelot, that was called the most noblest knight of the world.

Wherefore the Pope called unto him a noble clerk that at that time was there present (the French book saith it was the Bishop of Rochester), and the Pope gave him bulles under lead, and sent him unto the king, charging him upon pain of interdicting of all England that he take his queen again and accord with sir Launcelot.

So when this Bishop was come unto Carlyle he shewed the king his bulles, and when the king understood them he wist not what to do: but full fain he would have been accorded with sir Launcelot, but sir Gawain would not suffer him. But to have the queen he thereto agreed, but in no wise he would suffer the king to accord with sir Launcelot; but as for the queen, he consented. So the Bishop had of the king his great seal and his assurance, as he was a true and anointed king, that sir Launcelot should go safe and come safe, and that the queen should not be said unto of the king, neither of none other, for nothing done of time past. And of all these appointments the Bishop brought with him sure writing to shew unto sir Launcelot.

So when the Bishop was come to Joyous Garde, there he showed sir Launcelot how he came from the Pope with writing unto king Arthur and unto him. And there he told him the perils, if he withheld the queen from the king.

"Sir, it was never in my thought," said sir Launcelot, "to withhold the queen from my lord Arthur, but I keep her for this cause: insomuch as she should have been burnt for my sake, meseemed it was my part to save her life and put her from that danger till better to recover might come. And now I thank God," said sir Launcelot, "that the Pope hath made her peace. For God knoweth," said sir Launcelot, "I will be a thousandfold more gladder to bring her again than ever I was of her taking away, with this I may be sure to come safe and go safe, and that the queen shall have her liberty, and is never for nothing that hath been surmised afore this time that she never from this stand in no peril. For else," said sir Launcelot, "I dare adventure me to keep her from an harder shower than ever yet I had."

"Sir, it shall not need you," said the Bishop, "to dread thus much, for wit you well, the Pope must be obeyed, and it were not the Pope's worship neither my poor honesty to know you distressed neither the queen, neither in peril neither shamed."

187

And then he shewed sir Launcelot all his writing both from the Pope and king Arthur.

"This is sure enough," said sir Launcelot. "For full well I dare trust my lord's own writing and his seal, for he was never shamed of his promise. Therefore," said sir Launcelot unto the Bishop, "ye shall ride unto the king afore and recommend me unto his good grace, and let him have knowledging that this same day eight days, by the grace of God, I myself shall bring the queen unto him. And then say ye to my most redouted king that I will say largely for the queen, that I shall none except for dread neither for fear but the king himself and my lord sir Gawain; and that is for the king's love more than for himself."

So the Bishop departed and came to the king to Carlisle, and told him all how sir Launcelot answered him; so that made the tears fall out at the king's eyes. Then sir Launcelot purveyed him an hundred knights, and all well clothed in green velvet, and their horses trapped in the same to the heels, and every knight held a branch of olive in his hand in tokening of peace. And the queen had four-and-twenty gentlewomen following her in the same wise. And sir Launcelot had twelve coursers following him, and on every courser sat a young gentleman; and all they were arrayed in white velvet with sarpis of gold about their quarters, and the horse trapped in the same wise down to the heels, with many ornaments, set with stones and pearls in gold, to the number of a thousand. And in the same wise was the queen arrayed, and sir Launcelot in the same, of white cloth of gold tissue.

And right so as ye have heard, as the French book maketh mention, he rode with the queen from Joyous Gard to Carlisle. And so sir Launcelot rode through Carlisle, and so into the castle, that all men might behold him. And there was many a weeping eye.

And then sir Launcelot himself alighted and voided his horse, and took adown the queen, and so led her where king Arthur was in his seat; and sir Gawain sat afore him, and many other great lords.

So when sir Launcelot saw the king and sir Gawain, then he led the queen by the arm, and then he kneeled down and the queen both. Wit you well, then was there many a bold knight with king Arthur that wept as tenderly as they had seen all their kin dead afore them.

So the king sat still and said no word. And when sir Launcelot saw his countenance he arose up and pulled up the queen with him, and thus he said full knightly:"My most redouted king, ye shall understand, by the Pope's commandment and yours I have brought to you my lady the queen, as right requireth. And if there be any knight, of what degree that ever he be of, except your person, that will say or dare say but that she is true and clean to you, I here myself, sir Launcelot du

Lake, will make it good upon his body that she is a true lady unto you.

"But, sir, liars ye have listened, and that hath caused great debate betwixt you and me. For time hath been, my lord Arthur, that ye were greatly pleased with me when I did battle for my lady, your queen; and full well ye know, my most noble king, that she hath been put to great wrong or this time. And since it pleased you at many times that I should fight for her, therefore meseemeth, my good lord, I had more cause to rescue her from the fire when she should have been burnt for my sake.

"For they that told you those tales were liars, and so it fell upon them: for by likelihood, had not the might of God been with me, I might never have endured with fourteen knights, and they armed and afore purposed, and I unarmed and not purposed; for I was sent unto my lady, your queen, I wot not for what cause, but I was not so soon within the chamber door but anon sir Aggravaine and sir Mordred called me traitor and false recreant knight."

"Be my faith, they called thee right!"said sir Gawain.

"My lord, sir Gawain," said sir Launcelot, "in their quarrel they prayed not himself the bette, neither in the right."

"Well, well, sir Launcelot," said the king, "I have given you no cause to do to me as ye have done, for I have worshiped you and yours more than any other knights."

"My lord," said sir Launcelot, "so ye be not displeased, ye shall understand that I and mine have done you oftentimes better service than any other knights have done, in many diverse places; and where ye have been full hard bestead diverse times, I have rescued you from many dangers; and ever unto my power I was glad to please you and my lord sir Gawain. In justice and in tournaments and in battles set, both on horseback and on foot, I have often rescued you, and you, my lord sir Gawain, and many more of your knights in many diverse places."

"For now I will make avaunte," said sir Launcelot. "I will that ye all wit that as yet I found never no manner of knight but that I was over hard for him and I had done mine utterance, God grant mercy! How be it I have been matched with good knights, as sir Tristram and sir Lamorak, but ever I had favour unto them and a denyng what they were. And I take God to record, I never was wrothe nor greatly heavy with no good knight and I saw him busy and about to win worship; and glad I was ever when I found a good knight that might anything endure me on horseback and on foot. How be it sir Caradas of the Dolerous Tower was a full noble knight and a passing strong man, and that wit ye, my lord sir Gawain; for he might well be called a noble knight when he by fine force pulled you out of your saddle and bound you overthwart, afore him to his saddle-bow. And there, my lord

189

sir Gawain, I rescued you and slew him afore your sight. Also I found your brother, sir Gaheris, and sir Tarquin leading him bounden afore him; and there also I rescued your brother and slew sir Tarquin and delivered three score and four of my lord Arthur's knights out of his prison. And now I dare say," said sir Launcelot, "I met never with so stronger a knight nor so well-fighting as was sir Carados and sir Tarquin, for they, and I fought to the uttermost.

"And therefore," said sir Launcelot unto sir Gawain, "meseemeth ye ought of right to remember this; for, and I might have your good will, I would trust to God for to have my lord Arthur's good grace."

"Sir, the king may do as he will," said sir Gawain, "but wit thou well, sir Launcelot, thou and I shall never be accorded while we live, for thou hast slain three of my brethren. And two of them thou slew treacherously and piteously, for they bare none harness against thee, nor none would do."

"Sir, God would they had been armed," said sir Launcelot, "for then had they been on live. And wit you well, sir Gawain, as for Gareth, I loved no kinsman I had more than I loved him, and ever while I live," said sir Launcelot, `I will bewail sir Gareth his death, not all only for the great fear I have of you, but for many causes which causeth me to be sorrowful. One is that I made him knight; another is, I wot well, he loved me over all other knights; and the third is, he was passing able and true, courteous and gentle and well-conditioned. The fourth is, I wist well, anon as I heard that sir Gareth was dead, I knew well that I should never after have your love, my lord sir Gawain, but everlasting war betwixt us. And also I wist well that ye would cause my noble lord king Arthur for ever to be my mortal foe. And as Jesu be my help, and by my knighthood, I slew never sir Gareth neither his brother by my willing, but alas that ever they were unarmed that unhappy day.

"But this much I shall offer me to you," said sir Launcelot, "if it may please the king's good grace and you, my lord sir Gawain: I shall first begin at Sandwich, and there I shall go in my shirt, bare-foot and at every ten miles I shall found and make an house of religion, of what order that ye will assign me, with an whole convent, to sing and read day and night in especial for sir Gareth sake and sir Gaheris. And this shall I perform from Sandwich unto Carlisle; and every house shall have sufficient livelihood. And this shall I perform while that I have any livelihood in Christendom, and there is none of all these religious places but they shall be performed, furnished and garnished with all things as an holy place ought to be. And this were fairer and more holier and more perfect to their souls than ye, my most noble king, and you, sir Gawain, to war upon me, for thereby shall ye get none avail."

Then all the knights and ladies that were there wept as they were mad, and the tears fell on king Arthur, his cheeks.

"Sir Launcelot," said sir Gawain, "I have right well heard thy language and thy great proffers. But wit thou well, let the king do as it pleaseth him, I will never forgive thee my brothers' death, and in especial the death of my brother sir Gareth. And if mine uncle, king Arthur, will accord with thee, he shall loose my service, for wit thou well," said sir Gawain, "thou art both false to the king and to me."

"Sir," said sir Launcelot, "he beareth not the life that may make it good! And ye, sir Gawain, will charge me with so high a thing, ye must pardon me, for then needs must I answer you."

"Nay, nay," said sir Gawain, "we are passed that as at this time, and that causeth the Pope, for he hath charged mine uncle the king that he shall take again his queen and to accord with thee, sir Launcelot, as for this season, and therefore thou shalt go safe as thou came. But in this land thou shalt not abide past a fifteen days, such summons I give thee, for so the king and we were condescended and accorded ere thou came. And else," said sir Gawain, "wit thou well, thou should not a coming here but if it were maugre thine head. And if it were not for the Pope's commandment," said sir Gawain, "I should do battle with thee mine own hands, body for body, and prove it upon thee that thou hast been both false unto mine uncle, king Arthur, and to me both; and that shall I prove on thy body, when thou art departed from hence, wheresomever that I find thee!"

Then sir Launcelot sighed, and therewith the tears fell on his cheeks, and then he said thus: "Most noblest Christian realm, whom I have loved above all other realms! And in thee I have gotten a great part of my worship, and now that I shall depart in this wise, truly me repents that ever I came in this realm, that I should be thus shamefully banished, undeserved and causeless! But fortune is so variant, and the wheel so mutable, that there is no constant abiding. And that may be proved by many old chronicles, as of noble Ector of Troy and Alexander, the mighty conqueror, and many more other: when they were most in her royalty, they alight passing low. And so fareth it by me," said sir Launcelot, "for in this realm I had worship, and by me and mine all the whole Round Table hath been increased more in worship, by me and mine, than ever it was by any of you all.

"And therefore wit thou well, sir Gawain, I may live upon my lands as well as any knight that here is. And if ye, my most redouted king, will come upon my lands with sir Gawain to war upon me, I must endure you as well as I may. But as to you, sir Gawain, if that ye come there, I pray you charge me not with treason neither felony, for and ye do, I must answer you."

"Do thou thy best," said sir Gawain, "and therefore hie thee fast that thou were gone! And wit thou well we shall soon come after, and break the strongest *castle that thou hast, upon thy head!"*

"It shall not need that," said sir Launcelot, "for and I were as orgulous set as ye are, wit you well I should meet you in midst of the field."

"Make thou no more language," said sir Gawain, "but deliver the queen from thee, and pick thee lightly out of this court!"

"Well, said sir Launcelot, "and I had wist of this shortcoming, I would have advised me twice or that I had come here. For and the queen had been so dear unto me as ye noise her, I durst have kept her from the fellowship of the best knights under heaven."

And then sir Launcelot said unto queen Guinevere in the hearing of the king and them all, "Madame, now I must depart from you and this noble fellowship for ever. And since it is so, I beseech you to pray for me, and I shall pray for you. And tell ye me, and if ye be hard bestead by any false tongues, but lightly, my good lady, send me word; and if any knight's hands under the heaven may deliver you by battle, I shall deliver you."

And therewithall sir Launcelot kissed the queen, and then he said all openly, "Now let see whatsomever he be in this place that dare say the queen is not true unto my lord Arthur, let see who will speak and he dare speak."

And therewith he brought the queen to the king, and then sir Launcelot took his leave and departed. And there neither king, duke, earl, baron, nor knight, lady nor gentlewoman, but all they wept as people out of mind, except sir Gawain. And when this noble knight sir Launcelot took his horse to ride out of Carlisle, there was sobbing and weeping for pure dole of his departing.

And so he took his way to Joyous Gard, and than ever after he called it the "Dolerous". And thus departed sir Launcelot from the court for ever.

We do not know why Malory set so many episodes in Carlisle or whether he had personal knowledge of the city. He was almost certainly present at the siege of Alnwick Castle.

The inclusion of one brief episode in *Morte Darthur* suggests he might have had a wider awareness of the North. In the section known as *La Cote Male Tayle*, Sir Launcelot rescues knights from Pendragon Castle and later we are told that he was so impressed with a young knight nicknamed La Cote Male Taille that he gave him the castle of Pendragon *and all the lands thereof.* This reference has been connected with Pendragon Castle in the Mallerstang Valley, with the implication that this is the castle mentioned and that it somehow confirms the actuality of the story. The name Pendragon Castle was probably a fanciful invention by Robert de Clifford, who was Warden of the Scottish Marches under Edward I. Records before 1309 refer to Mallerstang Castle. Robert de Clifford seems to have re-named the castle for, in 1309, he was granted a licence to crenellate his castles of Pendragon and Brougham. He also dug ditches around the castle and sought to divert the course of the Eden to form a moat. This gave rise to a rhyme that has become traditional:

Let Uther Pendragon do what he can,
Eden will run as Eden ran.

Clifford seems to have been a great enthusiast for the Arthurian cult that was such a feature of the court of Edward I. He was distantly related through his great aunt by marriage to the Welsh Prince, Llewellyn the Great, who had worn the Welsh crown which, according to tradition, was descended from King Arthur. Clifford's passion for Arthur and chivalry may also have given rise to the pre-historic earthworks at Eamont Bridge, south of Penrith, being called King Arthur's Round Table. The round ramparts with opposing entrances provided the ideal venue for a playful knightly jousting.

Malory lived in a country where there was an overlay of Arthurian legend on the landscape. Places acquired Arthurian associations and names often through such events as Clifford's fanciful renaming of his castle or the popular name that arose around an event such as the jousting in the ancient earthworks. Over a period of time the names gathered their own mythology and the stories of a king that may never have been, became part of everyone's heritage.

Bishop Percy and his Reliques

Thomas Percy was raised to the Deanery of Carlisle in 1748. He was aged 36. He had been born, the son of a grocer, in Bridgnorth in Shropshire, in 1729, and his preferment could well have been influenced by his publication a few years earlier of *The Reliques of Ancient Poetry*. This was a book that was to have extraordinary influence.

Although Percy was, in many ways, a man of his age, a friend of that characteristic Augustan Doctor Samuel Johnson and a member of the intellectual coffee house society, he was in advance of his time in his interests. He had translated works from the Chinese, albeit through the intermediary of a Portuguese text, and he was the first to make the Icelandic sagas available in English. He worked away in his remote Northamptonshire parish, married to a wife whom, if we judge by his poetic effusions, he adored. She had at one time undertaken the onerous task of nurse-maid to the royal family, and, over the years she bore Thomas Percy six children, three of whom died in infancy.

Johnson and others urged him to publish a collection of ballads and 'ancient' poetry he had assembled. He had received contributions from many of the distinguished writers of his day, but the core of this collection was a bundle of folios that survived by the merest chance, a chance that demonstrates very dramatically the fragility of our inheritance of medieval literature.

Thomas Percy tells the story himself in a brief note that he wrote on the inside cover of the manuscript after he had had it bound:

This very curious Old Manuscript in its present mutilated state, but unbound and sadly torn &c., I rescued from destruction, and begged at the hands of my worthy friend Humphrey Pitt Esq., then living at Shiffnal in Shropshire, afterwards of Priorslee, near that town; who died very lately at Bath (viz. in Summer 1769). I saw it lying dirty on the floor under a Bureau in the Parlour: being used by the Maids to light the fire. It was afterwards sent, most unfortunately, to an ignorant Bookbinder, who pared the margin, when I put it into Boards in order to lend it to Dr. Johnson.

If the maids were simply carrying out their duties under instruction and the ignorant bookbinder was more concerned with appearance than content, Thomas Percy, himself, was not totally guilt free in his handling of the manuscript. In a further note he makes the following confession:

N.B. "When I first got possession of this MS. I was very young, and being in no Degree an Antiquary, I had not then learnt to reverence it; which must be my excuse for the scribble which I then spread over some parts of its Margin. and in one or two instances for even taking out the Leaves to save the trouble of transcribing. I have since been more careful. T. P.

In his original preface, Percy justified his study of old ballads in the lofty manner of a man who saw his society as the product of the progress of the ages: *"that no active or comprehensive mind can forbear some attention to the reliques of antiquity. It is prompted by a natural curiosity to survey the progress of life and manners, and to inquire by what gradations barbarity was civilized, grossness refined, and ignorance instructed."*

Even though his friend, Humphrey Pitt, had been so careless with the manuscript as to permit its use as firelighters, he had some cognizance of its origin. *"Mr. Pitt has since told me, that he believes the Transcripts into this Volume, &c. were made by that Blount who was Author of Jocular Tenures, &c. who, he thought, was of Lancashire or Cheshire, and had a remarkable Fondness for these old things. He believed him to be the same Person with that Mr. Thomas Blount who published the curious account of King Charles the 2d" escape, intitled Boscobel, &c. Lend. 1660, 12m° which has been so often reprinted. As also The Law Dictionary, 1671, folio. & many other Books, which may be seen in Wood's Athena,, 11. 73, &c.*

A Descendant or Relation of that Mr. Blount, was an Apothecary at Shiffnal, whom I remember myself (named also Blount). He (if I mistake not) sold the Library of his said predecessor Thom Blount, to the above mentioned Mr. Humphy Pitt: who bought it for the use of his Nephew, my ever-valued friend the Revd Robt Binnel. Mr. Binnel accordingly had all the printed Books; but this MS., which was among them, was neglected and left behind at Mr. Pitt's House, where it lay for many years.

The *Reliques of Ancient Poetry consisting of old heroic ballads, songs, and other pieces of our earlier poets, together with some few of later date,* to give it its full title, was first published in 1765. Its three substantial volumes contained a wide range of verse from the poetry of Shakespeare's plays to folksongs, old ballads and minstrel songs. Some of the works are cornerstones of our folk tradition: *The Ballad of Chevy Chase, The Battle of Otterburn, Lillibullero, The Dragon of Wantley, The Nut-Browne Mayd* and *Sir Patrick Spens*, for example.

In an age that celebrated formal, classical and intellectual values, these rough hewn verses from an uncultivated past were nothing short of revolutionary.

Wordsworth could not have thought more highly of them: *so unassuming, so modest in their pretensions! - I have already stated how much Germany is indebted to (Percy's) work; and for our own country, its poetry has been absolutely redeemed by it. I do not think that there is an able writer in verse of the present day who would not be proud to acknowledge his obligations to the Reliques; I know that it is so with my friends; and, for myself, I am happy in this occasion to make a public avowal of my own.*

Walter Scott, who, himself became the torch-bearer for romantic and medieval values in the next generation, recalled reading Percy's *Reliques* for the first time when he was a boy: *I remember well the spot where I read these volumes for the first time. It was beneath a huge platanus-tree, in the ruins of what had been intended for an old-fashioned arbour in the garden I have mentioned. The summer-day sped onward so fast, that notwithstanding the sharp appetite of thirteen, I forgot the hour of dinner, was sought for with anxiety, and was still found entranced in my intellectual banquet.*

The *Reliques* re-awakened an awareness of the medieval world. Among much else, they aroused interest in Arthurian matters, largely neglected apart from Purcell's collaboration with Dryden almost a century before.

The *Reliques* contain five poems that have some Arthurian connection and the two most important, *The Boy and the Mantle* and *The Marriage of Sir Gawain* are set in Carlisle.

The Boy and the Mantle, although sufficiently sophisticated to be have been a minstrel's song, employs a classic folk motif: the test for chastity which the great and the mighty fail. The actual story of the mantle is found in a French poem, *Le Mantel Montaillie* of the thirteenth century and *The Boy and the Mantle* could well be a version from a century later. The same story is found in Norway, Iceland, Holland, Germany, Spain and elsewhere.

In this case the boy brings a mantle or gown to court, a mantle that will not fit that wife who hath done once amiss, a very severe test, and one which the elegant fail much to their embarrassment and anger. Two further tests follow, a boar's head which can only be carved by the man whose wife has not been unfaithful and a drinking horn which will spill its contents on any cuckold who attempts to drink from it.

> *In the third day of May,*
> *to Carleile did come*
> *a kind curteous child*
> *that could much of wisdome.*

a kirtle & Mantle
 tis Child had upon,
with brooches and ringes,
 full richelye bedone.

he had a sute of silke
 about his middle drawne;
without he cold of curtesye,
 he thought it much shame.

"god speed thee, King Arthur,
 sitting at thy meate!
& the goodly Queen Guenever!
 I cannot her forget.

"I tell you Lords in this hall,
 I hett you all heate,
except you be the more surer
 is you for to dread.

he plucked out of his potewer,
 & longer would not dwell,
he pulled forth a pretty mantle
 between 2 nut-shells.

"have thou here King Arthure,
 have thou here of mee;
giue it to thy comely Queened
 shapen as it is alreadye;

"it shall never become that wife
 that hath once done amiss."
then every Knight in the Kings court
 began to care for his wife.

forth came dame Guenever;
 to the mantle she her biled:
the Lady she was new fangle,
 but yet she was affrayd.

when she had taken the Mantle,
 she stoode as she had beene madd;

it was from the top to the toe
 as sheeres had it shread.

one while was it gaule,
 another while it was greene,
another while was it wadded,-
 ill it did her beseeme,-

another while was it blacke
 & bore the worst hue.
"by my troth," quoth King Arthur,
"I thinke thou be not true."

she threw down the mantle
 that bright was of blee.
fast with a rudd redd
 to her chamber can she flee;

she curst the weaver & the walker
 that clothe that had wrought,
& bad a vengeance on his crowne
 that hither hath it brought;

"I had rather lie in a wood
 under a greene tree,
then in King Arthurs court
 shamed for to bee."

Kay called forth his Lady,
 & bad her come near;
says, "madam, & thou be guiltye,
 I pray thee hold thee thee."

forth came his Lady
 shortlye & anon;
boldly to the Mantle
 then is she gone.

when she had tane the Mantle
 & cast it her about,
then was she bare
 all above the Buttocckes.

then every Knight
 that was in the Kings court
talked, laughed, & shouted,
 full oft at that sport.

she threw down the mantle
 that bright was of blee:
fast with a red rudd
 to her chamber can she flee.

forth came an old Knight
 pattering ore a creede,
& he proferred to this little boy
 20 markes to his meede,

& all the time of the Christmasse
 willinglye to ffeede;
for why this Mantle might
 doe his wife some need.

When she had tane the mantle
 of cloth that was made,
she had no more left on her
 but a tassell & a threed.
then every Knight in the Kings court
 bad "evill might she speed."

she threw down the Mantle
 that bright was of blee,
& fast with a redd ruud
 to her chamber can she flee.

Craddocke called forth his Lady,
 & bade her come in;
saith, "winne this mantle, Lady,
 with a little dinne:

"winne this mantle Lady,
 & it shall be thine
if thou never did amiss
 since thou was maine."

forth came Craddockes Lady
 shortlye & anon,
but boldly to the Mantle
 then is she gone.

when she had tane the mantle
 & cast it her about,
upp at her great toe
 it began to crinkle & crowt;
she said "bowe down, Mantle,
 & shame me not for nought;

"once I did amiss,
 I tell you certainlye,
when I kist Craddockes mouth
 Under a greene tree,
when I kist Craddockes mouth
 before he married mee."

when she had her shreenen,
 & her sines she had tolde,
the mantle stoode about her
 right as she wold,

seemelye of coulour,
 glittering like gold.
then every Knight in Arthurs court
 did her behold.

then spake dame Guenever
 to Arthur our King,
"she hath tane yonder mantle,
 not with wright but with wronge!

"see you not yonder woman
 that maketh her selfe soe cleare?
I have seene tane out of her bedd
 of men fiveteeene,

"Preists, Clarkes, & wedded men
 from her by-deene!
yet she taketh the mantle

& maketh her-selfe cleane!"

then spake the little boy
 that kept the mantle in hold;
says "King! Chasten thy wife!
 of her words she is to bold.

"she is a bitch & a witch,
 & a whore bold!
King, in thine owne hall
 thou art a Cuckold!"

A little boy stoode
 looking over a door;
he was ware of a wyld bore
 wold have werryed a man.

he pulld forth a wood kniffe;
 fast thither that he ran;
he brought in the bores head,
 & quitted him like a man.

he brought in the bores head,
 and was wonderous bold:
He said, "there was never a Cuckolds kniffe
 carve it that could."

some rubbed their knives
 upon a whetstone;
some threw them Under the table,
 & said they had none.

King Arthur & the Child
 stood looking them upon;
all their knives edges
 turned backe againe.

Craddocke had a little knive
 of Iron & of steele;
he birtled the bores head
 wonderous weele,
that every Knight in the Kings court

had a morssell.

the little boy had a horne
 of red gold that rouge;
he said, "there was noe Cuckolde
 shall drinke of my horne,
 but he shold it sheede
 Either behind or beforne."

some shedd on their shoulder
 & some on their knee;
he that cold not hitt his mouth
 put it in his eye;
& he that was a Cuckold,
 every man might him see.

Craddocke wan the horne
 & the bores head;
his Lady wan the mantle
 unto her meede.
Everye such a lovely Lady,
 God send her well to speede!

And so sentimental virtue is rewarded and the pretensions of the court, of the rich and powerful, are subject to coarse mockery. Bishop Percy published the original ballad with a few minor bowdlerizations - the *Buttocckes* were excised. However, he seems to have been sufficiently taken with it to have written his own somewhat smoother, more elegant and balanced version: *as revised and altered by a modern hand.*

We find Guenevere a little more dignified when she is open to mockery:

 "I had rather live in desarts
 Beneath the greenwood tree:
 Than here, base king, among thy groomes,
 The sport of them and thee."

When the old knight tries to bribe the boy the poem acquires a contemporary coziness:

 "And all the time of Christmas
 Plumb porridge shall be thine,
 If thou wilt ley my lady fair
 Within the Mantle shine."

Guinevere's spiteful outburst at the success of Craddock's virtuous wife, becomes the more restrained accusation:

> *"See yon shameless woman,*
> *That makes herself so clean:*
> *Yet from her pillow taken*
> *Thrice five gallants have been."*

and the boy's splendid exposure of the truth:

> *"she is a bitch & a witch,*
> *& a whore bold!*
> *King, in thine owne hall*
> * thou art a Cuckold!"*

emerges very tamely as:

> *"Of speech she is too bold,*
> *Of carriage all too free;*
> *Sir king, she hath within thy hall*
> *A cuckold made of thee."*

The two versions present an interesting contrast in tastes and sensibilities. They demonstrate how courageous Percy was in publishing his *Reliques* and why, perhaps, he sometimes appeared patronizing and condescending towards work that he obviously relished.

If Thomas Percy found it necessary to make minor alterations in some poems and produce alternative versions of his own, his other Arthurian poem set in Carlisle was particularly challenging. Half of nearly every page had been used by that parsimonious housemaid as kindling and he found himself with one of the strongest pieces of his collection in severely mutilated form. His solution seemed sensible, but it caused great controversy in its day and gave a particular romantic colouring to the Arthurian story for later generations. Percy made his approach very clear:

THE MARRIAGE OF SIR GAWAINE is chiefly taken from the fragment of an old ballad in the Editor's MS., which he has reason to believe more ancient than the time of Chaucer, and what furnished that bard with his Wife of Bath's Tale. The original was so extremely mutilated, half of every leaf being torn away, that without large supplements, &c. it was deemed improper for this collection: these it has therefore received, such as they are.

He was severely censured, and quite rightly so, by the dyspeptic antiquarian, John Ritson, for his lack of respect for his original materials.

When he published the fourth edition of his book, he added the sentence: *They are not here particularly pointed out, because the Fragment itself will now be found printed at the end of this volume.*

He defended himself when he introduced the mutilated fragment in this edition, as follows: *The second poem in this volume, intitled The Marriage of Sir Gawaine, having been offered to the reader with large conjectural supplements and corrections, the old fragment itself is here literally and exactly printed from the editor's folio MS. with all its defects, inaccuracies, and errata; that such austere antiquaries, as complain that the ancient copies have not been always rigidly adhered to, may see how unfit for publication many of the pieces would have been, if all the blunders corruptions, and nonsense of illiterate reciters and transcribers had been superstitiously retained, without some attempt to correct and amend them.*

This ballad had most unfortunately suffered by having half of every leaf in this part of the MS. torn away; and, as about nine stanzas generally occur in the half page now remaining, it is concluded, that the other half included the same number of stanzas

> *Kinge Arthur lives in merry Carleile,*
>   *And seemely is to see,*
> *And there he hath with him Queene Genever,*
>   *That bride soe bright of blee.*
>
> *And there he hath with him Queene Genever,*
>   *That bride soe bright in bower,*
> *And all his barons about him stoode*
>   *That were both stiffe and stowre.*
>
> *The King kept a royall Christmasse*
>   *Of mirth and great honor,*
> *And when . . .*
>
> *[About Nine Stanzas wanting]*
>
> *"And bring me word what thing it is*
>   *That a woman most desire.*
> *This shal be thy ransome, Arthur," he sayes,*
>   *"For Ile have noe other hier."*
>
> *King Arthur then held up his hand*
>   *According thene as was the law;*
> *He tooke his leave of the Baron there,*
>   *And homward can he draw.*

And when he came to merry Carlile,
  To his chamber he is gone;
And ther came to him his cozen Sir Gawaine
  As he did make his mone.

And there came to him his cozen Sir Gawaine,
  That was a curteous knight:
"Why sigh you soe sore, uncle Arthur," he said,
  "Or who hath done thee unright?"

"O peace, O peace, thou gentle Gawaine,
  That faire may thee beffall,
For if thou knew my sighing soe deepe,
  Thou wold not mervaile at all.

"For when I came to Tearne Wadling,
  A bold Barron there I fand
With a great club upon his backe,
  Standing stiffe and strong.

"And he asked me wether I wold fight,
  Or from him I shold begone -
Or else I must him a ransome pay
  And soe depart him from.

"To fight with him I saw noe cause,
  Methought it was not meet,
For he was stiffe and strong withall,
  His strokes were nothing sweete.

"Therefor this is my ransome, Gawaine,
  I ought to him to pay:
I must come againe, as I am sworne,
  Upon the New Yeers Day.

"And I must bring him word what thing it is . . .

[About Nine stanzas wanting]

Then King Arthur drest him for to ryde
  In one soe rich array
Toward the foresaid Tearne Wadling,
  That he might keepe his day.

And as he rode over a more,
  Hee see a lady where she sate
Betwixt an oke and a greene hollen:
  She was cladd in red scarlett.

Then there as shold have stood her mouth,
  Then there was sett her eye;
The other was in her forhead fast,
  The way that she might see.

Her nose was crooked and turnd outward,
  Her mouth stood foule awry;
A worse formed lady than she was,
  Never man saw with his eye.

To halch upon him, King Arthur,
  This lady was full faine,
But King Arthur had forgott his lesson,
  What he shold say againe.

"What knight art thou," the lady sayd,
  "That will not speak to me?
Of me be thou nothing dismayd
  Tho I be ugly to see.

"For I have halched you curteouslye,
  And you will not me againe;
yet I may happen, Sir Knight," she said,
  "To ease thee of thy paine."

"Give thou ease me, lady," he said,
  Or helpe me any thing,
Thou shalt have gentle Gawaine, my cozen,
  And marry him with a ring."

"Why, if I help thee not, thou noble King Arthur,
  Of thy owne hearts desiringe,
Of gentle Gawaine . . .

[About Nine Stanzas wanting]

And when he came to the Tearne Wadling
  The Baron there cold he finde,
With a great weapon on his backe,
  Standing stiffe and stronge.

And then he tooke King Arthurs letters in his hands
  And away he cold them fling,
And then he puld out a good browne sword,
  And cryd himselfe a king.

And he sayd, "I have thee and thy land, Arthur,
  To doe as it pleaseth me,
For this is not thy ransome sure:
  Therfore yeeld thee to me."

And then bespoke him noble Arthur,
  And bad him hold his hand,
"And give me leave to speake my mind
  In defence of all my land."

He said, "As I came over a more,
  I see a lady where she sate
between an oke and a green hollen;
  she was clad in red scarlett.

"And she says, 'A woman will have her will,
  And this is all her cheef desire.'
Doe me right, as thou art a baron of sckill:
  This is thy ransome and all thy hyer."

He sayes, "An early vengeance light on her!
  She walkes on yonder more -
It was my sister that told thee this,
  And she is a misshappen hore!

"But heer Ile make mine avow to God
  To doe her an evill turne,
For an ever I may thate fowle theefe gett,
  In a fyer I will her burne."

[About Nine stanzas wanting]

The Second Part

Sir Lancelott and Sir Steven bold
 They rode with them that day,
And the formost of the company
 There rode the steward Kay.

Soe did Sir Banier and Sir Bore,
 Sir Garrett with them soe gay,
Soe did Sir Tristeram that gentle knight,
 To the forrest fresh and gay.

And when he came to the greene forrest,
 Underneath a greene holly tree
Their sate that lady in red scarlet
 That unseemly was to see.

Sir Kay beheld this ladys face,
 And looked uppon her swire:
"Whosoever kisses this lady," he sayes,
 "Of his kisse he stands in feare."

Sir Kay beheld the lady againe,
 And looked upon her snout:
"Whosoever kisses this lady," he says,
 "Of his kisse he stands in doubt."

"Peace cozen Kay," then said Sir Gawaine,
 "Amend thee of thy life.
For there is a knight amongst us all
 That must marry her to his wife."

"What! Wedd her to wife!" then said Sir Kay.
 "In the divells name anon,
Gett me a wife where ere I may,
 For I had rather be slaine!"

Then some tooke up their hawkes in hast,
 And some tooke up their hounds,
And some sware they wold not marry her
 For citty nor for towne.

And then bespake him noble King Arthur,
  And sware there by this day:
"For a little foule sight and misliking . . .

[About Nine stanzas wanting]

Then she said, "Choose thee, gentle Gawaine,
  Truth as I doe say,
Wether thou wilt have me in this liknesse
  In the night or else in the day."

And then bespake him gentle Gawaine,
  With one soe mild of moode,
Sayes, "Well I know what I wold say -
  God grant it may be good!

"To have thee fowle in the night
  When I with thee shold play;
Yet I had rather, if I might,
  Have thee fowle in the day."

"What! When lords goe with ther feires," she said,
  "Both to the ale and wine?
Alas! Then I must hyde my selfe,
  I must not goe withinne."

And then bespake him gentle Gawaine,
  Said, "Lady, thats but a skill:
And because thou art my owne lady,
  Thou shalt have all thy will."

Then she said, "Blesed be thou gentle Gawain,
  This day that I thee see,
For as thou see me at this time,
  From hencforth I wil be.

"My father was an old knight.
  And yet it chanced soe
That he married a younge lady
  That brought me to this woe.

"she witched me, being a faire young lady,
  To the greene forrest to dwell,
And there I must walke in womans liknesse,
  Most like a feeind of hell.

"She witched my brother to a carlish B. . . .

[About Nine Stanzas wanting]

"That looked soe foule, and that was wont
  On the wild more to goe.

"Come kisse her, brother Kay," then said Sir Gawaine,
  "And amend thé of thy liffe:
I sweare this is the same lady
  That I married to my wife."

Sir Kay kissed that lady bright,
  Standing upon his feete;
He swore, as he was trew knight,
  The spice was never soe sweete.

"Well, cozen Gawaine," sayes Sir Kay,
  "Thy chance is fallen arright,
For thou hast gotten one of the fairest maids
  I ever saw with my sight."

"It is my fortune," said Sir Gawaine.
  "For my uncle Arthurs sake,
I am glad as grasse wold be of raine,
  Great joy that I may take."
 Sir Gawaine tooke the lady by the one arme,
  Sir Kay tooke her by the tother;
They led her straight to King Arthur
  As they were brother and brother.

King Arthur welcomed them there all,
  And soe did Lady Genever his Queened,
With all the knights of the Round Table
  Most seemly to be seene.

King Arthur beheld that lady faire
  That was soe faire and bright.
He thanked Christ in Trinity
  For Sir Gawaine that gentle knight.

Soe did the knights, both more and lesse,
  Rejoyced all that day,
For the good chance that hapened was
  To Sir Gawaine and his lady gay.

Percy's supplemented version, the one that aroused so much interest at the time and created a far more fairy-tale Arthurian world than that of the original more earthy ballad, stayed fairly close to the original, where it existed, except for smoothing out the versification. However, when Percy added new stanzas to replace those gaps of nine stanzas, where the paper had proved so useful in kindling the fire, Percy gave free rein to his imagination.

A fair damsel enters and asks Arthur for:

A boone, a boone, 0 kinge Arthure.
I beg a boone of thee;
Avenge me of a carlish knighte,
Who hath shent my love and mee.

At Tearne-Wadling his castle stands,
Near to that lake so fair,
And proudlye rise the battlements,
And streamers deck the air.

That image of proud battlements and streamers decking the air, the creation of Percy's imagination, was the one that stayed with readers and was constantly quoted in guidebooks and tourist's journals. They imagined the castle, which is not mentioned in what we have of the original text, and they thrilled to Percy's description of the grim baron:

Noe gentle knighte, nor Lady gay,
May pass that castle-walle :
But from that foule discurteous knighte,
Mishappe will them befalle.

Hee's twyce the size of common men,
Wi' thewes, and sinewes stronge,

211

And on his backe he bears a clubbe,
That is both thicke and longe.

Percy also introduced the idea of magic ground:

On magicke grounde that castle stoode,
And fenc'd with many a spelle :
Noe valiant knighte could tread thereon,
But straite his courage felle.

His footnote continues the distortion of the extensive stone remains into a medieval, if not an Arthurian, castle:

Tearne-Wadling is the name of a small lake [in Inglewood Forest] near Hesketh in Cumberland, on the road from Penrith to Carlisle. There is a tradition, that an old castle once stood near the lake, the remains of which were not long since visible. Tarn, in the dialect of that country, signifies a small lake, and is still in use.

The *grimme barone* has borne away the lady's love and *sore misused* her. Arthur immediately calls for Excalibur and rides to Tarn Wadling.

And when he came to Tearne Wadlinge
Benethe the castle walle :
" Come forth; come forth; thou proude barone,
Or yielde thiself my thralle."

On magicke grounde that castle stoode,
And fenc'd with many a spelle :
Noe valiant knighte could tread thereon,
But straite his courage felle.

Under the effect of the magic, King Arthur's sturdy sinews lose their strength. He has the choice of yielding to the baron or fighting him or returning in a year's time having solved the riddle.

And bringe me worde what thing it is
All women moste desyre;

Percy has missed out the whole section where Arthur tells the story of the bold Barron to Gawain as he has already told the story of the encounter. The original Arthur was not magicked, but chose caution as the better part of valour.

The answers Arthur receives are summed up in a neatly-turned verse:

Some told him riches, pompe, or state;
Some rayment fine and brighte;
Some told him mirthe; some flatterye;
And some a jollye knighte.

Percy can't resist expanding verses to make the loathly lady yet more loathly:

> *Her haires, like serpents, clung aboute*
> *Her cheekes of deadlye hewe :*
> *A worse-form'd Lady than she was,*
> *No man mote ever viewe.*

She states her terms if she is to provide the solution to the riddle:

> *Now this shall be my paye, sir king,*
> *And this my guerdon bee,*
> *That some yong fair and courtlye knight,*
> *Thou bringe to marrye mee.*

In the original Arthur very generously offers the gentle Gawain without being asked.

Percy has Arthur prick over hill and dale to *the barone's bowre.* In the original the baron bears *a great weapon on his backe* and pulls out *a good browne sword.* Percy insists on his *clubbe.*

Gawain volunteers to marry the loathly lady, but Arthur offers polite resistance:

> *Nowe naye, nowe naye, good sir Gawaine;*
> *My sister's sonne yee bee;*
> *This lothlye ladye's all too grimme,*
> *And all too foule for yee.*

Gawain is his usual courteous self:

> *I'll marry her, unkle, for thy sake,*
> *And I'll thy ransome bee.*

When Gawain said, *Thou shalt have all thy wille."*

> *Hee sawe a young Lady faire.   . . .*
> *Sweet blushes stain'd her rud-red cheeke, . . .*
> *The ripening cherrye swellde her lippe, . . .*
> *And all her necke was snowe.*

She and her brother have been enchanted:

> *But now the spelle is broken throughe,*
> *And wronge is turnde to righte;*
> *Henceforth I shall bee a faire lady"*
> *And hee be a gentle knighte.*

Those proud battlements with streamers decking the air and the giant with thews and sinews strong was to make an instantaneous impression on Percy's contempories. Its high romantic vein, so removed from the witty toughness of the original, corresponded to the eighteenth century's escapist fantasy of the Middle Ages.

Percy may have written a totally different poem. His alterations and additions turned the poem from a popular entertainment of the Middle Ages, direct and rumbustuous, into an a sophisticated eighteenth-century antiquarian's concept of the Middle Ages. That different poem touched a nerve. Tarn Wadling and its giant were celebrated. Arthur was woken from his Enlightenment sleep. And, in its own small way, *The Marriage of Gawain*, contributed to the birth of the Romantic revolution.

Tarn Wadling was celebrated. Directories, tourist guides and gazeteers all quoted Percy's version of the ballad, saying it was a ballad as old as Chaucer, and making particular point of mentioning the giant, the castle battlements and the enchanted ground.

The tarn's international reputation and the romantic enthusiasm felt towards it is well illustrated by an American tourist's comments in 1826:

Ten miles from Penrith, we passed a pretty little sheet of water, called Tarn Wadling, on the margin of which are situated the ruins of Castle Hewin, which was once a regal fortress possessing great strength. Its aspect at present is very different from what it seems to have been in the days of good King Arthur, when it was the seat of knighthood, and is thus alluded to in a ballad of that age:

> *'In Tearne Wadlinge his castle stands,*
> *All on a hill so hye,*
> *And proudlye rise the battlements,*
> *And gaye the streamers fly.'*

N.H. Carter: *The Journal of a Tour Through Ireland, England, Scotland, France, Italy and Switzerland in the Years 1825, '26. and '27.*

Carlisle, on the strength of Percy's *Reliques,* had become the home of King Arthur.

The Real Arthur
in the Carlisle of the Imagination

We constantly mythologise our past. We render and re-render the distancing content of history into an imaginative past, where actions and emotions are clarified and writ large. The contradictory, muddled individuation of ordinary lives becomes the narrative line of the selected past. The ordinary and the everyday is forgotten. We give a gloss to the past that is very little different from the fictions we create to re-envisage ourselves.

The legends of Arthur have played a peculiar role in this process of continuous re-invention. The legends of the Celts, of their racial tragedies and of the heroism and the blood-lust of their warriors, came to express a communal defiance, a projection of racial triumph and glory in the face of persistent defeat as they were driven ever westwards. Once they had been powerful. An Arthur had conquered and ruled and ushered in a reign of peace and order. The legends offered a racial pride. They became a cornerstone of identity.

When lands were invaded and the Celts were pushed ever westwards the legends migrated with them. The Gododdin from Lothian carried the stories of their sad prince Dristan south and replanted it in Cornwall. Llywarch Hen, once a prince of Rheged, became a bard in Powys. Celts, in the sixth century, crossed the Channel and settled the Armorican Peninsula and renamed it Brittany. They took their culture and legends with them and re-imagined a distant past in a now forsaken land. The people of Rheged would have found themselves pushed into the hills as the Anglo-Saxons settled the valleys and then, later, as the Norsemen, who had sojourned in Ireland, came to establish their thwaites and homesteads. They may have retained something of their identity. The names Carlisle, Cumberland and Cumbria suggest a persistence of Celtic identity, perhaps even into the eleventh and twelfth centuries.

Breton minstrels carried their native tales throughout Europe. There are eleventh century carvings of Arthur and Guinevere and Gawain and Tristan on the tympanum of an eleventh-century arch in Modena Cathedral.

With the Norman Conquest, the legends of the Celts re-emerged in a paradoxically dominant role. The Bretons provided support to their Norman neighbours and the Norman conquest brought with it Breton soldiers and nobles and minstrels. There may have been something of a re-melding of Celtic romance. The stories that had been told for centuries in Brittany may have been heard alongside their counterparts which had evolved in the intervening centuries in Cornwall, Wales, Cumberland and Scotland.

Geoffrey of Monmouth may even have embodied the process in his very person. He was of Welsh or Breton parentage, reared in Wales and served a Norman establishment. His imaginative enthusiasm was politicized to give legitimacy to Norman Rule. The mystical transformations of the Celts were straight-jacketed in the narrative of 'evidential' history. Arthur became the antecedent of England's rulers and then, through another Celtic metamorphosis, the king, who had resisted the Anglo-Saxons, became an English hero. Wace transmuted Arthur into Norman French, and Layamon, speaking the English of a conquered people, but employing their heroic verse forms, and, living on the Welsh border, and perhaps drawing on a Celtic hinterland, added imagination and fantasy to a harder political vision.

During the same century, if Arthur's political role had been inverted, his cultural role was to undergo something of a parallel revolution. Stories, that were once the religious projections of a Celtic culture, may have lost their mystical and religious elements to become the imaginative stories of a far more refined and civilized people as they remade themselves and found newly sophisticated ways of feeling and self-expression. Marie de France and Chretien de Troyes explored worlds of feeling and love, toyed ironically and sentimentally with refined emotions that were far removed from the brutal heroism and fantastic nature worship of the Celtic tales they employed. The Breton fantasies enabled them to engage imaginatively in a secular fable that was neither ethically pre-determined, as in the lives of saints and stories of religion, nor politically determined, as with the stories of Charlemagne or the chronicle histories by Geoffrey and Wace.

The political Arthur of Geoffrey resides in an actual world of cities and castles, of arms and battles, dates and history. Chretien and Marie created worlds that dwelt on the edge of dreams. Life, love and death were played out somewhere other, where neither space nor place had significance. This was even more so with the evolving story of the Grail and in such works as Wolfgang von Eschenberg's *Parzival*.

The evolving Story of the Grail became a vehicle for religious aspiration, a parable and paradigm of the Christian life. The verse romances in the generations following Chretien provided entertainment and were works of burlesque and rough humour and wild imagination. The imaginative source fed two divergent streams: the prose romance became the central parable of a spiritual age and the verse romances were secular parodies of a hierarchical society, poems where the actions of rulers were sometimes celebrated, but more often parodied and lampooned.

These stories circulated throughout western Europe. In England, they were known by the Anglo-Norman rulers, who continued to speak French until the fourteenth century.

The English Arthurian poems emerged two hundred and fifty years after Geoffrey fabricated his fertile history. The poems in the alliterative tradition are unusually conservative. The fashionable poetry of the day, by Chaucer and Gower and others, took its form and content from the advanced, humanist literature of contemporary Italy and France. Their work introduced the metrical forms and rhyme that became the mainstay of English poetry. The alliterative poets, provincials to a man, living in the Midlands and the North of the country, were reinvigorating, if not reinventing, the traditional forms of the language. They may have been conservative in employing a metre based on alliteration, but, within that tradition, they were endlessly enterprising.

The alliterative *Morte Arthure* took its story from the chronicles of two hundred years previously and selected and shaped the narrative into a coherent, though still episodic form. The story was no longer a legitimation of Norman rule, but a tragic tale that raised moral questions about the nature of kingship and heroism. *The Awntyrs of Arthure* pushed the complexity of technique to the utmost to create an insistently moral tale that questioned the values of the ruling elite.

The ballads, in their demotic manner, challenged the pretensions of the age. *The Wedding of Gawain* and the *Marriage of Gawain* exposed the courtly manners; *The Avowyng of Arthure* was a brutal attack on the fantasy manners of chivalry; *The Boy with the Mantle* mocked pretensions to sexual morality. *The Carle of Carlisle* challenged the hierarchical structure of society.

The stanzaic *Morte Arthur* humanized its heroes, revealed their tragedy. Malory understood the tragedy inherent in the flawed nature of human kind. He may have claimed to be writing of a time when people's emotions and actions were very different, *for love that time was not as love is nowadays,* but he understood the destructiveness of emotions and the impossibility of the ideal.

In whatever Celtic legends there were in the centuries before the Normans, Arthur may have held his court in Carlisle. The little we know suggests the possibility of the city having a continued importance that might have given it mythographic significance. The poets of Rheged would have known a ruined city very similar to the one that was settled by their Anglo-Saxon successors. Across the troubled lands of Northern England, this commanding city of the Roman Wall, the city that Bede described, might have appeared as a city fit for Arthur. We do know that the legend of Owain/Ywain/Yvain, originated in an historical personage who lived somewhere in the north-west. This legend persisted and mutated to become whatever legend Chretien heard from the Bretons, and, possibly, a parallel Welsh one that became the tale of *The Lady of the Fountain* in *The Mabinogion*. And Peredur/Perceval, Tristan and Merlin may owe something to originals in the North of England and the Borders. The Welsh folk memory of the *Gwyr Gogledd*, the men of the North, testifies to the power and persistence of a strong sense of racial loss. It needs to be said that the names in the landscape from Pendragon Castle to Arthur's Stone Circle offer no evidence whatsoever, and, similarly, false equivalents are found throughout the country.

The battles listed by Nennius four centuries after Arthur might have lived, do not exclude the possibility that Arthur fought in the north. Legends, and modern arguments persist, that would attach Arthur to the Gododdin and make him a hero of the Elidon Hills.

In 1092, William Rufus *went northward with a great army, and set up the walls of Carluel, and reared the castle, and drove out Dolfin, who ruled the land, and garrisoned the Castle, and went south again. then he sent many peasant folk with their wives and cattle to dwell in the land and till it.* The city William Rufus captured and settled may have been very different from that recorded by Bede. Florence/John of Worcester talks of the city having lain waste after having been destroyed by the Danes in 875, but there is contradictory archaeological and other evidence. The wooden fort William built may have overlooked a small, poor settlement among some remnants of ruins from the times of the Romans. John Denton, writing in 1610, said that *it lay waste for the most part of 200 years before the last Conquest saving a few cottages among the ruins inhabited by Irish Scots.* He also writes that Waldieve gave to the priory *a mansion near St Cuthbert's church where at that time stood an antient building called Arthur's chamber taken to be part of the mansion house of King Arthur the son of Uterpendragon, of memorable note for his worthiness in the time of antient kings.* William of Malmesbury mentions an arch and an inscription. It is possible that the Bretons, who accompanied the Normans, may have seen the ruins in the midst of an impoverished and comparatively desolate land, and sensed a once great king. Legends of Arthur might still have circulated among whatever Celtic settlements remained in the more remote parts of the area, in the fells and on the marshes.

In 1122, Henry I visited the city and funded the building of a stone keep and city walls and provided the land for the building of an Augustine Priory. Ten years later the diocese of Carlisle was created. At the same time both the Franciscans, the Greyfriars, and the Dominicans, the Blackfriars, built friaries in the city. The city prospered as the political, military and spiritual centre of the west borders, and its economic importance was enhanced by the presence of a mint for the silver mined at Alston. The only other mints in the north were at York and Durham. Carlisle received its charter in 1158 from Henry II.

The legends as they re-emerged in the writings of Chretien and Marie imply that the name of Cardoel was already current among the Bretons. The form is Norman/Breton, not Welsh or English. Neither poet would have much cognizance of a northern city. Chretien probably had no concept of it at all, and Marie, if she was the Marie attached to the English court, would have been aware of it as a garrison town involved in Henry II's border wars. It certainly was not her sunlit city of beautiful ladies. Their imaginary tales required a city removed in time and place and their knowledge of Carlisle did not contradict the Cardoel of their imaginations.

However, the Carlisle of the time may have had some resonance in the wider world. Jordan Fantosme wrote *A Chronicle of the Wars between England and Scotland in 1173 and 1174* in which he describes a siege of the city in such a way that it might come from an Arthurian romance:

> *Away goes king William with his great gathered host*
> *Towards Carlisle the fair, the strong garrisoned city.*
> *Lord Roger de Mowbray and his chivalry*
> *And lord Adam' de Porz joins himself to his Border-men.*
> *The earls of Scotland lead the hated people,*
> *Who never had any repugnance to do fiendish things.*
> *They make such progress, I know not what more to tell you,*
> *That they could see Carlisle full of beauty;*
> *The sun illuminates the walls and turrets.*
> *He who has a merry banner, gladly displays it;*
> *And sound the trumpets in every rank:*
> *You might hear noise in the shuddering city;*
> *But lord Robert de Vaus gently begs them*
> *Not to be dismayed nor act cowardly;*

It has been suggested that Cardoel might have been a careless mis-transcription of Caerleon from Geoffrey or Wace, a casual mis-hearing or forgetting. Chretien probably had sufficient awareness of southern England to know of Caerleon and not to confuse it, and Marie certainly knew Caerleon as she mentions it elsewhere in her *Lais*. She is also very specific in her location of Kardoel as a place of fighting against the Picts and the Scots. Arthur makes his court in several places in the romances and there is no need to argue for one place. Geoffrey may wilfully have mis-read Carduel for Caerleon and given his near-native city precedence.

The Arthurian stories that followed throughout the thirteenth century were set in a landscape that was as a mirror to the writers' own world. It corresponded to the world they knew in the fashions and the manners of the people. Physical laws of hurt and death rarely applied. They may not have made the imaginative leap that connected Cardoel with Carlisle.

And yet, Froissart, the Chronicler, who wrote *Meliador*, the last of the French Arthurian romances, did know the city. In his *Chronicles* he wrote of a *Carlisle, which is well inclosed with walls, towers, gates and ditches: king Arthur formerly resided here more than elsewhere, on account of the fine woods which surround it, and for the grand adventures of arms which had happened near it.*

The one exception is Guillame le Clerc and *Fergus of Galloway*. Guillame certainly knew the area thoroughly. His geography is more precise than that in any other Arthurian romance, but his story is set in a far different world. It is a poem that totters on the edge between heroic and mock heroic. Various political parallels have been suggested for the poem, none of which can be anything, but informed guesses. The poverty of rural Galloway, the drizzling streets of Carlisle and the hazards of the Queensferry have the ring of truth. A hunt that pursues a stag across the south of Scotland from Geltsdale to Ayr is as unlikely as Gawain and Ywain devotedly holding hands or a bemused King Arthur whittling a stick.

If the topography of most of the French romances was imaginary, the English romances are very precise in their locations. The poet of the alliterative *Morte Arthure* must have had his road atlas open in front of him, working out the routes taken and measuring the distance. He knew how long it took to ride from Carlisle to Sandwich. Geography was important to him. In his text he clearly rejected Caerleon as a setting for Arthur's court, and specifically placed one of the great dramatic scenes in Carlisle Castle. It was a scene of great symbolism in which Britain asserted its independence over Rome.

The Carlisle he chose, probably sometime around 1400, was very different from the prospering city that Chretien and Marie barely apprehended. Edward I had held his Parliament in the city in 1307, when the city was in the forefront of the wars with Scotland. Ten earls, seventy-six barons and 248 knights were present and the city's population more than doubled while the ailing king recuperated at Lanercost. The king's household spent £2,895 in the city during their few weeks residence and the burgesses of Carlisle must have felt themselves very affluent. It was not to last. Edward I died on Burgh Marsh looking across the Solway to Scotland. Within years, Robert the Bruce was laying waste the country around Carlisle. In 1315, during days of torrential rain, he besieged the city, but his siege engines were bogged down in the quagmire, and he retreated after the able defence led by Andrew de Harcla.

The country, and consequently the city, was impoverished by continuing Scottish raids, by disastrous harvests and cattle disease. A description of Carlisle during the attacks of 1345, suggests a city very different from Arthur's imperial capital: the air *was so corrupted and tainted by dung and manure heaps and much other filth put in the streets and the lanes that the men dwelling there and coming to the city for its defence are stricken with a dreadful horror.*

A truly dreadful horror was to descend on the city within a few years. In 1349 the Black Death killed between one third and two thirds of the inhabitants. The plague returned with terrible regularity in 1361, 1369, 1379 and 1391. On May 4th in that same year, 1391, the largely wooden city was swept by fire. In 1402, an army of 12,000 Scotsmen did *what evil they could* in the vicinity of Carlisle. It wasn't until 1424 that a truce was signed and, even then, the Borders remained a troubled and restless place.

The poet of the alliterative *Morte Arthure* may have been recalling those days a hundred years earlier when Edward I made Carlisle the de facto capital of England. The city's shrunken population and broken walls would not correspond to the opulence of his contemporary picture of feasting, fashion and arms. The mythology invoked a city that might once have been.

The poet of *The Awntyrs of Arthure* portrayed the darkness of the age in the ghost of Gaynor's mother. Her shrunken eyes and black bones might have been wracked by the plague. Her moral ferocity seems to come from a time of severe tribulation. Inglewood is swept by a storm and the social order of the hunt is rendered chaotic by the forces of nature. The king's hunting echoes that great hunt in 1280 when, so the *Lanercost Chronicle* tells us, Edward I killed more than two hundred fallow deer in Inglewood Forest.

The ballads set in Inglewood mark it out as a strange territory. Normal settlement and development was forbidden by the forest laws and this vast tract of land was reserved for the protection of game, especially deer. The forest, with its few inhabitants and fewer routes through it, must have seemed like a mysterious territory, where the normal order of society was suspended. It was the abode of outlaws as is evidenced by ballads such as *Adam Bell, Clym of the Clough and William of Cloudesly* and by place names such as Wragmire and Thiefside Hill. Abandoned strongholds such as Castle Hewin may well have been the resort of bands of outlaws at any time throughout the Middle Ages. It is not surprising that Inglewood Forest attracted stories to it, where kings were threatened by knights who suddenly rose up out of the undergrowth, where land disputes were settled by near mortal combat and knights found that they were subject to insult and testing. It was a place where authority was usurped and questioned.

Tarn Wadling is an even more remarkable case. This quiet pool, famous for its carp and bilberries, probably in the ownership of the nuns of Armathwaite, must have had something exceptional about it in the way of atmosphere or tradition that is now forgotten. Its singularity, perched on higher land between the valleys of two rivers, half way along a dangerous road, its shallowness and its sinking island and a set of associations that may be indicated by a name related to early Irish settlement might be sufficient to prompt accumulating legendary associations.

Thomas Malory may have known Carlisle. He probably served with Warwick at the siege of Alnwick Castle in 1461 and he could have travelled more widely in the north. Bad harvests and persistent warring across the Border meant that the city never really prospered and the siege of 1461 wrought much destruction. The internecine fighting throughout the north in those years may have been paralleled in the civil war between Arthur and Lancelot and we might imagine Lancelot and Guinevere with their 150 knights riding through a city impoverished by war, but Carlisle would not have seemed a city worthy of Arthur and the Round Table.

The mysterious aura of Tarn Wadling was further enhanced by Thomas Percy's intervention. The abode of a threatening and unruly man became a fairy tale giant's castle with battlements and pennants flying and it was this image that so attracted the nineteenth century romancer.

In the century that followed, Walter Scott set his *Bridal of Triermain* in north Cumberland, Tennyson, staying as a guest in Mirehouse, may have imagined the samite-sheeted hand reaching out of Bassenthwaite to grasp Excalibur and Edward Burne Jones was commissioned to paint his masterpiece, *The Death of Arthur*, to hang on the walls of Naworth Castle. For Burne Jones the bare windswept hills about Hadrian's Wall were the landscape of Arthur. The picture remained his contemplative recourse for over twenty years and was unfinished at his death. This tragic masterpiece now hangs in the heat and sun of Puerto Rico rather than in a medieval chamber in Naworth. Ernst Chausson set his grand opera, *Le Roi Arthur*, in Carlisle.

The landscape of the north stretching from Carlisle to Blanchland was the landscape of Arthur for that enthusiastic Arthurian, Jessie L. Weston, whose book, *From Ritual to Romance*, charted the transformation of the story of Arthur from early Celtic religious mythology into the Romance of the Holy Grail. T.S. Eliot, in his notes to *The Waste Land*, cites Jessie L. Weston as the source of his imagery of the Fisher King.

Wilson Armistead, in 1890, in a book retelling *The Tales and Legends of the English Lakes*, demonstrates how readily the hard realities of everyday can be transformed by the wilfull imagination:

No one versed in ballad lore - no reader of old poetry and romance, can approach Carlisle for the first time without pleasurable emotion. Carlisle is the border city - the city of King Arthur and his knights. It has been the scene of many a stout siege and bloody feud; of many a fierce foray, and mournful execution, and of many a just punishment upon traitors and reivers. It is, consequently, not to be pictured to the imagination without unusual interest. Old traditions of events like these have made it among the most remarkable of the cities of England; and it would be difficult to name another around which are clustered so many memories of such various degrees of attraction to the poetical and historical antiquary. Its approach from the south, though striking, gives no idea of its antiquity and former feudalism. It is situated in an extensive plain, surrounded in the distance by mountains, amongst which Saddleback, Skiddaw, and Crossfell, are prominent; and from afar off, with the smoke of its households hanging over it, does undoubtedly impress the imagination with ideas of the romantic.

Nearer approach, however, dissipates this illusion. We lose sight of the valley, being in it, and of the mountains, in the presence of immediate objects. Tall chimneys rear their heads in considerable numbers, pouring forth steam and smoke, and with square buildings and their numerous windows, prove incontestably that modern Carlisle is a manufacturing city, and has associations very different from those of its former history. On entrance, the contrast between the past and the present becomes still more vivid. We see that its walls and gates have disappeared; that its streets are clean, wide and comfortable, which no ancient streets in England ever were; and that it has altogether a juvenile, busy, and thriving appearance, giving few signs (to the eye at least) that it has been in existence above a century. It is true that two venerable relics, its castle and its cathedral, remain to attest its bygone grandeur and glory; but these are not immediately visible, and have to be sought out by the enquiring stranger; whilst all around him is modern and prosaic; and a mere reduplication of the same characteristics of English life and manners that he must have seen in a hundred other places.

Still, however, it is "merry Carlisle," and "bonnie Carlisle," although, like all other mundane things, it has been changed by time; and is quite as much King Arthur's city as England is King Arthur's England; and brimful of associations which the traveller will be at no loss to recall, of the crime and sorrow - the "fierce wars and faithful loves" of our ancestors, from the year 800 downwards to 1745. Not that Carlisle is only a thousand years old. It has a much earlier origin than the year 800, having been founded by the Romans. By them it was called Luguballium, or Luguvallum, signifying the tower or station by the wall, and was so named from its contiguity to the wall of Severus. The Saxons, disliking this long and awkward name, abbreviated it into Luel; and afterwards in speaking of it, called it Caer-luel, or the city of Luel; from whence comes its present designation of Carlisle. It is supposed to have been during the Saxon period, if not the chief city, the frequent residence of that great mythic personage, King Arthur, where he

> *With fifty good and able Knights*
> *That resorted unto him*
> *And were of his round table*
> *Did hold his jousts and tournaments,*
> *Whereto were many pressed,*
> *Wherein some knights did far excel*
> *And eke surmount the rest.*

Having quoted that awful piece of doggerel, Armistead goes on to retell the story of *The Marriage of Gawain* in Percy's elaborated version.

A more proportionate view of Arthur was provided at about the same time by the eminent Victorian historian, Mandell Creighton. He was born and raised in Castle Street in Carlisle. He sums up the connection between King Arthur and Carlisle very neatly:

We only gather that, in the long period of warfare against the English, the Britons fought bravely and were strong in a feeling of nationality. This national feeling took shape in a mythology, which may have had an historical basis in the past or may have expressed merely the military ideal of the race. The legend, however, of Arthur seems to have been the possession of the Celtic race, though it took new forms and was localised afresh wherever the race was hard pressed in conflict with its fierce enemy. We need not claim for the Borderland the possession of an historic Arthur to the exclusion of the claims of Brittany, or Wales, or Cornwall. The Arthurian legend was common to them all, and Arthur's Seat, and Chair, and Round Table are all to be found within a few miles of Carlisle, the Cardueil of Arthurian romance.

In the century or so since Mandell Creighton, our knowledge of the historical Arthur has advanced little. There is no evidence to connect him with Carlisle.

Yet, the real Arthur, who is the Arthur of the imagination of the ages, will forever be associated with Carlisle. Lanval's transcendently beautiful lady will ride towards the castle on her Spanish palfrey; Ywain will be told of the knight of the mysterious fountain and Perceval will fight with the Red Knight; Arthur will proudly disdain the Roman ambassadors at a magnificent banquet; Gawain will lie in the darkness beside his loathly lady; Lancelot and Guinevere will lie together within the castle chamber and hear the resentful clamour of Agravain and his fellow knights; Guinevere will be rescued from the flames by an impassioned Lancelot and, together, they will lead that slow procession of knights bearing olive branches along the streets towards where Arthur waits in Carlisle Castle.

Some of these stories can lay claim to being amongst the greatest stories in world literature. Marie de France is celebrated as the writer of the most exquisite tales; the imagination of Chretien de Troyes transformed the world of chivalry and prompted the most fertile romance of the Middle Ages; the alliterative *Morte Arthure* is one of the finest war poems in English; the Gawain romances are at the heart of our folk literature and Malory's *Morte Darthur* is one of the most celebrated works in our literature.

It is a truly remarklable heritage.

King Arthur may well live in Merrie Carlisle.

Further Reading

The best overall guide to Arthurian Literature is R.S. Loomis: *Arthurian Literature in the Middle Ages: A Collaborative History*. (Oxford 1959). James Douglas Bruce: *The Evolution of Arthurian Romance* (Slatkine 1974) is an exhaustive summary of medieval Arthurian literature. *The Arthur of the English* edited W.R.J. Barron (University of Wales 2003) brings together current research and Derek Pearsall: *Arthurian Romance* (Blackwell 2003) is a succinct contemporary overview. Francis James Child: *The English and Scottish Ballads* (Dover 1965) is the indispensable guide to English folk poetry

The major works referred to are to be found in:
Geoffrey of Monmouth *The History of the Kings of Britain* translated Lewis Thorpe (Penguin 1982)
The Lais of Marie de France translated by Glyn S. Burgess & Keith Busby (Penguin 1986)
Chretien de Troyes: Arthurian Romances translated William Kibler (Penguin 1991)
Fergus of Galloway translated by D.D.R. Owen (Everyman 1991)
King Arthur's Death translated Brian Stone (Penguin 1988)
King Arthur's Death: The Middle English Stanzaic Morte Arthur and Alliterative Morte Arthure edited by Larry Benson. (Bobbs-Merrill 1974)
Sir Gawain: Eleven Romances and Tales edited by Thomas Hahn (Medieval Institute Publications, 1995)
Sir Thomas Malory: *Works*. Edited by Eugene Vinaver (Oxford 1954)
Thomas Percy: *Reliques of Ancient English Poetry* (Dover 1966)

The medieval history of Carlisle is exhaustively covered in Henry Summerson's masterly *Medieval Carlisle: The City and the Borders from the Late Eleventh to the Mid-Sixteenth Century. C.W.A.A.S. 1993,* and admirably summarised in Mike McCarthy's *Carlisle: History and Guide* (Alan Sutton 1993). Mike McCarthy, with David Weston, edited *Carlisle and Cumbria: Roman and Medieval Architecture, Art and Archaeology* (The British Archaeological Association 2004)
William Hutchinson: *The History of the County of Cumberland* (reprinted E. P. Publishing 1974) is a superb source for the county's history and Mandell Creighton's *Carlisle* in the Historic Towns series (Longman Green 1889) is a delightfully written overview of the city's history.
Marjorie Rowling: *The Folklore of the Lake District* (Batsford 1976) is an excellent and well referenced summary of the area's folklore.
A.M. Armstrong, A. Mawer, F.M. Stenton and Bruce Dickens: *The Place Names of Cumberland* (Cambridge 1971) is an essential reference.

The best web-site for Arthurian literature is The Camelot Project at the University of Rochester at www.lib.rochester.edu/camelot, which provides most English language texts on Arthur, with useful introductions.